This collection of essays plunges the reader ... postcolonial Philippine history and the most hope .... brutal Marcos dictatorship was overthrown by a peaceful, popular uprising. The writers were all participants in the stirring events of 1986, and come from diverse social, professional and ideological backgrounds. The multiple literary genres – factual narrative, personal anecdote, political analysis and theological reflection – model how the past should be recovered for the sake of understanding and acting in the present. It will humble, encourage and enlighten all who continue to struggle today in the Philippines and in other parts of the world with political repression and the non-fulfilment of political dreams.

Vinoth Ramachandra, PhD
Secretary for Dialogue & Social Engagement, IFES

This is a significant book edited by a long-time friend, Dr Melba Maggay. This book focuses on the postcolonial identity of the Philippine people during the puppet rule of Marcos and beyond. Marcos used romantic justification for his martial law to shut out opposing voices and peoples. EDSA revolutions gave a glimpse of hope that never delivered, because the people in all social strata did not change in their deep-structure psyche. Today the "populist rule" of Duterte would be a regression and unapologetic savagery without accountability.

What happened to the Philippine people from the 1970s till now is relevant to the world at large, especially for those struggling in the post-colonial era in Africa, Latin and South Americas, and Asia. This book is insightful for it operates on two levels: the stark reality of encroaching evils on the personal level and the reflection of the cultural deep-structure that let these things happen. It is especially rare for a book such as this to even explore these dimensions from a theological and Christian perspective.

Wing Tai Leung, PhD
Founding President, Lumina College, Hong Kong
Former General Secretary, Breakthrough Youth Ministry

"There is an unseen hand that works for the good of those who try to stand for God's original purposes for society and its institutions." The editor herself gives us the clue to read this intelligent, intense and inclusive narrative. The contemporary political and social context in the Philippines, which mirrors what occurred in the 70s and 80s, has closely the same past in Latin America: authoritarian regimes and dictatorship under martial law. Previously, they were illegal regimes; today, the leaders are democratically elected but have "authoritative natures," along with populists and violent nationalists. This is actually a global phenomenon. It's a book urgently relevant.

Marcelo Vargas A.
Centro de Capacitación Misionera, Bolivia, Latin America

Three decades after the ruthless rule of Ferdinand Marcos ended, this diverse collection of personal essays gives a revealing and timely insight into the dark days of martial law in the Philippines, the subsequent "people power revolution" and ongoing consequences in the 21st century for the first Southeast Asian nation to declare itself a democratic republic. These are important stories of struggle, resilience and faith amid a convoluted interplay of ideological politics and social change.

Rev Tim Costello, AO
Chief Advocate, World Vision Australia

To Be in History: Dark Days of Authoritarianism is simply a remarkable work. Its style – testimonies and reflections of people from diverse social and professional backgrounds and divergent ideological commitments from a very dark period in the history of the Philippines – make it a compelling read. Everyone's story is marked with fear, loss and grief. And yet resounding in all is faith and hope, inspiring courage and perseverance in their struggle to end impunity and oppression.

The integrity with which each tell their story, how they confronted and were confronted with issues, questions and struggles of faith and life in a repressive and oppressive regime, at personal, community and institutional level, is refreshing. It is amazing how their story mirrors our story in the dark days of despotic rule in Africa in the 1970s and 1980s.

To Be in History is relevant today, not least for us in Africa, who, like the Philippines, are faced with the resurgence of authoritarianism. The enthralling stories, and reflections on the lessons from those dark days, provide encouragement and challenge the activist generation today, that fearful as the times may be, hope must triumph.

As one who is involved in civic-political activism, working for a non-violent end to militarism and authoritarian rule in my home country of Uganda and the continent of Africa, reading *Dark Days of Authoritarianism* is energizing and challenging at the same time. I am so glad that I have the book as a resource for the difficult journey ahead.

Bishop David Zac Niringiye, PhD
Civic-Political Activist
Senior Fellow, The Institute of Religion, Faith and Culture in Public Life
Author, *The Church: God's Pilgrim People*

The longing for freedom and for social justice lies deep in the human psyche. This moving book tells us the story of true events in the Philippines and how different groups sought to bring about change. In particular, it shows how committed Christian men and women can seek the good of their society, the power of prayer, and the grace of God. A prophetic voice for our times.

Rose Dowsett
Missiologist

To Be in History

Dark Days of Authoritarianism

To Be in History

Dark Days of Authoritarianism

General Editor

Melba Padilla Maggay

Langham
GLOBAL LIBRARY

© 2019 The Institute for Studies in Asian Church and Culture (ISACC)

This Philippines edition published by permission, published in the Philippines by ISACC under the title "To Be in History".

Published internationally under the title "Dark Days of Authoritarianism"
Published 2019 by Langham Global Library
An imprint of Langham Publishing
www.langhampublishing.org

Langham Publishing and its imprints are a ministry of Langham Partnership

Langham Partnership
PO Box 296, Carlisle, Cumbria, CA3 9WZ, UK
www.langham.org

ISBNs:
978-1-78368-485-4 Print
978-1-78368-486-1 ePub
978-1-78368-487-8 Mobi
978-1-78368-488-5 PDF

British Library Cataloguing-in-Publication Data
A catalogue record for this book is available from the British Library

ISBN: 978-1-78368-485-4

Cover & Book Design: projectluz.com

CONTENTS

By Way of a Prologue xi
  Melba Padilla Maggay

Part I: Years of Authoritarian Rule

1   The Awakening of Miss Goody Two Shoes. 3
     Elizabeth Lolarga

2   Life under Authoritarianism: Why It Should Never Happen Again . . 17
     Mary Racelis

3   The NatDem Front: A Historian Looks Back 35
     Fe B. Mangahas

4   Truth in a Revolution: Notes from the Underground 55
     Mario I. Miclat

5   A Peek from behind the Bamboo Curtain 69
     Alma C. Miclat

6   Uncle Sam behind the Scenes: A View from the Corridors of Power . . 87
     Willie B. Villarama

Part II: Days of People Power

7   Snap Elections 1986 103
     Melba Padilla Maggay

8   Seventy-Five Long Hours 109
     Adrian Helleman

9   Onward, Soldiers of Faith 115
     Rolando Villacorte

10   Diary from the Barricades. 125
     Melba Padilla Maggay

11   The Darkest Moment 133
     Rolando Villacorte

Part III: The Morning After: Views from the Margins

12 Thoughts on the Aftermath. 149
       Willie B. Villarama

13 A Nonviolent Revolution 157
       Adrian Helleman

14 On Historical Babies, Paradigms and Miracles 169
       Melba Padilla Maggay

15 A Gift for Millennials. 181
       Mary Racelis

Epilogue: Putting an End to Our Unfinished Revolutions 193
       Melba Padilla Maggay

About the Contributors 205

By Way of a Prologue . . .

"To be in history is to be in a place somewhere and answer for it."

Walter Brueggemann

By the look of it there was nothing portentous about that fateful day in September 1972. The sun was shining, there was the usual crowding round jeepney stops, and the wires between electric posts crisscrossed the sky like a mad artist's tangled lines. I was about to head to the *Manila Chronicle* office, where I was learning to be a cub reporter, my first job after university.

But then the minutes of waiting for a ride turned into almost an hour, for the jeepneys were few and far between. The boy behind the newspaper stand had no paper to sell that morning, and the corner of the sidewalk where the cigarette vendor held court, her radio blaring, was unusually silent. The sun beat down with increasing heat, and the crisscrossing electric wires above the roofs of houses seemed to lacerate the sky and hurt my eyes.

I gave up the idea of working that day and turned back home. As I reached the threshold I heard the stentorian voice of President Ferdinand Marcos, and soon enough his face showed up on TV as he intoned solemnly that he had declared martial law "to save the Republic and build a new society." Anxiety snatched at my heart and I quickly grabbed the phone to call my friends. Most lines were strangely busy, and those who did answer only said "hello" and then the line went dead. Much later, I learned that some of my friends had gone underground, gone to the hills and caught malaria, or been killed in an encounter with government troops.

I spent the first three months of martial law visiting my editor and friends who were rounded up under what came to be known as "preventive detention." It was the regime's invented tool for arresting without warrant and clapping in jail political oppositionists without charges.

The *Chronicle* was one of the first newspapers to get shut down. I found myself suddenly without a job. It took time to get my bearings after this shock. I could not, in conscience, work for *The Daily Express*, the only newspaper that had not been closed down because it belonged to a Marcos crony. I shifted to writing mostly innocuous speeches for cabinet ministers.

At first, martial rule did seem to bring some order to what looked like the beginnings of a "new society." I was caught jaywalking across a busy street in

San Juan, along with others hurrying to go to work. We were fingerprinted, had to pose for mug shots, and were told to sweep the market and the streets clean by way of punishment. It seemed that the government was dead earnest in enforcing its slogan *Disiplina ang kailangan*.[1] The skyline changed as new buildings rose up, numerous infrastructure projects got underway, and the papers were full of foreign investments pouring in.

But then what I read and heard within the walls of power was not quite what I was experiencing on the ground. I would hear of a friend from my activist days in the university being tortured and raped while in detention. A cousin in the provinces mysteriously died in jail without knowing what he was there for. It was like being in the land of the novelist Kafka, where one gets thrown behind iron doors and there is no one to address questions to, no one to turn to for redress or at least some clarity as to the abstract technical reasons for which one languishes in the castle dungeon.

Now and again, I would hear of bright young men and women getting killed at the foot of some lonely mountain or being discovered lying in a ditch by the wayside. These would have been leaders of our generation, those of us who were part of what has come to be known as the "First Quarter Storm," that wave of student protests and unrest in the early 1970s which was eventually used by Marcos as part of the reason why he declared martial law.

Unlike today's steep descent into outright barbarism alongside the creeping but systematic dismantling of checks and balances in our institutions, Marcos was forthright in declaring martial rule and he took the trouble to coat with finesse and a veneer of legality the abolition of Congress. The judiciary was captured and the Supreme Court was reduced to a stamping pad for the plethora of presidential decrees issued. The atmosphere of prosperity and progress, the cultivated sophistication symbolized by the Cultural Center and other such artifacts of the "edifice complex" of Marcos's wife Imelda, the soporific effect of a controlled press that pacified our questionings and subdued our critical instincts into acquiescence – all these combined to mask and keep below the radar screen the brutality and the massive raid on the country's coffers that was going on.

The telltale marks of the regime's excesses could not be prevented from showing, however. Its dirty fingerprints were stamped indelibly on language and popular culture. Words changed lexical meanings; for example, "detention" and "detainee" in ordinary circumstances mean holding an arrested person in temporary custody, but this was stretched to prolonged and indefinite

---

1. Discipline is what is needed.

incarceration as the powers saw fit. "Salvage," which in ordinary English means to rescue or save from total destruction, in the context of that time became the opposite: a murder marked by torture and mutilation. The victim was hogtied, the eyes were gouged out and the tongue cut, the mouth was stuffed with a newspaper crumpled into a ball and the body was dumped in a river or a field overgrown with *talahib*.[2] "*Na-salvaged*."

New names had to be invented to adequately describe the wholesale plundering and extravagant lifestyle of the Marcoses and their proxies; "*kleptocracy*" was coined, for instance, and "*Imeldific*" became synonymous with ostentatious spending, grossly lavish parties and grandiose extravaganzas.

It is not an accident that the first thing a would-be autocrat does is to clamp down on dissent by muzzling media – or, in today's technologically mediated social environment, simply run fake news campaigns and make them go viral through an army of trolls. Constant exposure to the subliminal messages of media round about us eventually lulls people into a kind of stupor, passively induced into uncritical acceptance of outright and even outrageous lies. Hitler's propaganda minister Joseph Goebbels once shrewdly observed that "If you tell a lie big enough and keep repeating it, people will eventually come to believe it."

To this day, the big lie persists that the martial law period under Marcos was a good thing. This is the revised history that the Marcos family and their loyalists wish us to believe.

By sheer repetition and constant reiteration, they wish to mesmerize many into their collective auto-suggestion that this period in our history was in fact a golden era presided over by a strong and heroic leader.

Unlike South Africa, which set up a Truth and Reconciliation commission to investigate the truth of what happened during the days of apartheid, we have continued to suffer the consequences of not having closure over the reported abuses of power by the Marcos regime. We have yet to come to some consensus on what exactly happened. No guilt has been assigned, no sin owned, and instead there is a blithe denial that something terribly wrong was ever done.

The failure to pin down accountability has led to a continuing divide in the nation, a political fissure that now and again surfaces with issues like burying Marcos in the *Libingan ng mga Bayani*,[3] or Bongbong Marcos contesting the ballots cast for the vice presidency. Depending on what is expedient, free-floating forces align themselves either with the pro-Marcos loyalists seeking a

---

2. A tall, perennial grass, growing up to three meters in height, which is native to the Indian subcontinent.

3. The sacred burial ground for the nation's heroes.

return to power, or with the anti-Marcos forces that surfaced at EDSA and are now derisively labeled by President Rodrigo Duterte as "*dilawan*."[4]

The restoration of democracy, or at least the semblance of what passes for democratic institutions, has yet to bring the country back to a stable party system and the rule of law. Instead, we are treated to shifting alliances and mass migrations to the party that holds the levers of power. Today, the fragile institutions that rose up out of the ruins of authoritarian rule are once again under threat of being either dismantled or slowly eroded as mere instrumentalities at the bidding of the ruling autocrat.

An enduring legacy of the martial law years has been the mystique of the strongman, fed by the mythology that the culture is, at bottom, authoritarian. The people need – and want – a strong iron hand. Nothing gets done, it is said, because the country suffers from "too much democracy," as the late Singaporean statesman Lee Kuan Yew put it.

There are many shades of gray to this, however.

First of all, we do not account to culture what are really functions of a social stratification rigidified by centuries of colonialism.

Inferiorized and disempowered, our people learned to bow down obsequiously to whoever happened to be in authority. Read properly, this is a maladaptation to asymmetrical power relations. It is not a preferred orientation toward authoritarian rule but a malfunctioning of one of the culture's most basic instincts: accommodation. On the surface, this accommodative bent looks like servile subservience to those in power. But scratch deeper and it may simply be a strategy of survival on the part of those trapped in powerlessness who can only hang onto the coattails of those in power.

Second, evidence from the remaining scraps of our indigenous culture shows that the traditional idea of a leader is not the strongman but the *silongan*, from the root word *silong*, "roof" – the term used by Cordillera peoples for the clan chief under whose capacious roof people seek protection and shelter. The *silongan* took care of those under his *sakop*, his acknowledged sphere of responsibility. This structure of communal responsibility and authority broke down, however, during the Spanish period when the chieftains were co-opted and became *gobernadorcillos*.[5] This drove a wedge between ruler and people. Thus was created a thin layer of a local ruling elite – the *principalia* –

---

4. "Yellow," the color used by the allied forces that gravitated around Cory Aquino in the campaign to oust Marcos.

5. The local governors who served as instrumentalities of the Spanish regime.

whose sense of accountability was no longer to their people but to their colonial masters.

The Americans cemented this ruling elite into an oligarchy, shifting to themselves its misplaced sense of obligation and loyalty by a deliberate policy of "benevolent assimilation." *Pensionados* were sent to the US to study so as to create a professional class laundered into an "American way of life." The bureaucracy was patterned after an American style of governance, meant to make us "a showcase of democracy in Asia."

We now know that "democracy" – or at least the structures and institutions that make it work within the cultural contexts of the West – is not exportable. Billions of dollars may be poured into "institution-building" in places like Iraq or Afghanistan. But unless there are supportive norms within the local cultures that would make it operative, the ruling ethos behind the democratic mechanisms put in place will still be the cult of the strongman, the *caudillo*. Elections will remain merely contests for power among rival clans, tribes and warlords.

The fledgling democracies that have emerged after experiences of authoritarianism in Latin America, Africa and other places bear this out. As Guatemalan sociologist Bernardo Arevalo puts it: "We have the hardware of democracy, but the software of authoritarianism."

It needs noting, however, that there is in this country a subterranean strain of consensus-building practice in our indigenous leadership that has yet to be paid attention to. If sufficiently studied and surfaced as a serious product of inquiry, it could yet serve as a seedbed for democratic institutions to flourish.

The tribal council of elders, like the *dap-ay* of the Kankanaey in Sagada, or that of the Ikalahan in Nueva Vizcaya, is a living remnant of the old ways of conflict resolution and collegial governance. Unfortunately, this has been submerged under the overlay of modern electoral practices. In Tubo town in Abra, for instance, after political rivalries intensified in the 2007 and 2010 elections, the elders of the *dap-ay* resorted to the old tradition of *butong*, a consensus-based arrangement in choosing leaders. The 200 elders of the Dap-ay di Tubo drew up a charter governing elections and the criteria for selecting candidates. They then presented the council's choice to the people for their approval. To date, all selected candidates in ten villages in Tubo are running unopposed, and Barangay Tabacda, which is included in the watch list of the Cordillera police, had not seen poll-related violence since 2013.[6]

---

6. Kimberley Quitasol, "Amid Hot Spots, Abra Town Keeps Politics Bloodless Thru 'Butong,'" *Philippine Daily Inquirer*, 13 May 2018, A14.

Experiences of immersion in grassroots communities also show that the most effective leaders tend to be those who quietly go alongside people, usually behind the scenes, listening and building consensus toward whatever needs resolving or doing. These consensus-builders are usually silent; they do not talk too much in meetings. Those who seem to be strong leaders are usually found unable to bring people together. The people may seem acquiescent, but come time to do things, they passively resist compliance by inattentiveness, lackadaisical implementation and eventual abandonment of projects.

Unfortunately, it is the *trapos* – the "traditional politicians" – who often know how to smooth out conflict and craft give-and-take compromises that might bring all stakeholders to the table. From the point of view of those used to open conflict, this is seen as backroom "wheeling-and-dealing" and lacking in transparency. *Naluto na*, as they say, already "cooked" in the back kitchen or in smoke-filled rooms. However, it may be that those schooled in Western governance processes will need to pay attention to those informal domains where force of personality and interlocking relationships count far more than formal rules and roles. In a culture of personalism, what works is often in that realm where a dense network of kinship ties and connections to power centers is brought to bear on the business at hand.

Clearly, there is a need to be "hermeneutically suspicious," as the Latin Americans say, as to how we read the patterns of our political behavior. Are we looking at these from theoretical frames borrowed from the outside, or are we looking at them from the inside, entering into the universe of meaning embedded in the artifacts, language and life systems of the culture?

For instance, what frames our understanding of recent history – the so-called Marcos "dictatorship" and the "People Power" uprising that came in its wake? Both of these have been analyzed through various lenses, depending on the ideological commitments of those writing. In this book, we do not attempt to construct or deconstruct interpretive frames that have been used in making sense of what has happened. The approach is simple: we each tell our story, what the British don C. S. Lewis called "primal history" – that primitive experience of reality as we have lived it, as against ideas and images constructed for us by anonymous authorities in newsrooms, theorized over by academia and spread by invisible trolls behind computer terminals.

The memories recounted in this book are an unlikely collection, and so are the writers. From various social and professional backgrounds and even divergent ideological commitments, we have come together to bear witness to a very dark period in our history as we have lived it.

The stories are written by people who tried their best to "be in history," to locate themselves *in situ*, within a social space whose poverty and gross inequalities called for an answer. Within their limited spheres of competence and influence, they tried to navigate with wisdom and integrity through the constraints of a regime that could knock on your door one night, pick you up and make you disappear into the shadows.

The usual tales of horrific torture and other human rights abuses during that period are now dismissed by some as having been suffered by only a few; and anyway, they were rebels, and the state had the right to put them in jail.

The following stories show that one-man rule cast a dark shadow, not just on a small number of dissidents, but on the whole fabric of society during that period. While largely quiet and undramatic, the stories speak of the general stain of corruption, a contamination spread by the rot at the center of power, including by those within circles seeking radical changes.

The first part of the book contains textured stories about the martial law years. A journalist of "bourgeois" background writes of her awakening, and what it was like to cover the cultural pursuits of Imelda, then empress of the arts, and at the same time help in the propaganda needs of the underground movement. A respected social anthropologist details some of the thousand and one ways in which the tentacles of monocratic rule tightly wrapped themselves even round the halls of academia. From the corridors of power, a politician and civil servant who served a cabinet minister under the Marcos regime tells firsthand the covert role of the US in ending the reign of the Marcoses, lending pathos to his last desperate effort to hold on to power.

A counterpoint to these narratives is at least three stories that reveal startling facts about the ideological underside of the National Democratic Front, then seen by mostly young and idealistic elements as the bearer of revolutionary change and the only alternative force to the violence of the regime.

A student activist who signed up early to the movement tells the story of his journey into truth, a search that began by embracing the ideological absolutism of the local Marxist movement, only to find that the road to its vision was littered with ruthless draconian measures, such as the bombing of Plaza Miranda in 1971 which almost decimated the leadership of the Liberal Party. This was blamed on Marcos then, a spark that he exaggerated as a conflagration and used for his own purpose of perpetuating himself in power. The bombing was justified by the communist movement's leadership as midwifery; it was to "hasten the birth pangs" of the coming revolution. This strategy of mayhem and hard pragmatism eventually waylaid its good intentions and sent it adrift without ethical moorings.

A historian who, along with her husband, was jailed for her revolutionary activities looks back at her involvement with the "NatDem." She speaks candidly of her early discomfort with its ideological framework, and traces the movement's failure to a faulty social class analysis and lack of spiritual and cultural dimensions in its purely materialist ethical system.

A writer and wife talks of her life and mission as representative of the Communist Party of the Philippines (CPP) behind the bamboo curtain, witnessing firsthand its socialist experiment. She was told at the end of her sojourn to simply forget all she had heard and seen in China, a warning against copycat movements.

The second part of the book is a cluster of gripping stories on the events leading to our People Power "revolution." The snap elections of 1986 and the four days of unarmed resistance at EDSA are told and analyzed from the various vantage points of actual participants.

A Canadian missionary details his experience of the "seventy-five long hours" during the days of the barricades. A newspaperman tells the tale of what it was like behind military lines, and how the darkest moment of the revolution turned into joy when the pilots of the Sikorsky gunships defected. This signaled to the public the wave of defection that was then already going on quietly among the military ranks. The head of ISACC (the Institute for Studies in Asian Church and Culture), which organized the evangelical presence at the barricades under the banner of KONFES (*Konsiyensiya ng Febrero Siete*),[7] has written a day-to-day account of what it was like to be among the millions who added to the body count at EDSA and stood unyieldingly before the advancing tanks.

The third and last part of the book is initial reflections on these and subsequent events.

There is a strong note of disillusionment in "Thoughts on the Aftermath," which sees EDSA 1 not as a miracle from heaven but as a product of a conspiracy hatched elsewhere that therefore did not yield the desired effects. "A Nonviolent Revolution" theologizes on the efficacy of active nonviolence as an alternative to the idea of a "just war," even as the author concedes that it does not necessarily lead to better results. It also raises questions on the missional role of foreigners, whose dual identity is such that they are both mere guests of the country who should not interfere with internal politics, and also missionaries called to stand in solidarity with the people among whom they serve.

---

7. Literally, "Conscience of February 7," the day of the historic snap elections that signaled the toppling of the regime.

"On Historical Babies, Paradigms and Miracles" examines the underlying theoretical frames behind many of the analyses already offered on the significance and meaning of what happened at EDSA. It outlines some fresh ways of looking at it from a more biblical perspective, and suggests that it is best seen not as a "restoration of democracy" within a liberal meaning frame, but as continuous with an older, indigenous tradition of fusing religion and revolution. "A Gift for Millennials" is a distillation of learnings from a wise and revered anthropologist who has immersed herself for decades in urban poor communities. She warns of the need to be vigilant when there is a narrowing of the democratic space, and she offers insights on the Duterte brand of populism, as well as practical advice for the next generation on how exactly to walk with the poor and see real change.

The book is capped by an epilogue that maps the paths the authors have taken and the lessons and insights they are taking with them for the onward journey.

It is said that history is told by the winners. No, we are only survivors. No one who goes through such a dark period emerges unscathed; we are all battle-scarred. We bear in our bodies and collective memory the wounds and marks of wrestling with insidious forces that again and again sought to defeat us by making an assault on that place where the battle between good and evil begins: our own inner spirit.

We are just wizened old soldiers grateful that we are still here to tell the story.

Melba Padilla Maggay, PhD
Editor

Part I

Years of Authoritarian Rule

1

The Awakening of Miss Goody Two Shoes

Elizabeth Lolarga

What good is it, my brothers and sisters, if someone claims to have faith but has no deeds? Can such faith save them? Suppose a brother or a sister is without clothes and daily food. If one of you says to them, "Go in peace; keep warm and well fed," but does nothing about their physical needs, what good is it? In the same way, faith by itself, if it is not accompanied by action, is dead. (Jas 2:14–17 NIV)

Overheard from former activist-political detainee Nympha Saño at the 2013 reunion of the Women against Marcos and for Boycott (WOMB): "*Pasalamat tayo kay Marcos. Dahil sa kanya, naging exciting buhay natin.*"[1] I tend to agree that there is reason to be thankful for the late dictator Ferdinand Marcos. Were it not for his martial law regime, our lives might have been humdrum, and we might not have taken the exciting risks that we did.

Speaking for myself, I might still be writing little angst-filled poems that reflect my "petit bourgeois" background were it not for that unique milieu that shaped me. In a visit to my English and life mentor Nieves B. Epistola in her cottage on the University of the Philippines (UP) campus in the mid-1970s, I met law professor Merlin Magallona's wife. I was introduced to her as a young poet. She asked point-blank, "Do you write progressive poetry?"

---

1. "Let us thank Marcos. Because of him, our lives became exciting."

3

Mrs E. (short for Epistola) answered gently for me, "No, she writes love poems, as where all poets must begin." But her husband Silvino, playing devil's advocate, couldn't help interjecting: "She writes about women's problems which she wouldn't be writing about if she wasn't so *burgis* [bourgeois]!"

Reviewing my diaries during the early martial law years, I see a girl of seventeen waking to the sound of her father's irritated voice asking if she had tinkered with his transistor radio the night before because he couldn't find his usual news stations. All he could get was static sounds and the Air Force channel. Our copy of *The Manila Times* did not arrive. We thought that the delivery boy was late. Beyond that, there was nothing unusual about that fair September morning in 1972; no portent of the darkness about to cover the land.

At St Paul College Quezon City, our high school principal, Sr Auguste Sartre, spoke before the general assembly, urging us to contact our parents/guardians so we could go back home. She announced that martial law had been declared. Our quarterly long exam scheduled for that day was postponed for another day. Classes were indefinitely suspended until things "normalized."

Subversive Materials

Our Student Catholic Action (SCA) advisor hoped the declaration applied to Metro Manila only and for a temporary period. My co-SCA officers met with her to find out if our seminar-workshop for newbie SCAns would push through (it wouldn't). I had brought mimeographed readings about the theology of liberation by Desmond Tutu and excerpts from the nationalist writings of, among others, Renato Constantino. Little did I know that under the new circumstances, these would be enough to put one in jail for possession of subversive materials.

Elsewhere in school, Sr Auguste unlocked the glass-encased bulletin board of the SCA to tear down its large recruitment poster with some seemingly harmless aphorism on freedom done in cut-out color paper. "We can't mention freedom. For now, we don't have freedom," she explained as I protested. Even the high school student council, responsible for our discipline in forming flag ceremony queues and silence in the classrooms and chapel, was abolished.

High school segued to college years at the University of the Philippines Diliman, still under martial law. Bag inspections at the different entrances of Palma Hall were carried out long before it was SOP to open one's bag at malls and hotels to be poked by security guards. Big grilles, where there had been none in the pre-martial law years, now lined the corridors of the first floor of Palma Hall. Midway upon entering University Avenue, the bus we rode on would be flagged down by guards in khaki uniforms who'd get on board to look at each of our faces. It felt like living in a state of siege for others, but in time these precautionary measures became, yes, SOP.

Among the organizations allowed to operate in 1973 was the UP Student Catholic Action (UPSCA). Its hangout was Delaney Hall below the Chapel of the Holy Sacrifice. I applied to be a member but dropped out later. One time, a senior member, Lorna Patajo (now Kapunan), asked if I'd like to join her to meet a political detainee on day release for a dental appointment. My curiosity aroused, and having time between classes, I went with her and came face to face with what in my eyes was my first rebel. I kept my surprise to myself. She was frail of build, had a soft speaking voice and *mestiza*[2] features probably darkened by what I imagined to be forced labor in the detention center. All the time Lorna conversed with detainee Carol Pagaduan (now Araullo), a lady guard stood at a discreet distance.

Politicization

From my high school SCA days the name of former Theresian Marisa Aguila had stood out. I looked up to her because she was one of those rare creatures: a politicized former *colegiala*.[3] We kept in touch through letters and cards. In one New Year's card dated 1974 she wrote the following (these may be her words or she may have been quoting someone else):

we are tired of
    "piece-of-paper peace"
we want the real thing!

aggressors may draft
    "peace agreements"
    with a lot of tongue work;

and despotic rulers
    may impose "peace"
    by decree . . .

but can we ever live
    in real tranquility
      . . . while we are kept

---

2. Mestiza means mixed parentage, Spanish-Filipino, so mostly white, not brown.

3. This means convent-bred, raised in a Catholic girls' college that tends to be exclusive and cloistered.

> hungry
> . . . and while our fists
>   (and even our tongues!)
>   are bound in heavy chains?

> brothers & sisters,
>   unite and join the cause . . .

> struggle for real peace!

But getting further politicized wasn't in my plans. I was in my early twenties when I encountered Mrs Magallona and her provocative question. I was mindful of my goal as a dutiful daughter – namely, get an education followed by a stable job. Being the first of eight children, I had taken it upon myself, with Mrs E.'s recommendation, to be a working student in my senior year. I wanted to be less of a burden to my parents and to help them with household expenses.

My first job was as a reporter for a crony-owned newspaper (the Marcos buddy was businessman Roberto Benedicto) *Philippines Daily Express*. There was no alternative media yet like *We Forum* or *Mr and Ms Special Edition*, unless you counted the underground press that produced *Liberation* and *Ang Bayan*.

Not yet a month into my work of helping put to bed the "Life and Leisure" pages, I was called out for the caption head I wrote for a photo showing the tourism secretary's wife, Amparo Aspiras, sampling a new pastry named after First Lady Imelda Romualdez Marcos. The caption head I had used and that saw print was: "A BITE OF IMELDA." My editor, Tere Orendain, said she had nightmares of being called out by Malacañang (Palace) or being invited to Camp Crame for questioning.

"Next time, Babeth," she said, "remember to use the name of Mrs Marcos with respect."

A few years before I had joined the *Daily Suppress*, as the paper was sarcastically referred to, the news desk there had had to put up with nightly visits from a military censor in fatigue uniform. He answered to the name of Col Camilo Curameng. His job was to go over the paste-up of the next day's news pages to see if everything toed the Marcosian line. In time, the news desk learned to practice self-censorship and thus the need for a Col Curameng became superfluous.

I'd have to hand it to Mrs Marcos that I found some joy in the performances put on at the Cultural Center of the Philippines, fruit of her so-called "edifice complex," a term I first heard in class from my political science professor, Francisco "Dodong" Nemenzo Jr. I watched my first full-length opera, *Madame*

Butterfly, in the Main Theater. I was stunned by the psychedelic effects that served as lighting and scenery for the Alwin Nikolais Dance Theater. At the Folk Arts Theater I caught Martha Graham's dance company and Alvin Ailey American Dance Theater in different years. Memorable was tall, noble-looking dancer Judith Jamison emerging dramatically from a basket in *Cry*. After her performance the audience rose in a spontaneous standing ovation. Most of the time, the tickets were complimentary ones for members of the press.

The "Life and Leisure" post was, I heard, a coveted one. But I felt hemmed in there, not being fashion savvy, and not having any passion for cooking, gardening and other homemaking skills. That holds true for me up to the present.

I'd feel a measure of pride when managing editor Neal H. Cruz would use my occasional news story, like my coverage of the International PEN (Poets, Playwrights, Essayists and Novelists) Conference in December 1977. A resolution was passed appealing to President Marcos "to order the release of writers under detention, including Behn Cervantes and Edgar Maranan; to enjoin the appropriate authorities henceforth to refrain from arresting and detaining writers on account of their writings; and to ensure that writers facing charges be henceforth heard and tried before civilian judges, in civilian courts." The resolution was attested by F. Sionil Jose, PEN secretary general.

Mr Jose, or Manong Frankie as I later learned to address him, sent a handwritten note thanking me for the PEN coverage. Along with it came a book, Ivan Illich's *Deschooling Society*. Manong wrote, "Hold on to the book. He will come to Manila next year for a series of lectures. You may want him to autograph it then."

I can't remember if Illich came, but there were great writers like Günther Grass, Mario Vargas Llosa and Mochtar Lubis who did, and the Philippine Center of International PEN hosted their visits. The top floor of Manong Frankie's Solidaridad Bookshop seemed to me a Freedom Center where writers and journalists converged to speak and smoke freely.

Writer's Business

But what did I learn from this exposure to the greats? That the writer's business is not to worry about bylines, prizes or reviews. Rather, one should be aware of the gift of language one is fluent in: one speaks for others who do not know how to express themselves. In this way, one becomes an instrument of something greater – something divine, perhaps?

I was reading Thomas Merton's *Seeds of Contemplation* then. He wrote that writers who write for God reach many people, while writers who write for human beings reach a few, make a little noise and earn some money – but only for a while. Writers who write for themselves will look at what they have written, be disgusted with it in ten minutes and wish they were dead.

I wrote in my journal how it was good to strive to be a vehicle like the one described by novelist Erica Jong: a river that flows while readers try to fish for their dinner and hopefully catch a reflection of themselves on the water.

After I left the *Express*, while being interviewed for another job, and based on a reading of some submitted poems, I was told that my works were "subjective, personal and inward-looking." The interviewer couldn't reconcile this with the image of the Ms Lolarga he had heard about from some *Express* staffers he socialized with at the National Press Club (NPC). My former officemates described me as nursing sympathies for the Left, a closet activist. Surprised, I said the girl they described might not be me. The interviewer tended to agree, as the tone in my poems indicated that I had not witnessed something violent outside myself enough to move me to record the incident in verse.

A bit bothered by what the man said, I consulted Mrs E., who said that poetry, especially lyric poetry, concerns itself with love while prose deals with justice. She said that, although I might be sympathetic to the Left, my poems remained subjective, adding, "Your first five hundred poems will be mostly or all love poems, and when you eventually write about justice, your work will read like a prose poem."

Noise Barrage

Sometimes, windows of defiant expression would suddenly open. A diary entry dated 6 April 1978 described the Batasan Pambansa election campaign fever that infected our quiet neighborhood in Barrio Kapitolyo, Pasig. The noise barrage made it feel like it was New Year's Eve as our neighbors, our family included, showed sympathy for the oppositionist party Lakas ng Bayan (LABAN).

My brother Junic and I stepped out of our house, yelling, "Laban! Laban!" and clapping our hands until they were sore. Lots of car horns honked in the street to a deafening decibel. Junic brought out the posters that he had made earlier, proclaiming, "Laban!" He also fetched our tin wash basin and whacked it several times, hitting it to the beat of the two-syllable Filipino word for "fight" as I screamed "Laban! Laban!" at the top of my voice.

I wrote, "I don't feel tired or weak at all. I feel exhilarated by the racket in the neighborhood. There seems to be unity among us after all. It's way past the five-minute limit for the noise barrage. Yet we can still hear sporadic cries of 'Laban!' A healthy opposition is indeed needed."

The noise barrage on that Thursday night proved a huge success, judging by how nervous the law enforcers became, arresting the demonstrators, led by former Sen Lorenzo Tañada, for breach of peace. But you can't bottle up pent-up emotions and convictions. I hooted and clapped my hands to express my protest over a political regime that had stifled truth.

Still, I continued to plod on as a workaday newspaperwoman at *People's Journal*, followed by *People's Tonight*, both owned by Marcos's brother-in-law Benjamin "Kokoy" Romualdez, whom we addressed as "Gov" (short for governor). When he was in our office at Port Area, Manila, he liked to sit with us at the news desk and shoot the breeze. Later, I felt bothered by the way he was shuffling editors around like helpless pawns. He called it a "guided Cultural Revolution" involving the promotion of some editors at the expense of others. Life at the *Journal* felt like that line from the TV series *Lou Grant*: it's not anymore a question of what's right or what's wrong that should happen to a newspaper; its bottom line now revolves merely round questions of profit and loss.

One time, my editors, Gus Villanueva and Vergel Santos, refused to attend a conference of editors from all the dailies called by Information Minister Greg Cendaña. They said it was just an occasion to distribute *payola* (bribe money) so the papers would write more flattering things about the Marcos administration.

Vergel mused how he would rather be out of the office chasing and writing stories again, even for a little magazine, so long as he could enjoy the freedom to write. He thought aloud, "What good will come from teaching good values to my children if I accept bribes in the form of watches or a car?"

Art Cariaga, another desk person, told me, "The only way to remain a clean newspaperman is to keep your needs as simple as possible." That meant no aspirations for designer clothes, imported shoes, travel to Europe and elsewhere, and the like.

At the Desk

I shared with Mrs E. the happenings at the news desk: the stories that were killed, the behind-the-scenes squabbles between media and government, the governor's remarks, the office power struggles. She suggested that I keep a separate diary to record all that and call it "At the Desk." My boyfriend, Rolly

Fernandez, who worked in the competing *Daily Express* as a copy editor, scoffed at Mrs E.'s suggestion. He said that in these times, idealism no longer had value, and I shouldn't entertain delusions that my jottings would be of use to a historian someday. However, he didn't tell me to quit keeping a diary.

I rode on the media merry-go-round – or was it musical chairs? After two years at the *Journal*, I resigned to join the publications group of the Population Center Foundation (PCF) under former newsman Vicente Tirol. PCF was a project of Mrs Marcos's to stem the tide of population growth. Even though I was just a contractual worker, I counted my blessings. I had the weekends off, compared to my newspaper jobs when we enjoyed only one day off and you worked on Christmas or Good Friday if your day off didn't fall on those days. PCF offered a shuttle service to and from the workplace, which was on the border of Makati and Taguig. Work, again compared to the daily pressure of a newspaper, was light, with a bi-weekly news and feature packet, and bi-monthly and quarterly magazines as outputs.

It was around this time (1981–1983) that the excesses of the Marcos regime – forced disappearances, hamlettings, political imprisonment and torture, and high-level corruption, among many others – were being leaked and reported in small publications that dared, like *Who* magazine. I contributed mainly cultural articles to *Who*.

One Christmas season, Cristina del Carmen (now Pastor), a former college chum and *Who* staff writer, and I decided to contribute our bit to the human rights cause by selling cards and pendants with handwritten quotes about freedom and carved out of beef stew bones. These were made by political prisoners from Camp Bagong Diwa in Bicutan, Taguig. The office of Task Force Detainees of the Philippines in Quezon City consigned these items to us. Cristina and I sold, and even bought for ourselves, said items to friends, relatives and co-workers, and returned the unsold ones in January the following year.

I joined the Women Writers in Media Now (whose acronym is WOMEN), at first thinking that its workshops would aid in improving my work, craft-wise, but I realized later that it was raising my political awareness. We met for workshops at the old Heritage Art Center in Cubao, QC. WOMEN also organized December visits to the Bicutan detention center, where I met Satur Ocampo and his comrades. On the blackboard was scrawled "Sison's Greetings," a reference to Jose Ma. Sison, the top political prisoner of the time and one of the founders of the outlawed Communist Party of the Philippines. The common toilets and baths had been scrubbed clean in time for WOMEN's visit. As for the double-decker cots and the prisoners' few worldly possessions, they were arranged neatly.

The atmosphere was convivial, as though it was one big get-together of kindred spirits. Only as we were about to leave and there was a community singing of "Bayan Ko" did it hit me how these prisoners didn't deserve to be where they were. There was something about the prisoners' collective mien: there was no pain or bitterness written on their faces. As one of the WOMEN members put it, it was as though the men had been through a cleansing rite, given the ordeals they'd gone through. Hence their ascetic look. Such was their appreciation of our visit that they gathered by the bolted and heavily guarded gate, waving their hands or clenching their fists until the van that ferried us away disappeared from their view.

What I found strange was that the prisoners from the Light-a-Fire Movement, who were identified as Social Democrats and who occupied the ground floor of the detention center, didn't mingle with the prisoners identified with the National Democratic Front (NDF). It seemed that they were not on speaking terms. We only saw and met the Light-a-Fire prisoners when they emerged from their silence as we prepared to leave.

As one raised to be a good Catholic girl, I thought I was fulfilling what Christ the King had said in Matthew 25:37–40:

> Then the righteous will answer him, "Lord, when did we see you hungry and feed you, or thirsty and give you something to drink? When did we see you a stranger and invite you in, or needing clothes and clothe you? When did we see you sick or in prison and go to visit you?" The King will reply, "Truly, I tell you, whatever you did for one of the least of these brothers and sisters of mine, you did for me." (NIV)

Duty done, I gave myself a pat on the back.

Aquino Assassination

That is, until former Sen. Benigno "Ninoy" Aquino Jr. was so blatantly assassinated. To me, that was the catalyzing event that truly woke me up, along with maybe hundreds of thousands of what the historian Fe B. Mangahas called "the Middle Forces." The assassination was just so dastardly – the height of *kababuyan*,[4] as a friend described its shoddy execution. No, to me it wasn't enough just to be Little Miss Goody Two Shoes. When the flatbed truck carrying Aquino's coffin passed by South Superhighway on its way to

---

4. Meaning like the behavior of a dirty swine.

the Manila Memorial Park, I again stood at the sidelines shouting, as though promising the slain oppositionist, "*Ibagsak ang rehimeng Marcos!*"[5]

Months before, Jerry Araos, sculptor, carpenter and former political prisoner who had links with the underground (UG) resistance, tried to recruit me to their cause. I had declined, explaining that I was basically a pacifist and was not in favor of a violent overthrow of the regime. I had a personal low tolerance of bloodletting. Besides, there was that sixth commandment to follow: "Thou shalt not kill."

Jerry didn't persist, but I opened the door to other forms of help. So he'd contact me when, for example, a pregnant underground worker needed a safe house. I'd also ask for the assistance of trusted friends in these "missions." One time, however, after I asked a co-worker, who I thought I could trust, if he could help find me a safe house, I was told to my face, "Aren't you afraid that you're being used?"

That did it! Sore with disappointment that my good intentions were being misread, I brooded over those remarks and examined my life so far. After a night of tossing and turning, I came to a decision. The term "comfort zone" wasn't in vogue yet, but I was of a mind that I should maybe step out of that zone, maybe begin truly to live, albeit a little dangerously; to take risks where I had hardly done before. The prospect was tantalizing. Thus far, I realized, I had had a sheltered life, a fortunate one, too; I had, in a way, to spread the blessings.

I contacted Jerry and told him I was ready to embrace a more radical course of action. He was like an elder brother to me. He had tried to convince me to go "more UG than the average UG" – whatever that meant. Maybe it meant I would be protected somehow, or I wouldn't be on the radar of the military. This was after he had dropped me off at Farmers' Market in Cubao, Quezon City, after dinner one evening at his house at UP Village.

Things moved fast. As a prelude to my exposure-immersion, I met a couple of Jerry's comrades at his home. They interviewed me on my background and skills. I felt uncomfortable; their line of questioning made me think that coming from a petit bourgeois background was something to be ashamed of, apart from the fact that I lacked experience in resistance work.

One senior comrade, however, was more understanding, assuring me that the movement was made up of human beings and that I should be forgiving if human mistakes were committed.

By February 1984, I was aboard a Philippine Airlines flight to Cebu under a false name. From Cebu, a comrade and I boarded a ship that took us to Cagayan

---

5. "Bring down the Marcos regime!"

de Oro. The rough waters ensured no sleep. After reaching Cagayan de Oro, I was taken to the United Church of Christ office where, after a thorough bath to remove the dust and tiredness of travel, I buckled down to edit documents. Later, the pastor's wife inquired if I felt "oppressed" because she had put me to work immediately. I told her that that was what I was there for: to be useful.

I lived with the pastor's family for a few days before moving to an apartment where a couple and a deaconess were staying. I cooked our meals and washed my own clothes. A few days later, I was told to prepare clothes enough for a week in a carry-all shoulder bag. The comrades were all my teachers. I was a wide-eyed innocent, so when I was asked what identification papers I had on me, I fished out from my wallet my membership card in Imee Marcos's Experimental Cinema of the Philippines. The comrade assigned to me smiled broadly and said it was the perfect cover. In case I ran into police inspectors along the highway, I could always say I was a documentary film writer.

No other information was given on where we were headed. My journal from the period got lost in the frequent changes of address, but editor Ester Dipasupil managed to run excerpts from it in *Sunday Malaya* magazine in 1984. I recall travelling by day in a bus, jeep and on a motorcycle, and by night on foot through rain and mud. My sneakers would be yanked out every time my feet sank into the mud, delaying our trek. I swore so many times that it became a joke among the trekkers, especially with the leader. By this time I was assigned the assumed name of Aida.

NPA Camp

Later, when we reached the New People's Army camp in a forested area, the team leaders compared notes about how the first-timers like me were faring. One leader said his young member must be a *señorita* because she kept exclaiming "*Puñeta!*"[6] My leader said I was from another class because of my frequently uttered swear words during the journey.

But it's a small world. I saw the familiar face of photographer Alex Baluyut who, before the word "embedded" was in vogue, was closely following the NPA with his camera. We had neighboring hammocks, and when we had run out of things to talk about, we passed his nail clippers between us to trim our finger and toe nails.

I must've been at the camp for at least ten days. There I learned to bathe in the open air in a stream with armed guards whose backs were turned against

---

6. This is a Spanish curse word; used by upper classes.

us women. What was more difficult was taking a poop in holes dug in the ground. When one squatted, there were flies buzzing about. I was constipated throughout that period of immersion and exposure.

Our shared meals were rice and salt, sometimes with small green or red chilies, sometimes with the rarer *tuyo*.[7] One time, someone opened a big can of Skyflakes crackers. The contents were rationed among us with no seconds for anyone. Food that I had always taken for granted was precious. There was even a young soldier with the *nom de guerre* of Habagat, nicknamed Habbie, who requested me to think of him when I left the forest and bought a bottle of Royal Tru-Orange. He said to drink it with him in mind and make a toast to freedom.

In the forest I heard the "Internationale" sung in commemorative rites for the comrades who perished when the MV *Doña Cassandra* sank in November 1983. The voices came from a more elevated part of the forest, and the hair on my arms rose as the singers reached the chorus:

> *Ito'y huling paglalaban*
> *Magkaisa nang masaklaw*
> *Ng Internationale*
> *Ang sangkatauhan.*[8]

Visitors like me picked up information on a need-to-know basis. It wasn't my business to be an inquisitive reporter. I just did what I was told, then kept my ears peeled for info like that about the nun who served as treasurer of the NDF Mindanao. She was one of the *Cassandra* casualties. The bank passbook had been with her at the time of the sea accident.

In the same place somewhere in Agusan del Sur, I also ran into Roz Galang, who had preceded me by a few years at my former workplace, PCF. I knew it was her when she inquired about my colleagues, from Amadis Ma. Guerrero to Vic Tirol. I had heard stories about how she had been released from political prison, then worked at PCF for a while, before deciding to go underground again. Vic helped her get as much pay as possible from her vacation and sick leaves from PCF.

Roz became my "supervisor" for the tasks I did in Mindanao that had me traveling with her from Cagayan de Oro until she "settled" me in Davao City. She asked me to go over the political news and feature stories printed in the booming alternative media (*Malaya, We Forum, Signs of the Times, Veritas*) and

---

7. Dried fish.

8. This is the end of battle; unite so the scope of the international, spans the whole of humankind.

sum these up further in précis form. I worked for a week, at the end of which she picked up these typewritten summaries, folded them several times, sliced a sanitary pad lengthwise and inserted the rolls of paper into it.

I was able to make a return trip to Manila to succor a friend who was going through a marital crisis. I took this chance to solicit goods (medicines, prenatal vitamins and secondhand clothes) for the members of the house collective and for the comrades in the forest. I filled up a *balikbayan*[9] used box that my family and donors, including a godmother who owned a hospital, thought was going to a Christian mission in the south.

Members of my collective were surprised when, on Sundays, I'd dress up for Mass. One of them even suggested that if I wanted to persist in this practice, instead of going to the neighborhood's parish church in Barrio Obrero, I'd be better off visiting the Redemptorist Church where the priests gave more progressive homilies. She called the priests there "Reds" for short. I went there one Sunday but was late for Mass – the people were streaming out. I went around the church and found a small side chapel. There I prayed and meditated, treasuring my brief solitude away from collective life.

Alone in the chapel, conversing with my Creator, I felt my soul soothed. I felt that I had a conversation partner I could be at home with. In my collective I was the odd person out, the one who had not yet fully studied and imbibed Marxist-Leninist-Maoist thought. I asked God for relief from these feelings of "ideological inferiority."

In Davao, Roz introduced me to Jinky Yap, who would later go on to head Gabriela, a radical women's organization named after Gabriela Silang, a famous heroine of the revolution against Spain. My new assignment was to help her put out a feminist newsletter. With time on my hands, my tendency to brood or overthink got the better of me. I missed my family and the friends I could be thoroughly open with. In a collective setting, I felt I had to be careful about what I said in case I betrayed my true self too much. Soon I was sinking into depression. I feared it would turn to something graver with my history of depressive episodes, so I deemed it time to leave.

My boyfriend Rolly sent me my airfare back to Manila. After a brief recuperating period in my grandmother's home in Baguio, I returned to work. The voice of conscience could not be stilled, however. Comrades called to see me and asked for support – for safe houses or a meeting place. I even offered our own Pasig home for meetings.

---

9. *Balikbayan* is our term for our overseas workers scattered abroad, who have the famous habit of sending home a huge box of goodies during Christmas or special occasions; you can see these *"balikbayan* boxes" being checked-in at any airport where Filipinos are passengers.

Once, I handed over my spare front door key to Rolly's and my first home in Antipolo to an officer of the National Democratic Front. I couldn't refuse him. There was a need inside me to be useful to something higher than myself. It was one way to combat my melancholy nature. It was another way to glimpse the glory of the Kingdom in the unlikeliest of ideologies.

People Power

During the snap elections of 1986, my now-husband Rolly and I decided to follow the Left's call for a boycott. We believed in the Leftist analysis of the situation: that Corazon Aquino did not represent deep change but a possible restoration of the old oligarchy. It was a decision we quickly regretted as People Power took form in February 1986.

But still, Rolly had joined an anti-Marcos newspaper, the revived *Manila Times*. On the second day of People Power, I told my parents I was going to join the people on EDSA (Epifanio de los Santos Ave.) who were supporting the coup plotters against Marcos. By then I was a breastfeeding mother of an eight-month-old baby. I promised that I would be back in time for the next feed.

My sister Suzy and I bought packs of dinner rolls for the soldiers holed in at Camp Aguinaldo. We walked the length of EDSA, from where Robinson's Galleria now stands to the military camps and back. There was no crushing crowd but hundreds of people freely milling about outside the camps' gates. Suzy stepped on a live ember from the previous night's bonfire and had to get emergency treatment from a parked ambulance. That was what personally made the walk back and forth along EDSA memorable: Suzy's limping home.

Two days later, when news broke that the Marcos family had fled for Hawaii, the family joined in the nation's euphoria. Rolly had to sleep in the newspaper office to keep tabs on the unfolding story.

I've told confidantes how I wish I had had more youth and reckless foolishness to waste; then I might have had more to give. I was so busy being a dutiful daughter who was grasping at some form of financial and emotional stability, a poet trying to find her own voice, a wife and a mother, that I might have missed the chance to do more for the cause of justice. Perhaps I'm being too harsh on myself. But as for regrets, there are few, if none at all. Like many, I responded to a "call of the times," a call to put our convictions to work. And when one responds to that call, there can be no regrets.

2

Life under Authoritarianism

Why It Should Never Happen Again

Mary Racelis

It was the morning of Saturday, 23 September 1972. My Ateneo students and I had assembled by the gate along Katipunan Road awaiting a jeepney that would take us on a field trip to a community development project in an urban poor neighborhood. If it had been ordinary times, they would have been chatting and cracking jokes. But it wasn't ordinary times. We had awakened that morning to radio and television sets mysteriously silent. Was there a brownout? Why the eerie silence? What was going on?

The news erupted soon enough: President Marcos had declared martial law! Fear and alarm quickly took over since we did not know what to anticipate. I encouraged the students to go home as quickly as possible, while I returned to my office at the Ateneo's Institute of Philippine Culture to find out more from my faculty colleagues there.

The next six years, 1972–1978, dramatized the full meaning of what self-serving one-man authoritarian rule meant: the flagrant violation of civil and political rights, denial of the rule of law, governance by personal fiat and the crushing of democracy. Words like detention, torture and salvaging entered whispered conversations. Marcos's cronies took full advantage of their closeness to power to marginalize or eliminate competitors and augment their own personal wealth. It was a terrible time.

For many like me, martial law came across in different ways depending upon one's situation at any one particular time. In my academic roles, I faced it in the classroom and in my research on urban poor neighborhoods; I also faced it in my connections with community organizing NGOs as a staunch defender of human rights; and I faced it, not least, as wife, mother and daughter.

At the Ateneo, I continued teaching, doing research and working with NGO and community groups on the Tondo Foreshore in the midst of student protests, sham elections, summary searches and arrests, and ever destabilizing happenings. Personal relief came in 1978 when my children, my parents and I were able to leave the country for the USA, where I took a position in New York with UNICEF and later in its Kenya Regional Office. Fourteen years later, in 1992 and long after EDSA People Power, I came home for good.

This, then, is my account of the fateful years from 1972 to 1978 living under the Marcos dictatorship. Although my fourteen-year self-imposed exile away from the Philippines distanced me from events in the country, frequent communication and home leave every two years enabled me to keep in touch with friends and kin and to catch up with what was happening there. Returning in 1992 to become the country director of the Ford Foundation's Manila office meant re-engaging with longtime NGO and academic friends now heading government and civil society initiatives, as well as many new and younger movers and shakers on the Philippine development scene.

Reflecting on those years now, nearly a half century since the declaration of martial law and thirty-two years since EDSA's 1986 People Power, what lessons come to mind? Can the martial law experiences of my generation offer meaningful insights for today's young Filipinos poised to chart our nation's future?

Academic Dis-ease

After the first shock of dead radio and television stations had subsided and we had gotten used to the dizzying array of changes thrust upon us every single day, the "new normal" offered a certain stability. The patterns of governance – or misgovernance – were emerging. Some predictability was possible as to how one should operate in the context of a complex political reorganization. For most, that meant keeping one's head down and watching what one said publicly. Arrests of prominent political and economic leaders along with activists tagged as "Communists" continued. Trucks packed with armed military men became a common sight on the streets, along with experiences like waking up every day to the radio playing the *Bagong Lipunan* (or New Society) March.

One sociology alumnus and a former student of mine who was now a powerful person in the Marcos Administration invited key social scientists, mostly from Ateneo and the University of the Philippines (UP), to do research that would strengthen the government's social development programs. Many of the fifteen to twenty scholars who attended the meetings at the start did so for fear that their absence might condemn them as being uncooperative. During the course of a sumptuous breakfast week after week, the project director outlined the incentives: "Take a community, or any number of communities, to explore development options you want to test. Focus on your favorite theories. Money is no problem. We can fund whatever you propose."

I was appalled at this social engineering approach bordering on the unethical, and so managed to stall him at subsequent meetings. That turned out to be the major strategy of the academic participants: appear to be interested and discuss the various subjects he raised, but never reach any conclusions that would get an actual research project underway. It reminded me of James Scott's description of the weapons of the weak as everyday forms of resistance. His "foot-dragging strategies of the peasant" applied to us! Do just enough to get by with your boss, but not enough to produce anything significant along the lines he wishes.

Some five to ten meetings later, the numbers had dwindled down to a handful. I too joined the ranks of participants giving some kind of excuse – health problems, family needs or heavy academic workloads – to explain why we really could not continue attending those sessions. It was becoming apparent that unless you opted for the underground, you simply had to pretend to comply with the authorities, but you could in the process find unobtrusive ways of undermining the oppressor regime. When martial law ended many years later, the government project official found himself largely ostracized from the ranks of his fellow social scientists whom he had hoped to co-opt for his social engineering drive.

Classes nonetheless got underway, research plans were finalized and office staff carried out their normal routines. The student body was fragmented. Activists continued to agitate, with some disappearing into the ranks of the underground. Most continued their studies, trying to make sense of the political situation and devise less open ways of protesting which would not land them in detention centers. Others effectively stood back, held their breath, kept their heads down and tried to remain uninvolved and thus undetected.

I was particularly shaken by learning at the outset that some of my faculty colleagues were viewing martial law with cautious optimism. Strongman Marcos might after all restore discipline in the populace, they said, so that assisted by top-level technocrats, he would spur the government to move forward with the New Society's development agenda. "Let's wait and see," they counseled. Others on the faculty, however, adamantly rejected authoritarian rule and the crushing of democracy.

Fear became the dominant emotion of the day, with self-censorship as one outcome. What if during one of your lectures you made a comment that someone in your class – the child of a government or military official, perhaps – might interpret as critical of the government, causing him or her to report you? Although the University of the Philippines faculty were far more susceptible to that scenario since government officials and military personnel were more likely to be enrolled there, one was never certain, even at the Ateneo. There were also outside public lectures to give that called for self-censorship.

Having been invited to talk about Philippine rural society at the National Defense College of the Philippines – an invitation which I was afraid to refuse – I had to figure out how to talk about social class without appearing to be Marxist! Instead, I maneuvered through the patron–client discourse and functionalist analyses of Philippine values like *utang na loob*, *hiya* and *awa* (reciprocity, shame/shyness and pity or mercy). Those ideas were safe.

Public speaking in any lecture hall under martial law meant operating in a dual-think mode. One of my voices would be speaking to the audience; the other, silent voice was quietly checking on what my speaking self was saying. Could that last sentence be misconstrued and deemed subversive by some hidden enemy? The same double-think applied to telephone conversations. If someone were listening, might he or she detect something dangerous in my statements? This subtle self-surrender to an oppressive political environment became routine.

Only when our Filipino NGO delegation met on the steps of the University of British Columbia library at the 1976 UN Habitat meeting in Vancouver and began whispering the latest news from home did we realize what we were doing. All of us burst out laughing. "Why are we whispering? We are in Canada!"

Being on the Ateneo faculty in those days was affirming, but also sometimes problematic. Affirming to the activists among us was the theology of liberation developed in Latin America by Gustavo Gutiérrez of Peru, Leonardo Boff of Brazil and other Latin American theologians. They represented the alternative Catholic paradigm to Marxist ideology in condemning mass poverty and injustice, advocating a preferential option for the poor and prioritizing grassroots initiatives and action. Further influence on this rethinking came from *Pedagogy of the Oppressed* by Brazilian Paolo Freire, who saw the poor acting as co-creators of knowledge and praxis.

Activist Catholic priests, nuns, bishops and laity in the Philippines played significant roles in disseminating this new thinking. The language of oppression pointed to systemic sin in the structures of society that enabled elites to create and sustain poverty. To counter this evil, basic Christian communities or grassroots groups drew on the Bible as the framework for establishing their right to gain access to food, water, sanitation and electricity, and to basic services like health and education, and to have their voices heard. Organizing themselves to confront power nonviolently was key. Any similarities with Marxism quickly disappeared in the theology of liberation's rejection of violence and the concept of overthrowing the state, all the while maintaining a belief in God as central to the human presence on earth.

This religiously framed orientation took a political cast in that many Ateneo students and faculty with Jesuit support defined themselves as Social Democrats, or SocDems, in contrast to the Marxist-linked National Democratic Front, or NatDems, associated with our University of the Philippines counterparts. This opened the Ateneans to taunts of being *burgis* (bourgeois) and "clerico-fascists" out of step with the cries of the day – *feudalismo*, *capitalismo* and *imperialismo*. The battle lines fell into place between the Ateneo SocDems and the UP NatDems, even as each anti-Marcos set continued its grassroots mobilizing and teach-ins among labor groups and the rural and urban poor.

Much as I admired the Jesuits as intellectuals in the academic world and social action activists, especially in their Mindanao parishes, the more pragmatic side of Jesuit decision-making sometimes fazed me.

Soon after martial law was declared, two Ateneo professors, Dr Bienvenido L. Lumbera and Dr Dante C. Simbulan, went into hiding. When they did not return to their posts within the specified time, they were dismissed. As both were being hunted by the Marcos Administration because of their alleged ties with the Communist Party, a number of faculty members felt it unreasonable of the university to have demanded their return and fired them for noncompliance. Their supporters suspected that the stringent conditions stemmed from the university's unwillingness to tolerate faculty members suspected of having actively promoted Marxist thinking in the classroom. As the faculty representative on the board of trustees, I felt that their political orientations had to take a second place to their rights as faculty members in the context of academic freedom. My confrontational posture did not endear me to the Ateneo administration under President Jose A. Cruz, S.J. In the end, his views, supported by most members on the board of trustees, prevailed. Simbulan and Lumbera were out.

Lumbera was subsequently captured and imprisoned, and upon his release was warmly welcomed into the University of the Philippines faculty. The Ateneo thus lost its distinguished literature professor. In 1993, as a UP faculty member, Bienvenido Lumbera received the Ramon Magsaysay Award for Journalism, Literature and Creative Communication Arts, and in 2006 he was named National Artist for Literature. His ties of friendship with the Ateneo were, however, restored when in 2000 the university bestowed on him its Tanglaw ng Lahi Award. The designation recognized him as a person who had dedicated his life's work to the pursuit of Filipinism and the Filipino identity through literature and the arts.

As for Fr Jose A. Cruz, S.J., a Jesuit colleague told me many years later that as university president, Fr Cruz had wanted me dismissed too for my strong advocacy on behalf of Simbulan and Lumbera. Fortunately, a number of my Jesuit friends resisted that proposal and won.

Other sources of unease came from the apparent closeness of Fr Cruz as the university president to Ferdinand Marcos. Earlier, President James F. Donelan, S.J., a favorite of Imelda Marcos, had accepted her offer of a substantial scholarship fund donation to the Ateneo. The trade-off came in her protégé, pianist Van Cliburn, being awarded an honorary PhD at a special university convocation. Although again I objected to that proposal at the board, I was overruled. While accepting scholarships to support bright but poor students was surely a worthy aim, having to tolerate Mrs. Marcos's preening at being feted by the Jesuit university was, for me, too much. Incredibly, the welcome committee asked me as the faculty trustee and only woman on the board to present a bouquet of flowers to Mrs. Marcos upon her arrival for the ceremony. I promptly dismissed that request as repugnant and informed the administration that I was boycotting the event, which I did.

My antipathy toward Mrs. Marcos stemmed not only from her role as wife to the dictator but also from her own exasperatingly grandiose ambitions. As the social development member of PROS, an interdisciplinary planner group of architects, an engineer, a finance manager and a public administration specialist, I was called upon to join them when Mrs. Marcos summoned us to explore land development options for low-income Filipino households. The indignity of having to breathe in clouds of dust as her helicopter landed on the construction site while we respectfully awaited her below was anathema to me.

As the PROS architects were among her favored groups, that entailed having to endure time and again her two- to four-hour-long perorations on the City of Man. Her illustrations included drawing one vast modern development landscape in ever-expanding circles that extended from Manila on the South China Sea to Infanta on the Pacific coast. At the same time, she had no compunctions about fencing off informal settlement communities in

Metro Manila so they would remain unseen when participants of her large international conferences arrived in the city.

With hindsight, what I considered to be my principled stands vis-à-vis Jesuit decision-making may have been a shade naïve and triumphalist considering what intricate paths the Jesuit leadership had to negotiate in those days. My outspoken criticism of actions taken by them generated a tense relationship with the university president, Fr Jose A. Cruz.

Take, for example, the latter's reference that he wrote for me in connection with UNICEF's offer to me of a position in New York in 1977. The organization had asked him for a letter of reference, and he sent this directly to UNICEF. Years later, when staff members were allowed to examine their personnel files, I discovered his letter. Although he had given me fairly satisfactory ratings, I was chagrined to learn that he had ended his comments with something like, "However, Mrs Hollnsteiner [my then name] can sometimes be a problem." Fortunately, UNICEF did not take that detrimental statement seriously and recruited me anyway.

Only after I returned to the Ateneo in 2000 did I learn that Fr Cruz had been able to wield his considerable influence with Malacañang to get many individuals released from detention and to receive other favors granted by the dictatorship. He and I made our peace.

The political confrontations tearing society apart affected other groups on campus, including the Jesuits themselves. There were those passionately advocating grassroots social action and those favoring more sober academic approaches to understanding social reality. In 1969, Fr Frank Lynch, S.J., Resident Consultant of the Institute of Philippine Culture (IPC), was approached by the director of the Jesuit Institute of Social Order to undertake an exploratory study of the conditions of workers on the Negros sugar plantations. As the IPC director, I consulted our Policy Committee and got their support. Fr Lynch then met an inter-sectoral group in Bacolod, which included the bishop and representatives of government, education, labor and the planters. The National Federation of Sugarcane Planters (NFSP) agreed to fund a social science assessment of human conditions among the 320,000 workers whose livelihoods depended on sugar. The study would pinpoint the problem areas on the plantations and with additional data suggest ways of reforming inappropriate management and other practices so as to improve the lives of the workers.

Attacks from the Left citing sugar planters as the most oppressive elites in the Philippines questioned the credibility of this kind of research, especially when paid for by the sugar planters. Lynch affirmed the validity of establishing better relations on the plantations, insisting that many of the sugar planters were genuinely interested in that prospect. Moreover, he had the support of various concerned stakeholders in the area. While he explained that he would have discussions with the Survey Advisory Committee and various planters during the research to provide useful feedback and gain further insights into the data, the content of the report and its publication rights remained entirely in IPC hands. His task was to frame the problem as a need to benefit the workers, gather empirical data and report it accurately, and discuss it with all stakeholders with the intention of improving the conditions of thousands.

The resulting publication, *A Bittersweet Taste of Sugar*, revealed among many important findings that the larger and longer-established plantations tended to offer their workers better terms and conditions. The problem plantations turned out to be the smaller, often fly-by-night operations which took advantage of their workers in various ways. It was clear that the NFSP had to police its own ranks and weed out or pressure its offending members to change their ways in the interests of the workers and the industry itself.

At almost the same time, seminarian Arsenio "Jun" Jesena, S.J. published his report in a Manila newspaper on his weeks of having lived and worked alongside migrant sugarcane workers, or *sacadas*. He recounted harrowing stories of their poverty and maltreatment, and denounced their inhumane working and living conditions. A small war broke out on campus, mainly among the Jesuits themselves, dividing the supporters of Jesena and Lynch. The lay faculty mostly stayed back, perhaps remembering the African proverb that when elephants fight, it is the ants on the ground that get trampled. The divide stemmed from the undercurrent of animosity between those who favored social action versus the academic approach. The former insisted that Jesena's firsthand qualitative report told the real story; the academically inclined stressed the empirically solid results of the Lynch study, not least because Lynch was a highly regarded social scientist.

The martial law counter-rhetoric of *feudalismo* and *capitalismo* entered the scene in portraying Jesena as giving eloquent witness to elite oppression of the poorest. Lynch did not attack his Jesuit brother, recognizing that experiential accounts like Jesena's brought important and emotionally compelling insights into the situation. For widespread changes on the institutional level and policy reform purposes, however, research utilizing large-scale surveys and extensive key informant interviews was necessary. To achieve these aims, Lynch discussed the findings extensively with the planters and local groups, focusing on the changes that were needed toward better lives for thousands of sugar workers.

Ideological differences also emerged in controversies between the Ateneo de Manila and the University of the Philippines. These surfaced dramatically in the IPC research on the Tasaday people soon after they came to the world's attention in 1971. Then Presidential Assistant on National Minorities (PANAMIN) Manuel "Manda" Elizalde prevailed upon Robert Fox of the National Museum to become part of a team studying this recently discovered "Stone Age People." Fox encouraged Lynch to join, starting with a visit to the cave. In the months following, they brought in a varied group of specialists – anthropologists, a biologist, a linguist and other scientists – striving to establish who the Tasaday were and whether they had indeed been isolated for centuries from other people in the forest. The scientists exercised great care in describing their findings, concluding that the Tasaday had mostly remained isolated for some 150 years, living a hunting and gathering life which had only recently been enhanced by the introduction of metal tools brought in by a neighboring resident. To label them a "Stone Age" tribe was patently misleading, however.

Manda Elizalde nonetheless had his own ambitions, including fame and, some alleged, underlying intentions to exploit, with the support of Marcos and his cronies, the mining and logging potentials of the land. Despite strong protests from the scientists, Elizalde brought in a range of celebrities, like actress Gina Lollobrigida and air hero Charles Lindbergh. They in turn dramatized his sensational "Stone Age discovery" worldwide. Fox and Lynch both withdrew in disgust some months after they had started, and the area was closed off to visitors except for Elizalde and retinue.

The bitter controversy erupted a decade and a half later in 1986, when European and Filipino journalists visited the cave site. Reporting that the Tasaday were not only dressed in jeans and T-shirts but that two of them reported that they had been bribed to appear primitive during the Manda times, the news of a "hoax" set off a furor in the media. Even official anthropological circles abroad joined in calls for accountability.

A small group of UP faculty of the more radical tinge seized the opportunity to discredit the Ateneo-led researchers of earlier days. Although the latter were portrayed as possibly not actually complicit in the hoax, they were seen as naïve and as having played into Elizalde's hand by describing the Tasaday as simple hunter-gatherer cave-dwelling people utilizing stone and, more recently, metal tools. The real target of this onslaught was, of course, Marcos and his crony, Manda Elizalde. Yet by association the Ateneo-linked scientists who had fastidiously studied the Tasaday in the 1970s were vilified as toadying professionals. Ironically, none of the UP clique leading the offensive against their Ateneo-led counterparts had ever visited the Mindanao site. Undertones of the NatDem–SocDem thrusts affected people's opinions.

Much later, Tasaday members confessed that they had invented the hoax story because they had been bribed to do so by a translator, apparently responding to incentives from anti-Marcos forces eager to discredit Elizalde. By trying to destroy the Tasaday and all those who upheld their authenticity, including Fr Lynch and young Filipino anthropologists Carlos Fernandez IV and David Baradas, the small but vicious anti-Marcos UP faculty clique could sharpen their attacks on Elizalde and Marcos. In thinking typical of the Left, innocent individuals could be sacrificed for ideological interests. The wounds between Ateneo and UP created by the appalling events festered for many years. Only with the emergence of the next generation at both institutions have the unhappy memories of this blot on Philippine anthropology been largely buried.

The NGO World: Community Organizing and Human Rights

My entry into the world of NGO involvement with the urban poor occurred during a 1960s St Patrick's Day celebration organized by the then predominantly Irish-American Jesuits. Standing on the high school terrace, glass in hand, gazing in awe at the stars above and the lights of the Marikina Valley below, I noticed Denis Murphy, S.J. approaching.

"Happy St Pat's," came the greeting, followed by, "Mary, I want to invite you to join the board of PECCO." The Philippine Ecumenical Council on Community Organization, I learned, was composed of Catholic and Protestant clergy and nuns united to promote community organizing on the Tondo Foreshore. It was the first registered ecumenical group in the Philippines, so far as anyone knew, and marked a significant breakthrough in Catholic-Protestant relations.

I had come to the board's attention through published articles based on my fieldwork in an ordinary low-income Tondo neighborhood not far away. PECCO was expanding the board to bring in lay members. When I responded that I was already too overwhelmed with teaching and research tasks to consider any further outside engagements, I heard Denis counter with, "Mary, it's only one meeting every three months." With some misgivings, I agreed. Little did I know then that the "Yes" to Denis would initiate a turning point in my life.

Joining the board turned out to entail not only meetings but also immersing myself among the community's informal settlers struggling to resist ever-threatening evictions. PECCO was funding the training of Filipino community organizers, initially guided by pastor-trainer Herbert White, who had learned issue-based community organizing (CO) from American organizer Saul Alinsky of Chicago stockyards *Rules for Radicals* fame. Training entailed the CO learners' actual immersion in communities, starting with legwork and situation analysis, getting people together to discuss issues they identified, working out strategies and tactics, deciding on actions the people could undertake, role playing the likely scenarios, moving into nonviolent demand-based, conflict-confrontation action modes, reflecting on victories or defeats, and retooling for the next round.

What kind of research was I supposed to do? Denis clarified that I simply needed to be present, to listen and to learn. Perhaps I could make some suggestions in the organizing process if my opinion was sought. The new research reality, I realized, was that I should not attempt to speak for the people by playing the traditional role of academic researcher speaking about and publishing my findings on them. Rather, the people should represent themselves, with me in some way facilitating the process of their articulating their voices. The people were the experts on their lives, not I.

The tables were turned. Organized as ZOTO, or the Zone One Tondo Organization, a people's organization or PO, community members themselves established the frameworks out of which they would articulate their concerns, do their own analyses of data building on their indigenous knowledge and experience, and integrate information and insights gained from outside contacts. So that was what "praxis" in the theology of liberation was all about, I soon realized!

My intense admiration for poor people's capacities to organize around their interests grew exponentially over the coming months, and indeed continues to this day. Initially guided by community organizers (COs), who later became the Filipino trainers, the POs tackled "simpler" issues like demanding more public water taps and the city's hiring of ZOTO workers for construction projects. Gaining greater confidence through the experience of planning and follow-up action, they demanded a moratorium on evictions, secure tenure, onsite upgrading of their settlements, a health center on the premises, and more. Their effective resistance of the government's plan to resettle them outside the city despite many often violent attempts resulted in the government's eventually backing down. ZOTO confirmed that residents would remain onsite but would go through a re-blocking process for a more livable environment. They located additional land nearby to accommodate the overflow population displaced by roads and public spaces.

Crucial in their newfound resolve was the role of several priests from the Pontifical Institute for Foreign Missions (PIME), in particular, Frs Gigi Cocquia, Francesco Alessi and Joseph Vancio. Setting up a chapel right next to the dumpsite, they activated the praxis tenets of liberation theology. By enabling rather than instructing or preaching, they encouraged the people to incorporate their spirituality and prayer as central to their lives and actions. Participation in church events became intrinsic to people's community organizing actions. These priests later affirmed that they had learned what God meant by listening and being with the people. It came as no surprise when the two Italians among them were deported soon after the declaration of martial law.

It was mind-blowing to realize that ZOTO had the capacity, assisted by PECCO community organizers, to create clever nonviolent and successful confrontational strategies even under martial law. It was inspiring to see usually marginalized people realize their strengths in carefully planned democratic and collective efforts. My identification with their struggles led to a consultancy in the World Bank-supported Ministry of Human Settlements' onsite upgrading and nearby relocation process for the Tondo Foreshore. My tasks entailed participating in, designing, carrying out and analyzing the results of a survey of this largest informal settlement in Southeast Asia. In partnership with ZOTO through PECCO, I was supporting ZOTO's views in their negotiations with government. I felt like a double agent.

This ambivalence came to the fore at the United Nations Habitat International Conference on Human Settlements in Vancouver, Canada, in 1976. As part of the NGO delegation to the People's Forum, I gave a public presentation on the situation of the urban poor in the Philippines. This entailed a critique of government resettlement policies and their failure to address the real needs of thousands of urban poor families. I had often given that lecture in the Philippines, but as I left the hall, a Filipino political scientist friend warned me to watch out when I returned home. I had, after all, criticized the government in public abroad. "But," I protested, "I didn't say anything that I haven't said many times in Manila!" "Ah, but you're in Canada, and you are washing the government's dirty linen in public. That's different."

Sure enough, while no repercussions occurred immediately upon my return, I soon discovered that I was no longer receiving notices of meetings called by the Ministry of Human Settlements about Foreshore developments. I decided I should raise this with project director General Gaudencio V. Tobias, with whom I was on good terms professionally. Our conversation revealed that one of his staff, who had been in the Vancouver audience, had reported my remarks to him. After more discussion, I believe I convinced him that such critiques were standard fare for academics and should be visualized by managers as constructive criticism aimed at improving the project.

Not long after, I received an urgent call from the office of human rights lawyers Jose Diokno, Lorenzo Tañada and Francisco "Soc" Rodrigo asking me to come by. Co-PECCO board member Teresita (Tessie) Palacios, a social work faculty member at the University of the Philippines, received the same invitation. There we learned that these distinguished lawyers were organizing the defense at a military tribunal of ZOTO leader Trinidad Herrera,[1] who had been recently arrested and tortured. Would Tessie and I, they asked, be willing to write separate statements explaining community organizing as a standard approach accepted worldwide for people's development and not identified as communist? They said we could think about it and let them know, but time was of the essence.

Tessie and I talked it over, terrified at the prospect of, in effect, testifying against the military by writing those statements. Neither of our husbands knew how involved we were with PECCO and ZOTO, considering the dangers posed by the martial law context. If they learned about our participation through publicity about the trial, we could already anticipate the recriminations and the charges of irresponsibility in our failing to consider the safety of our families.

In the end, we decided that we had to write the statements to defend Trining. It was clear to us as academics who had worked on the Tondo Foreshore that we uniquely possessed the credibility needed by the defense lawyers. We were, after all, virtually the only academics who knew Trining well and could justify the lawyers' rejection of the military's contention that people like her engaged in community organizing were communists. If we chose not to help her in this time of need, we could never return to the Foreshore or continue serving as advocates of the urban poor. Our lives would forever be clothed in shame; when the moment of truth came, we had turned away!

Looking back, I consider the article I wrote for Trining Herrera's trial the most important paper I ever produced. Tessie and I quickly submitted our contributions to the legal team. A while later they showed us the rebuttal statement of a Marcos military ally, which decried CO in far from convincing ways. The lawyers did not ask us to write counter-statements. We never found out whether our tremblingly submitted papers actually made a difference for Trining, but we always hoped that somehow we had contributed to her eventual release.

---

1. Also known as Trining, a nickname.

We unpacked the small bags organized for the week of the statement writing, removing the extra clothing, nightwear, undergarments and toothbrush and toothpaste we had hidden away from our husbands' eyes. It took months before we stopped waking up trembling at hearing cars slow down or stop in front of our houses at 2 a.m. Would the next one bring a pounding on the gate? Fortunately, that never happened – and our husbands never found out.

As martial rule continued interminably on, PECCO began to experience internal problems. Unlike the truly impressive Protestant members at the beginning – Pastors Henry Aguilan and Ramon Tiples, labor leader Cipriano Malonzo, journalist Domini Torrevillas-Suarez and missionary Richard Poethig of the Urban-Industrial Mission – the two new younger recruits appeared to be more permissive in recommending new community organizers for training. Our policy regarding the political leanings of the COs emphasized that they had the right to follow whatever political thinking they favored. We would not, however, tolerate their taking orders or running errands for the Communist Party. If we learned of such behavior, they would immediately be dismissed.

The Catholics on the board began to suspect that the more radically oriented new Protestant board members were actively encouraging young people connected with the National Democratic Front to apply. By that time, Leftist organizers were already infiltrating the Foreshore and influencing residents to adopt more open protest actions. ZOTO leader David Balondo resisted these moves and was murdered in retaliation, it is believed, by the Left.

The increasing violence of some groups led to confrontations on the ground between our long-term COs and their Left counterparts. The former were seeing their years of successful nonviolent organizing efforts being consistently undermined by radical forces inciting the people to violence, inflamed by Marxist teach-ins. Inevitably, the resulting strategies brought military crackdowns and arrests. In effect, the Left reaped the harvest by taking over many of PECCO's organized networks. Our framework of "whatever people decide is what we support" could not compete with the far more structured Mao-Marxist framework.

Faced with this situation, the Catholic board members began to think about the need to dissociate themselves from the Protestant group. Denis Murphy, Sisters Victoria Pascasio and Rose Bacaltos, Fr Ted Butalid, Teresita Palacios and I recognized the importance of retaining the support of Catholic Church bishops and not jeopardizing their situations by tolerating possible NDF infiltration of our community organizer ranks. At many tense and highly emotional meetings, we argued these points and finally put the separation issue to a vote. The body was divided, and I as chair had agonizingly to cast the deciding vote.

That marked the end of PECCO. Cip Malonso wept at the dissolution of a truly ecumenical interreligious collaboration. All of us from the original membership felt equally distraught. However, there was some comfort in our agreement that in going our own way – which for the Catholics meant moving out of Manila to less dangerous provincial cities – we would continue to respect the others while still organizing people for power. Not long afterwards, the Catholic members of the now-defunct PECCO developed COPE, or Community Organization of the Philippine Enterprise, while the Protestant members created PEACE. Issue-based organizing became the template for CO as NGOs sprang up all over the country organizing communities after EDSA People Power in 1986.

Between teaching, research and continuing to work with COPE and community groups, I was comfortably settled at the Ateneo as the director of the Institute of Philippine Culture and teaching in the Department of Sociology and Anthropology. IPC had more than enough studies to keep us busy.

One day, the regional officer of the International Labor Organization came by to discuss a study on agricultural laborers that she hoped the IPC would carry out. After submitting the requested research proposal to her, we prepared the necessary contract documents. A few days later she returned, reporting that she was puzzled. Upon her routine submission of the project to the National Economic Development Authority for endorsement, the Director General had told her that, although he respected the work of the IPC and knew me well, there were some problems in having us do the study. As he was not specific about the objections, she came to ask me. I told her I was mystified.

It was then I realized that perhaps my reputation of criticizing government policies toward the urban poor was catching up with me. The regional officer very regretfully withdrew her request regarding the research. The signs were ominous. Clearly, I was becoming a liability to the IPC and future research grants. It was time to think of alternatives.

Family Concerns and Coming Full Circle

By the late 1970s, cries against the authoritarianism and violence generated by the Marcos dictatorship were mounting, although still necessarily muffled. Cronies close to the president were raking in huge corruption-supported profits and the country was suffering. Protesting, however, could bring severe reprisals.

My businessman husband, Helmuth Hollnsteiner, began to talk of leaving the country, but where to go? The only place suitable for him in the United States was California, because it was warm and offered good job prospects; but that was also the state with hippies and drugs – not a place to raise our five mostly teenaged children. Australia? Back to Austria, his country of birth? But he had become a Filipino citizen. Should I then respond positively to a query from the United Nations Children's Fund (UNICEF) in New York as to whether I would be interested in applying for a senior position there? We decided not for now.

Then, early in 1978, to my total surprise, Ministry of Social Welfare Estefania Aldaba Lim came to my office to inform me that I had been shortlisted for her position as she was taking a job abroad. Would I agree to be considered?

I was horrified at the prospect of serving in the Marcos Cabinet and alarmed at the thought of being on the Administration's radar screen (apparently they didn't know much about the Tondo Foreshore). As a subterfuge and delaying tactic, I asked for time to think. I knew I had to find a diplomatic way of rejecting the possible offer. It was then that I contacted UNICEF to inform them that I had reconsidered and was now interested in the New York position. They soon confirmed the offer, and a few months later I became UNICEF's Senior Policy Specialist for Women's Development, Community Participation and Family/Child Welfare.

So off to New York I went with four of my children – Susanna, Lisa, Peter and Theresa – stopping in several Southeast Asian cities on the way to complete my IDRC study grant on urbanization and the urban poor. My father, Ramon Racelis, stepmother, Edita Castro Racelis, and third daughter, Karin, joined us in New York somewhat later, while my husband opted to remain in the Philippines. In 1983 UNICEF posted me to Nairobi, Kenya, to head its Eastern and Southern Regional Office, a position I held for nine rewarding years. Instituting the participatory management processes I had learned on the Tondo Foreshore brought great approval and recognition to our region as the most dynamic and creative in UNICEF. I owed it all to my urban poor and NGO community organizer friends.

Contact with the Philippines in those years came through letters and home leave. In 1986 the Philippines exploded onto the world scene thanks to the worldwide television coverage of EDSA People Power. I couldn't get through on the telephone to daughter Karin, now married and back in Manila. On the one hand, I was afraid she was at EDSA, where television footage showed tanks rumbling forth and helicopters flying menacingly overhead. At the same time, seeing what looked like millions of people on the street calling for Marcos's ouster, I thought to myself, "I'll never forgive her if she isn't at EDSA!" She was.

Many of my admiring Africa staff, desperate at being similarly under authoritarian governance in their own countries, later plied me with questions as to how Filipinos had done it – overthrown a dictator without bloodshed! How proud I was of our people and country!

In 1992, some fourteen years after my escape from the Marcos dictatorship, I came home for good, initially to serve as country director for the Ford Foundation. That enabled me to meet the next generation of amazing and enterprising NGOs, academics and government officials. After the five-year stint, I taught at the UP Sociology Department and rejoined the NGO world. The new millennium found me again at the Ateneo as IPC Director and a faculty member in Sociology and Anthropology. I was really back, having come full circle!

3

The NatDem Front

A Historian Looks Back

Fe B. Mangahas

Only be careful, and watch yourselves closely so that you do not forget the things your eyes have seen or let them fade from your heart as long as you live. Teach them to your children and to their children after them. (Deut 4:9)

Introduction

For me, the period before martial rule was a time of both intense ferment and great awakening. Under the Constitution, President Ferdinand E. Marcos was on his second and last term. Philippine elections, characterized by vote-buying, fraud and violence, had reached their limits. The atmosphere was charged with clamor for radical change and not just reforms. People were getting tired of elections with the same results: persistent graft and corruption, growing urban and rural poverty, the rising cost of living and education, unrest in the countryside and crime in the cities.

The Philippine media, reputed to be one of the most free in Asia, was exposing and debating the issues of the day, offering various solutions to the serious economic, social and political problems of the country. Central to the discussion was nationalism: how to unite the people in a common goal toward genuine democracy and effective economic development for all. Political analysts and social scientists from many colleges and universities had joined in, further exposing the bankruptcy of Philippine politics and governance, and discussing what could be done about this seemingly hopeless situation.

As a young student majoring in Philippine history at the University of the Philippines (UP) in Diliman, it was impossible for me not to be part of this ferment of nationalist consciousness. UP by then had become the center for radical ideas about social change and national liberation from corrupt politics, massive poverty and foreign intervention. The successful revolutions in China and Cuba and the ongoing war in Vietnam were held up as models for countries like ours to emulate. Our readings and fora began with the ideas of Claro M. Recto, Lorenzo Tañada and Renato Constantino. These opened my eyes to US dominance and oligarchic control of our economy, politics and national security, and to the continuing mis-education about these social realities. Later, our teach-ins progressed toward the theory and practice of radical social change by Marx, Lenin and Mao Tse-tung.

I must confess that it took me a while to accept the ideas of socialism, especially communism. As a member of UPSCA (UP Student Catholic Action), I felt that these ideas were contrary to the Christian teachings of love and nonviolence in dealing with problems, whether personal or social. However, in the midst of the social unrest and the call for radical solutions to the deteriorating conditions in the country, I began to ask myself, where was my church? (The theology of liberation had not yet influenced UPSCA in my time.) Our UPSCA activities (devotional prayers, Holy Mass, annual retreats, catechetical work, choir rehearsals and concerts, and fundraising for charitable causes) certainly warmed my heart. These activities were good, but they were somewhat detached from what was going on. In fact, these seemed to me to be very much part of the status quo which was being shaken up. I felt deeply disturbed and sad. I earnestly wanted to do something for the country.

It was SCAUP (Student Cultural Association of UP), organized by Left-leaning professors, students and writers, which exposed and drew me to the "struggle for national democracy" as conceptualized and concretized by Jose Ma. Sison, the leading light of the movement. Its framework of analysis and solutions to the Philippine problem clarified for me why our economy was in constant underdevelopment and our politics and government were so corrupt. It also proposed the kind of nationalism we should develop to address these festering and debilitating problems. There was no reference yet to the radical ideas of Marxist, Leninist or Mao Tse-tung thought. These would come later as I became more involved in the movement for national democracy.

How, then, could we change this anomalous economic and political setup? The solution lay in the transformation of the people's mindset – enabling them to acquire in the process an advanced form of nationalism called national democracy. As I understand it, national democracy is a socio-economic, political and cultural setup whereby economic resources and political power are shared across the broad sectors of society, which is possible only when the people from below are enlightened and become organized enough to put pressure on the officials and the bureaucracy to pursue a national democratic agenda.

I can now recall only vaguely what the National Democratic (ND) Ten-Point Program was like in my time (and not necessarily in the original text and sequence). The list included the following goals:

1. Assertion of one's democratic rights to freedom of ideas, peaceful assembly and redress of grievances;

2. Formation of a nationalist and pro-people's education;

3. Genuine land reform and real industrialization;

4. Support for the peasants' and workers' rights to decent working and living conditions;

5. Advocacy of an independent foreign policy;

6. Protection and preservation of the environment and natural resources;

7. Support for the indigenous people's right to their ancestral lands and way of life;

8. Promotion of the Muslim Filipino's struggle for self-determination;

9. Call for the removal of US military bases and a ban on nuclear weapons on Philippine territory; and

10. Assertion of freedom of religion and respect for other faith-based traditions.

I found these goals of the struggle for national democracy (then and even now) acceptable to the broad sectors of our society. I also found the means of pursuing these goals acceptable to the majority. As I understood it, we were to promote these objectives through legal and democratic means. We were to discuss, debate and arrive at a consensus; organize openly and act peacefully to obtain the said legitimate demands. As I recall, it was a period of vibrant consciousness-raising on the campus. At this stage I also acquired skills in organizing – the discipline, diligence and patience of an activist-in-making. I still went to the UP chapel to attend Holy Mass, pray the rosary and talk to Jesus at the tabernacle. But at the same time I began to feel uneasy listening to the parish priests' homilies, which seemed irrelevant to my recent NGO commitments. I soon lost interest and dropped out of my UPSCA activities. Unfortunately, my faith could not connect my new-found activism with the Church.

A Social Volcano about to Erupt

After graduation, and while teaching the Rizal course and Philippine history at the University of the East (UE), I became a member of KAGUMA (*Kapisanan ng mga Gurong Makabayan*, or "Alliance of Nationalistic Teachers"). This started my radicalization as a NatDem activist. My readings and study now focused on Marxist, Leninist and Mao Tse-tung thought (MLTT) and their application to the Philippine situation as articulated by Amado Guerrero in his book *Philippine Society and Resolution*. (Amado Guerrero was the *nom de guerre* of Jose Ma. Sison.) I also found out that KAGUMA as an organization was among the NGOs inside the NDF (National Democratic Front). What was radical to the term NDF (now NDFP: National Democratic Front of the Philippines) was the theory and practice of social change as revolution. The "Front" referred to the support of all oppressed sectors of society for the "national democratic revolution" to end "imperialism, feudalism and bureaucrat capitalism" under the guidance of the new Communist Party of the Philippines (CPP) and its armed group, the New People's Army (NPA).

My knowledge of these theories deepened through discussion-study groups (DGs) with leading Leftist intellectuals of the national democratic movement on the following topics: culture and revolution, women and revolution, Marxism, Leninism and Maoism. These studies were conducted after classes in private homes, in student and faculty lounges or offices, and sometimes in coffee shops or restaurants. We had a great deal of freedom of thought and space then to learn about society and revolution. I count this period in my intellectual life as one of the most exciting and enriching. Our mentors were not only brilliant but active participants in many fora, debates and rallies on and off campus.

In our study on culture I became aware that our view of the Philippine problem was shaped by those who controlled our education, media, the church and family. These institutions made us believe that the roots of our social problems were the breakdown of morality, the absence of good manners and right conduct, parental neglect of families, being rich or materialistic in values, and so on. Through Marxism, I realized that these were simply symptoms or manifestations of a deeper cause – that of the economic divisions in our society due to "imperialism," "feudalism" and "bureaucrat capitalism."

"Imperialism" referred to foreign – especially US – control of our economy (owning big capital and industries, and control of markets and labor) in alliance with Filipino big capitalists and businessmen. "Feudalism" referred to the big Filipino landlords with their vast tracts of land tilled by poor tenants. The rest of the population was made up of landless tenants, agricultural workers and middle class people: petty farm owners, small to medium entrepreneurs and industrialists. "Bureaucrat capitalism" was the control of Philippine politics and government by the rich to acquire more wealth at the expense of the majority. When violent conflict arose, the state had at its disposal the police and the military, trained and supplied with arms, mainly by the United States.

The role of education, media, the church and family in sustaining these class divisions particularly impressed me. I realized that it was through these institutions that the general population was blinded, sedated and rendered passive when faced with an economic system based on unequal distribution and use of resources through free enterprise. I was particularly struck by the role of the church and religion as the "opium of the people." Henceforth I found myself increasingly missing Sunday Mass; I readily went only when invited to weddings, baptisms and burials. I seldom prayed the rosary and hardly visited the Blessed Sacrament. I was preoccupied with my DG studies and in helping organize students and faculty members in UE who were willing to join our KAGUMA exposure trips to urban poor communities. I also urged them to participate in the intensifying urban protest movement in the "university belt" which by this time had become a center for dissent and massive demonstrations.

Leninism and Maoism, on the other hand, exposed me to the need for a revolutionary party to guide the oppressed masses and with its own army fight on to victory – just like what happened in Russia, Cuba and China, and what was going on in Vietnam. This was premised on the materialist and historical experience of past revolutionary movements whereby the enemies of the people (imperialism aligned with the big bourgeoisie: big land owners and capitalists) would not, when threatened, simply yield their hold on the economy and government without the use of counter-revolutionary force or state violence. And the most reliable force that the revolution could rely on to resist to the end was that of the working class (Lenin) and the peasants (Mao). Together, the two sectors constituted the decisive force for the victory of the people's revolution. My initial reaction to this was to ask whether armed struggle was necessary in the fight for national democracy, to which our political officer (PO) assigned in KAGUMA gave a vague reply.

The succeeding events would eventually open my eyes to state violence. The teach-ins by university professors, student activists and full-time cadres of the NDF bore fruit. The first three months of 1970, called the First Quarter Storm, signaled the widening support of the NDF. This consisted of several protest rallies by students, teachers, professionals and workers, ending at Mendiola, a few steps away from the Malacañang Palace. I remember how tear gas would often reach our classrooms close to the streets along Gastambide Street. My students and I had to bring wet towels sprinkled with *kalamansi*[1] to cover our faces. My co-faculty and I sometimes joined the rallies just outside UE where we witnessed how students hurled molotov cocktails at the police, while the police, with heavy shields and wooden clubs, would mercilessly strike down the students at close range. We all cowered in fear of getting hurt.

It was at this time that I met Roger, an instructor of Filipino language and literature, also in UE. As members of KAGUMA we helped organize the successful faculty strike for salary increases and the defense of academic freedom. We soon discovered our common interest in the arts, literature and history. In time, amidst seemingly endless ND meetings, turbulent demos and fearless confrontations with the police and school authorities, our friendship grew into mutual admiration and finally to love and marriage (shortly before the declaration of martial law). It was a strange courtship without dates of the romantic kind, only activism and commitment to a common cause keeping us busy and together for the most part.

The demonstrations which followed were bigger and more violently dispersed. Students at the militant University of the Philippines took control of the campus in a siege lasting twelve days, known as the "Diliman Commune." Violence escalated in the regions and provinces, from Baguio, Davao and Cagayan de Oro to the Mindanao State University in Lanao del Sur.

The rest is history. The social volcano finally erupted. President Marcos called for a Constitutional Convention (ConCon) to amend the Constitution. People feared that this would change the important economic provisions in the 1935 Constitution as well as change the form of government to a parliamentary one, so Marcos could run again as Prime Minister. Then the horrifying Plaza Miranda bombing took place, which practically annihilated the Liberal Party candidates running for the Senate. Marcos blamed the CPP for this carnage as part of their August Plan to topple the government. Marcos reiterated his threat of declaring martial law. Finally, on 23 September 1972, Marcos announced the imposition of martial rule under P.D. 1081 (which was actually signed on

---

1. Lemon juice.

21 September 1972). Roger and I were among nine faculty members dismissed from the university for "subversion" and other unlawful activities. We were informed that our names had been posted at the university gates with the warning written in bold letters: "for arrest and detention."

"From the Masses to the Masses"

It was not just the nine of us who lost our jobs at the university. Four of my colleagues were also "suspended" – guilty by association with us in KAGUMA. For those of us in the movement, the initial weeks of martial law were ones of fear and danger. There were so many arrests, including those of senators and other officials from the opposition, critical members of the media, student and labor leaders, and well-known activist personalities. There was no Congress, judiciary or media. Military agents (then called "Ajax") proliferated, disguised as civilians. They were all over the place: in jeepneys, restaurants, marketplaces, grocery stores – everywhere. Whenever we went out to meet secretly with our "cellmates," we made sure no Ajax was tailing us. Once, sensing an Ajax was following me, I decided to waylay him by entering Quiapo church. I stayed there for about half an hour – at peace with the world. I tried to pray, but I felt strange and at a loss about what to pray for; I could only ask in my mind: "Lord, where are you during these dangerous and anguished times?" Feeling that I had lost the Ajax, I looked around me before leaving the church. I saw the familiar sight of people praying.

Roger and I decided to join the underground (UG) life of NatDem activists. For Roger and me (a newly married couple), martial rule was like a long dark night with no ray of dawn in sight. But it was different when we were with our ideologically advanced comrades from the Party, who informed us about latest developments. They said martial rule could lead to a revolutionary situation where the national democratic forces under repression and widening violence nationwide could expand, gaining more support for the struggle.

Our UG task was to sustain the NatDem educational work among the basic sectors away from our comfort zone as petty bourgeoisie/middle class NatDem. This meant working among the most oppressed and exploited class of people: the workers, peasants and urban poor. We were also assured of the growth of the New People's Army (NPA) in the countryside due to the Marcos reactionary army's abuses and ferocious attacks on those opposing martial law. Arms were also forthcoming from the People's Republic of China. All these emboldened us to continue in the struggle; they made us hopeful despite the many dangers we faced each day.

On 19 January 1973, while on our way to a meeting with NatDem comrades, Roger and I were apprehended and brought to Camp Aguinaldo. Though tense and nervous, we managed to appear calm during the initial hours of form-filling, fingerprinting and mug shots against a blank board. Then the most terrifying moments followed. We were separated and brought to separate rooms. We lost contact and I began to imagine the worst that could happen to us: Roger being tortured, and me being harassed or even sexually molested.

I was made to wait for a few minutes for the interrogation. I waited, my heart pounding heavily. I suddenly found myself saying a short prayer: "Lord, please help us!" I answered my interrogating officer as truthfully as I could, revealing names and places already known to them. The questioning seemed to last an eternity. At one point I stiffened as I felt something flowing between my legs. I was bleeding! Crouching from fear, I cried for help. "I'm three months pregnant! Please, I need a doctor," I pleaded in panic. The interrogating officer stood up quickly to make a phone call. After what seemed ages of waiting, I boarded an army jeep which brought me home. The following morning, my sister accompanied me to RM Medical Center where I underwent DNC. I had lost our first child, and Roger was nowhere where he could be informed.

Within a year of my release I had reconnected with my NatDem cell group. I was back at work, this time among the urban poor. There I learned to get used to the heat, dirt and stench of the slums. I was shocked at the miserable life the people lived, compared to the scandalously affluent lifestyle of the rich. And yet it was through my immersion with them that I learned how generous the poor can be with the very little they have – be it food, drink or a space to stay in. I also witnessed how brave and tenacious they could be in the underground struggle, ready to sacrifice all for the cause.

From the urban poor sector, I was later assigned to help the KM (Kabataang Makabayan) cadres in their literacy program for unschooled or out-of-school workers. This meant going to the workers' UG house to review with them basic reading and writing skills in Pilipino and English.

It was a hard but rewarding task for me because it helped make them literate enough to read and understand basic documents on the rights of workers and on the necessity to organize and join labor unions. But I soon felt uncomfortable going into their UG quarters near the factory. I sensed danger especially for me: a petty bourgeois who could easily be identified as a stranger to the place. I suggested to my companion NatDem Lery that perhaps we should move to a safer location. He informed our PO about my request. It was not easy to relocate. I then asked to be replaced. It turned out that there was a need for someone to work among writers and visual artists. As I had been a music graduate before I went into history, I was assigned to the group.

But less than a week after I left the workers' cell group, my fellow NatDem activist Lery was violently attacked by a group whom the neighborhood identified as drug addicts. Comrade Lery suffered thirty stab wounds which left him instantly dead. I hardly recognized his bloated face and body during the wake. But what really pained me was the denial by my fellow co-NatDem workers that his killers were Ajax or military soldiers. They firmly believed they were drug addicts as reported. I could not comprehend their reaction. Was there a difference between being killed by addicts and by the military agents? Why belittle or demean *kasamang* (comrade) Lery's heroic death?

My next task was to help raise the level of commitment among the visual artists. This meant emphasizing the need to accept armed struggle as the primary form of the NDF struggle alongside the basic sectors of peasants and workers. With me were two comrades (full-time Party members). By this time, I had been inducted as a candidate member (CM) of the Party. In an orientation with visual artists, the first speaker talked about the real situation of the ongoing revolution. He inspired our audience with how the UG movement under the NDF was not only surviving but actually growing in strength and numbers. The second talked about the movement's need to link up the urban center with the countryside. This would require more sacrifice on our part, to the extent of those capable and willing to do so joining the armed struggle. My talk focused on what specific talents they could contribute to the call of the hour. I ended with the idea that their best weapon was their art: their paints and brushes, canvases and frames, and their paintings as their very acts of revolutionary work. This did not sit well with my co-speakers. I was soon assigned to another group – this time among researchers and political analysts.

Roger had been released a long time before I got this task. He was back trying to earn a living for us by working as a part-time life insurance agent, freelance editor, and part-time scriptwriter for television and films. We also now had a child, a boy of five years we named after Karl Marx (Karlos Tagumpay) and nicknamed Tagúm. He seemed to us a precocious child growing up with activists who took turns looking after him while we met for our monthly DGs.

I will never forget how, when he was just nine months old, I had had to hold him tight while hiding behind thick bushes. A suspicious-looking jeepney had parked in front of our house. Sensing danger, I hurriedly but gently carried him while he was still asleep to hide behind our UG house where the bushes were thick, so the three men in the jeepney would think there was no one at home. I remember praying hard for God to keep Tagúm quiet and asleep.

After nearly one hour of hiding in the bushes, with heart pounding loudly throughout, I breathed a sigh of relief when the jeepney finally left. I feared these moments more for Tagúm than for Roger and me. UG life was no life for children born under martial rule.

This was the reason why I readily accepted the task to work above ground. I could live in a normal household with fewer risks. The research was to be about the middle class in Philippine society and its role in the national democratic revolution. By the early 1980s the violence of the Marcos dictatorship had reached its height due to the expansion of the UG resistance. The NDF thought of conducting a study on the middle class which, by this time, had also emerged as a force to reckon with. The Opposition had begun organizing for the first election to be held under martial law – the *Batasang Pambansa* election.[2] Although they lost, they found the courage to speak out and hold meetings *de avance*.[3] They also discovered new forms of resisting martial rule, such as noise barrage, prayer vigils, coffee shop fora[4] and the like. At that time, the powerful cronies controlled the media, so the opposition elements would publish political tracts by copying them by Xerox, known as "Xerox Journalism." Alternative magazines surfaced, denouncing Marcos and his cronies' kleptocracy, the abusive military and the absence of free, genuine elections.

The Church, too, was waking up from its complacency. Pope John Paul II, who was in the country, was quoted in the alternative media as saying (which I can only paraphrase now): "Whenever there is conflict between the state and the basic rights of the citizenry, this should be resolved based on the principle that social organizations exist for the service of citizens and the protection of everyone's dignity. A state cannot claim to serve the common good when the citizens' rights are not safeguarded and instead are trampled upon." I wondered then whether Jaime Cardinal Sin and the rest of the hierarchy took notice of what the Pope said.

At around this time our research team had completed the middle class study commissioned by the NDF leadership. The study had two main objectives: (1) to define and determine the size of the "middle class" as distinct from the upper and lower classes in our society; and (2) to determine the political orientation and tendency of the middle class at this stage of the anti-Marcos dictatorship and fight for national liberation of the CPP-NPA-NDF. This had

---

2. National Congress election.

3. The final large meetings organized in advance by contending parties just before the election.

4. Coffee shops became places for public discourse, these being banned in the media and other usual channels of debate.

become necessary because the last data on the size and political character of classes in Philippine society had been gathered by the Left between 1965 and 1970; this had been published in the 1971 edition of Amado Guerrero's *Philippine Society and Revolution* (PSR). Based on its estimates, the members of the classes were as follows:[5]

A – 1% foreign and local big capitalists, big businesses and big landlords

B – 7% middle class

C – 90% { industrial workers, tenants, agricultural workers

At first, we had difficulty defining who were the members of the middle class. *PSR* did not define them as a class in relation to the semicolonial and semifeudal mode of production in Philippine society. It simply described their composition, political tendencies and potential role in the national democratic revolution. For instance, the middle class or petty bourgeoisie, according to *PSR*, includes the "vast majority of the intelligentsia (teachers, student youth, low-income professionals, office clerks, and lower government officials); middle peasants; small businessmen; master handicraftsmen; carpenter-contractors; fishermen with their own motorized boats and implements; and relatively well-paid skilled workers."[6]

We had problems with this definition. It seemed to us that it was not far from the existing social science definition of the middle class based on education, occupation or property as well as income and lifestyle. As one could sense, these factors would vary across the members of the middle class identified by *PSR*. We asked ourselves in the study group: Was it the level of education, skills or amount of property that accounted for one's profession or occupation and therefore one's income and lifestyle? Not necessarily. Income and lifestyle, for one, varied across the members of *PSR*'s middle class. Similarly, possession of property and levels of education and skills varied across the sectors described as middle class. For instance, must the fishermen possess motorized boats to qualify? How about those with diplomas but unable to

---

5. Amado Guerrero, *Philippine Society and Revolution* (Hong Kong: Ta Kung Pao, 1971), 240.

6. Guerrero, *Philippine Society and Revolution*, 242.

find jobs, or receiving salaries way below their professions? and so on. After much deliberation, we came up with a refined definition of the middle class.

Our study defined three types of members of the middle class based on their position in relation to production:[7]

1. Those who continue to own and work using their own means of production (to include that of skills):
    •   traditional petty bourgeoisie (PB) or small business; based on family labor or hired labor; engaged in small production, small proprietors, small shopkeepers, market stalls, corner groceries;
    •   artisans and handicraftsmen (shoes, furniture, radio and TV repairs, and others);
    •   service (owners of dress shops, tailoring, beauty parlors, massage parlors, etc.);
    •   self-employed professionals (doctors, dentists, lawyers, accountants, etc.).

2. Those who do not own their means of production but sell their labor and do not engage in production:
    •   economic: their functions are related to the distribution and sale of commodities; they include salaried professionals and employees in marketing, financial, clerical and sales;
    •   political: their work is essential in the maintenance of the conditions keeping order and harmony in civil society; they include policymakers, supervisors, managers of production, police and armed forces, government employees, executive, legislative and judicial officials, etc;
    •   ideological and cultural functionaries: their work includes generation/creation and inculcation of values essential to the smooth functioning of the production process, in maintaining the status quo. They can be found in the following institutions: family, church, school, media, arts, entertainment, etc.

3. National bourgeoisie (Filipino businessmen and landowners). They are owners of the means of production and extractors of surplus labor but because of the contradictions brought about by foreign capital, there are instances when they can unite with the other oppressed sectors or even classes in society.

7. "Middle Class Study" (unpublished document, 1980–1982), 1–2.

Based on these definitions, our study had two significant results. First, the middle class thus defined was large enough to constitute almost half of the industrial workers and agricultural workers put together (see diagram).[8]

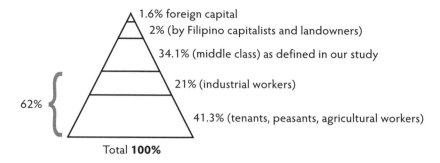

Thus, the size of the middle class was 34.1 percent, compared with 62 percent of the basic sectors of workers and peasants. But the "Findings of the Study" reported that "The size of the middle class is significant in relation to the number of the gainfully employed in the country. While much smaller, if compared to the size of the farmers and workers, still their size and number merit attention."[9]

The second result described the political character of the middle class. The "Findings" reported: "The economic condition of the middle class is deteriorating. It is increasingly becoming restive, their level of politicization and organization on the whole is still low. Repressive management and government policies block their efforts to organize themselves."[10]

Our study recommended that the "Churches and non-government institutions could direct some of their efforts and programs towards serving the Filipino middle class. They are an important component of the church of the poor. Program plans and aids could be channeled to them after making the needed adjustments in other fields of activity."[11] The NDF work, however, remained focused on the basic sectors (workers and peasants) and the primacy of armed struggle. We never asked ourselves up to what level the middle class could be politicized, or whether the middle class could act on its own for social change. Thus, we made no recommendation to politicize and organize

---

8. "Middle Class Study," 3.
9. "Middle Class Study," 4.
10. "Middle Class Study," 5.
11. "Middle Class Study," 6.

the middle class, as much of what we were doing was among the basic sectors of urban poor, workers and farmers.

From 1980 to 1981, Metro Manila, then the seat of government, was rocked by a protest movement principally from the middle class composed of professionals, media people, church people, businessmen, employees, members of the opposition parties and their constituents. This was different from the militant protest rallies from the late 1960s to the late 1970s led by the NDF composed of students, teachers, professionals, workers, the urban poor and peasants. As already noted in our middle class study, the middle class was already restive – due to the failed "economic enterprise" by Marcos as imposed by the IMF-WB and the harsh effects of dictatorial rule nationwide for almost ten years. What united the middle class was the desire to end martial rule through nonviolent means by pushing for an honest and genuine election.

Ninoy Aquino (Marcos's greatest political rival) was in the US for his heart operation courtesy of Malacañang. Marcos feared that if Ninoy died in jail, the people would blame Marcos and consider Ninoy a hero. To everyone's surprise, Ninoy decided to come home despite being warned that he would surely die in the hands of the military. He was killed as predicted. Gun shots met him as he was coming down from the plane. He fell dead on the tarmac. The whole nation was shocked, and news of the tragedy reached the rest of the world. Ninoy Aquino's wake drew thousands of sympathizers. Roger and I joined Ninoy's funeral, which was likened to a huge protest rally that took eleven hours to walk from Sto. Domingo church to the Parañaque memorial park.

The people's grief turned into rage when the Sandigan Bayan[12] ignored the results of the Agrava Commission and instead absolved the generals accused of the crime. Only the soldiers were charged and imprisoned. From then on, militant and widespread rallies openly defied the police and MetroCom. My NatDem comrades and I joined the middle class-led rallies. Side by side with the SocDems, LibDems, and so on, we bravely faced the police who were armed with tanks of water, tear gas and even guns to disperse us. This time, yellow ribbons and showers of confetti mixed with the red banners of the militant Left (the yellow ribbons were a reference to the song "Tie Me a Yellow Ribbon" popularized while Ninoy was abroad).

The NDF continued to expose the numerous violations of human rights which, according to Amnesty International, had reached 8,000 cases of "salvaging" (summary executions) and 50,000 kidnappings and disappearances.

---

12. The court where government employees accused of corruption and other malfeasance are tried.

It also listed some twenty major detention centers and safe houses (hidden quarters where suspected activists, subversives and communists were tortured). Almost every month, I heard of fellow NatDems being killed. I also noticed that more priests, nuns, pastors and church workers were in sympathy with us and the "rebels" fighting for democracy and an end to the dictatorship. Many from the religious sector, in fact, were being arrested, tortured or killed. Many women detainees were subjected to torture and rape.

My heart and mind were deeply affected by these horrifying events. More often than not I found myself in the company of "yellow" activists, especially the religious and church-based NGOs. One day I decided to join the NAMFREL (National Movement for Free Election) which was tasked to guard the snap presidential election that Marcos suddenly announced. When asked why, I finally had the courage to say what had been bothering me since the conclusion of our middle class study. I replied that I wanted to join the urban mass movement of the middle class. I no longer felt comfortable with the NDF, which to me had by then become neither national nor democratic. I felt that we, the petty bourgeois, were only part of the "Front."

My PO patiently explained why we should not take the electoral process seriously. He explained why the NDF must be faithful to the primacy of the armed struggle and reliance on the basic sectors as the vanguard of the national democratic revolution. I gently argued that for me, the road to socialism or communism was long and distant. I honestly confessed my commitment to national democracy as the transition stage and that in this the middle class had a vital role to play. Why a Front? Why not change NDF to National Democratic Forces? I must have said something terribly wrong or that was anathema to the NDF ideological framework as my PO (kind but firm in his commitment) said it was up to me, but I could no longer be part of the cell group. I could, however, remain a friend and ally of the movement. I had no reply. There was an uneasy silence followed by some small talk. Then we said our sad goodbyes.

EDSA People Power

No one ever imagined that the highway EDSA (previously called Highway 54) would play such a big role in the liberation of the people from the dictatorship. Named after a celebrated Filipino nationalist intellectual, Epifanio de los Santos, the highway served as the location of the country's major military camps – Camp Crame and Camp Aguinaldo. On that fateful day, 22 February 1986, at around 11 p.m., Radio Veritas of the Catholic Mass Media and the underground Bombo Radyo rattled the Metro Manila residents with the shocking news that

National Defense Secretary Juan Ponce Enrile and AFP Vice Chief of Staff Fidel V. Ramos, together with a group of soldiers belonging to the Reform the Armed Forces Movement (RAM), were holed up in Camp Crame.

Jaime Cardinal Sin was on the air pleading for people to go to EDSA to protect Enrile, Ramos and the rebel soldiers from the Marcos loyalist troops ready to attack them at any time. Stunned by the news, Roger and I hurriedly got dressed and proceeded on foot to EDSA, despite the curfew. We were amazed at what we saw. Crowds were gathered at several gates of both camps, exchanging news and views, fearful yet hopeful in the face of the exciting events. People Power had begun.

The next two days, 23 and 24 February, strange things happened along Morato Avenue where we lived. Makeshift altars suddenly sprouted. On several street corners we saw a crucifix and small statues of Mary on tables laden with flowers. Dimly lit by candles, people gathered around these "altars" to pray, sing hymns or simply exchange the latest news. The night seemed long and eerie when gunshots suddenly reverberated from ABS-CBN, the television station nearby. Then we heard the sound of tanks approaching. We all stayed close to one another. When one soldier asked for directions to the ABS-CBN stations, one person bravely pointed in the opposite direction. Apparently, the huge statues of Christ and Mary blocking Morato Avenue and Scout Rallos stopped the tanks from going through to their destination.

Our son Tagúm (by then nine years old) was with us. As we made our way to the radio/TV network to lend support to the "rebel" soldiers there, Roger and I noticed that Tagúm had picked up some broken branches from the avocado tree near our gate. He tied these up to form a cross. He also picked up some pieces of stone which he pocketed. He said, without our asking him, that these would ward off Satan and other bad spirits along the way.

On 25 February, Roger and I were back at EDSA. People from all walks of life were there, praying and singing patriotic songs and religious hymns, while vendors sold peanuts, cookies and drinks. Among the crowds were the images of the crucified Christ and the Virgin Mary. At one point the people offered food and drinks, rosaries and flowers to the unbelieving soldiers, to avert a bloody confrontation. In the long watch at EDSA, amidst barricades, Roger and I repeatedly sang with the people "Ang Bayan Ko." We became more militant when the troops from Malacañang began to penetrate the crowds, by then numbering about two million. The soldiers in the armed tanks began to move toward us but were unable to proceed, for it would mean running over dead bodies by the hundreds. The same thing happened when the helicopters were supposed to drop bombs on the millions at EDSA. Instead of following orders, the pilots landed their aircraft inside the beleaguered camp and joined the people.

On the evening of 25 February, we heard over the radio that the rebel soldiers had overrun Malacañang. The Marcos family was being transported by plane to Hawaii. The following morning, millions on EDSA rejoiced and celebrated their victory. I went to Morato Avenue to see what was going on. People were gathered with smiles of relief, joyful that the dark period of martial rule had at last come to an end. Overwhelmed by the sight and atmosphere, I leaped for joy, with the morning sun shining brightly in the clear sky!

The Middle Forces on My Mind

How does one interpret or even call the "people power" at EDSA? Given that it was composed of the broad mass of people led by the middle class, unarmed and empowered by faith and the desire to end the nearly twenty-year dictatorship and military atrocities, how could anyone call it a "revolution"? To the NDF, as Roger and I heard and read, it was not a revolution but merely a "convulsion" or "disturbance" at EDSA. To them, what happened was the restoration of our age-old liberal democracy back into the hands of the elite and its imperialist ally. I agree with this to a certain extent.

To me, however, the historic event at EDSA was symbolic of our people's capacity to rise up against tyranny and fight for democracy, maybe, not yet of the national democratic type under the leadership of a revolutionary party. But the people had decided to act in unison with courage and determination to topple the Marcos regime of lies and violence, armed only with prayers, songs and offerings of flowers and food. For me, the movement failed to appreciate the role of faith in God which is deep in our culture. Faith united the people in a nonviolent form of toppling the Marcos dictatorship. In restoring democracy, though imperfect, the country was freed from the terror and violence of martial rule.

I believe that the leadership in the movement failed to consider the people's deep spirituality as an integral element in the fight for national democracy. I remember wondering what had happened to the provision on the "freedom of religion and respect for faith-based traditions." It simply disappeared from the Ten-Point NDF program. I guess it was not considered important. The sense I got from what I had seen then was that Christian-Marxist members were considered more advanced in their commitment if they became more Marxist than Christian in the long run.

This brings me to the other lesson I have learned from EDSA People Power. Any struggle for social change can no longer be reduced to "class struggle" or planned economics. It is more complex than that. I saw in the EDSA phenomenon our deep Filipino values uniting our people toward a common goal. Such values as *damayan* (mutual help and compassion), *kalinisan at kababaan ng loob* (purity of intentions and humility) with *paninindigan* (commitment to a worthy cause) were very much alive and "caused our people at prayer to act peacefully," according to Teresita Obusan, whose study on Filipino spirituality goes back to the 1896 Philippine Revolution against Spanish colonial rule.[13]

At EDSA People Power I also witnessed the vital participation of the "middle forces" with many members coming from so-called civil society. They were significant not only in terms of number but also in their capacity to lead the people (including the basic sectors of the urban poor, workers and peasants). *PSR* had long since "recognized their political significance in the people's democratic revolution in shifting decisively the balance of power against the national and class enemies of the Filipino people."[14]

What a NatDem like me failed to realize was that the middle class participation would, in effect, make possible the Party's takeover of the state. In such a scenario, it would be the Party which would implement the NDF program toward socialism and its ultimate people's program under communist rule. No wonder I had to be just a friend or ally for my failure to comprehend this.

My Onward Journey

From Cory Aquino's presidency up to the present Duterte Administration, Roger and I have been consistent in our stance of "critical collaboration." We support whatever government policy or program will benefit all oppressed sectors of our society, especially the poor. At the same time, we resist any attack on our democratic rights and institutions as well as processes.

Today we meet once a week for Bible study in Church Café, an ecumenical group of friends and former comrades in the movement. I feel gratitude in my heart. I thank God that Roger and I are alive to witness the flowering in

---

13. Teresita B. Obusan, *EDSA: A New Paradigm in Revolution*, Series no. 5 (Manila: National Commission on Culture and the Arts, 1965).

14. Guerrero, *Philippine Society and Revolution*, 244.

the church – Catholic and Protestant alike – of the same spirit of struggle for social justice, national sovereignty and inclusive economic growth.

I see this in my present involvement as Fellow of the Institute for Studies in Asian Church and Culture (ISACC), as trustee of the Center for Community Transformation (CCT) and member of the Salt and Light for Christ Charismatic Community (SLCC). In Church Café, our brilliant and patient teacher, Pastor Sunil Stephens, instructs us about the Word not only through the verses in the Bible but as evident in the arts, philosophy, science, history and culture. We relish all this and apply what we learn among our small group and with others, especially our families. We learn as we enjoy coffee, food and wine in friendship and fun.

I guess I have come full circle at age eighty. I look forward to another "epiphany of the saints" (*epifanio de los santos*) when we as a people might, perhaps, come together again to bring about genuine social change.

The dream of National Democracy still lingers in my mind. Once, in a friendly jest, my Church Café mate Mario, reacting to my "reminiscences," said, "Ay, Fe, there was no national democracy as you imagined it." And we both laughed. I turned to listen to Manu's beautifully composed song to close our Bible study. Then we all prayed for each other, our families and friends, our country and the world. Each time I pray now I realize that what I have been through requires a continuous evaluation, not only of my idea of social transformation based on honest scholarship, but also of how I practice my faith and manner of preserving what is good and dynamic in our culture.

I trust that our youth – the millennials – will carry on with the task of making our people's lives better and more secure in the future. Unlike our generation, they have new and better technologies to communicate with: cellphones, the Internet, social media, and so on. They have access to diverse information which allows them greater freedom of choice as well as greater responsibility in using the information to recreate our society.

I hope, too, that what I have shared about life as a NatDem under martial law will add to the content and direction of their lives and the continuation of the daunting task of nation-building.

Patnubayan nawa tayo ng Manlilikha. May the Creator be our guide, that in all things God may be glorified.

References

Agoncillo, Teodoro A., and Fe B. Mangahas. *Philippine History*. Expanded and updated edition. Quezon City: C & E Publishing Inc., 2010.

Alaras, Consolacion R. *PAMATHALAAN*. Series no. 7 on Filipino Spiritual Culture. Manila: National Commission on Culture and Arts, 1995.

"Middle Class Study." Unpublished document, Manila, 1980–1981.

Obusan, Teresita B. *EDSA: A New Paradigm in Revolution*. Series no. 5. Manila: National Commission on Culture and Arts Culture Series on Filipino Culture, 1995.

Sison, Jose Ma. *Philippine Society and Revolution*. Hongkong: Ta Kung Pao, 1971.

4

Truth in a Revolution

Notes from the Underground

Mario I. Miclat

Why, O Lord, do you stand far off? Why do you hide yourself in times of trouble? (Ps 10:1 NIV)

Jesus Christ did not reply when Pontius Pilate asked him what truth was.

Searching for truth as a young man, I bumped into Lenin. He wrote not of truth per se, but of revolution: Force is the midwife of the old society pregnant with the new.[1]

Communists followed the Leninist dictum to overthrow capitalism the world over. Pursuing such a goal, Jose Ma. Sison (Joma) founded the "new Leftist" Student Cultural Association of the University of the Philippines (SCAUP) in 1959, to spite the "old Rightist" UP Student Catholic Action (UPSCA).

A Revolutionary Apprentice

I joined the SCAUP in 1967 when I was in my third year of a BS Foreign Service course. Before that, though, I had steeped myself in the anti-American writings of Senator Claro M. Recto. I had been intrigued by how the people of Olongapo, my hometown, had rejected him by a resounding zero vote when he ran for president. It was only my father who liked him, but Daddy was unable to vote. As the first Filipino manager of the Navy Exchange in the American base at

---

1. V. I. Lenin, *State and Revolution*.

Subic Bay, Daddy was bold enough to express his views. A man of integrity, his determination to assert Filipino workers' rights led to his dismissal. He lost his job, but luckily got another managerial position in Manila. A former Olongapo mayor told me that Recto was defeated in the polls because of his alleged collaboration with the Japanese during the war.

As a SCAUP applicant, I was asked to write an essay on current events, had to pass an interview and was assigned to the intermediate discussion group (DG) without having to pass through the beginners' course that covered essays by so-called nationalist senators Recto, Tañada and Jovito Salonga. I went straight to being a full member.

The SCAUP general secretary, Monico Atienza, a.k.a. "Togs," asked me to go with him and personally deliver a letter of invitation to Renato Constantino at his house. As we approached the historian's residence in a plush area in Quezon City, Togs whispered, "The united front includes the national bourgeoisie" (more on this term later. The Leftist movement used terms all its own. Togs, for one, was also called GenSec, short for "general secretary," in contradistinction to "secretary general" of the United Nations, which was perceived to be US-controlled). Constantino could not come to our induction traditionally dubbed as the "Recto Dinner." So it was Joma who had to deliver the dinner lecture at D&E Restaurant.

The intermediate course consisted of a fast review of essays by Constantino and Sison. It was followed by Maurice Cornforth books on communist philosophy, such as historical and dialectical materialism, a worldview that precluded the existence of the soul and God. Accounts of revolution, instead of textbooks or classic novels, became our reading fare. On top of the list was William Pomeroy's *The Forest*. Soon, I was assigned to handle a DG for applicants and new members. Practicing the so-called mass line (or the least common denominator), I had to limit our discussions to nationalism, not referring to communism at all. Togs then asked me to run in elections to the newly established Arts and Sciences Council (ASC). I became a council officer, and at the same time became the first editor of its college organ, *Sinag*. We used it as a propaganda arm of the Left. But the council became a mere debating ground between councilors Eric Baculinao and Rafael Baylosis on how to apply Roget's rules of order.

"Don't attend ASC meetings anymore, *kung ganyan rin la'ang nang ganyan*," Togs advised me.

Meanwhile, Togs made me join a small DG of four activists on Marxist–Leninist theories which centered on the need for a "correct" communist party leadership, as opposed to a "revisionist" one. We focused on the Little Red

Book, *Quotations from Chairman Mao Tse-tung*, which we bought from either Popular Book Store or Erehwon in Manila. Our group consisted of Beda Polig, Joe Cardenas and Charlie J. (not to be confused with Charlie D., who was suspected of being a government agent for having a father from the military or something, but was tolerated for being a good fundraiser and mimeograph operator. Activists were wont to suspect each other as spies and were wary of each other. A horrific incident was the death of Eddie Dasma at the hands of fellow activists upon Togs's orders, because he was suspected of being a government agent). Our discussions were then elevated to full articles by Mao from his four volumes, mostly on the philosophy of revolution following his doctrine "Political power grows out of the barrel of a gun."

SCAUP had a sister organization, the Kabataang Makabayan (KM). As I was a SCAUP member, it was assumed that I was a member of UP KM, too. Its activities extended to organizing unions and joining workers' strikes. Together with KM comrades from other chapters, we dressed down to blend with the workers.

I was preparing to go to our *tambayan* (or meeting area) at Vinzon's Hall (the students' building) where other SCAUP/KMs were gathering to man the strike at the US Tobacco Corporation, maker of Marlboro cigarettes. Union activities like this introduced me to a world I had never seen before. Discussions with workers in their ghettoes gave credence to our DGs about their plight as the oppressed proletariat. Before I could go out of my dorm at Yakal, though, Togs came to fetch me.

"Leave the strike to the Che Guevaras," he said. "We're going to Narra for a more profound ideological struggle."

Lenin wrote that giving more importance to workers' strikes than to ideological correctness was narrow syndicalism, that is, begging for palliative solutions like higher wages rather than addressing the main issue of having the working class capture political power on a permanent basis. Extending this principle, Maoists thought that the Cuban revolution led by Fidel Castro and Che Guevara was bound to fail for glorifying guerillaism rather than ideological correctness.

Togs brought me to Narra Residence Hall at the other side of the campus, where Joma had a speaking engagement. We arrived while some dormers were asking for his autograph. Then off we went with him in a car. The driver drove fast along the two-lane Katipunan Road and circled around Project 4, until I lost track of where we were. We ended up at the house of Ka Sam Rodriquez, an old communist who had just been released from prison and who spoke about his thoughts on the workers' movement. From there, we proceeded to Joma's apartment in Lepanto.

"Why did we have to go around in circles, only to end up in places where government agents were already waiting?" I asked Togs later. He said that the driver, labor leader Art Garcia, was "in ferment" or feeling agitated. Not directly answering my question, he said, "The government is getting more blatantly obstructive toward KM."

The incident somehow answered the criticism from SCAUP members as to why he now drove a "bourgeois" car instead of taking a "proletarian" jeepney.

Before long, Joma bade farewell as chair at a KM conference (not a usual congress) held at PPSTA Building in Quezon City. Nilo Tayag became his successor (Nilo was arrested in 1970 for organizing an armed group in Quezon province and, upon release, joined local clergy).

The Revolution Gets Murky

Unlike the nationalist-led nineteenth-century revolution that overthrew Spanish rule, Maoists believed that the struggle must be led by the working class steeped in communist ideology. The destitute peasants were supposed to be their reliable allies. The small owners and intellectuals, the so-called petty bourgeoisie, belonged to a united front that also included the native capitalists or the "national bourgeoisie." This explained Togs's attitude toward Constantino mentioned earlier. Without so much as analyzing the peculiarities of Philippine society, Joma copied the Maoist formulation hook, line and sinker.

Joma reestablished the Communist Party of the Philippines (CPP) in January 1969 (officially antedated to coincide with Mao's birthday on 26 December). Failing to meet erstwhile Huk leader Kumander Sumulong at their appointed time, he was later contacted by Bernabe Buscayno. Ka Dante, as he was fondly called, led a security group guarding Senator Benigno Aquino, Jr. at Hacienda Luisita. His group also handled some personnel who served as security guards at the Voice of America facilities in Tarlac. From his group arose the New People's Army (NPA). Sumulong, on the other hand, surrendered to Marcos at Malacañang.

Togs asked me to leave home and my studies and to start to live at Ka Dante's home barrio of Sta. Rita in Capas, Tarlac. My tutelage under Togs had come to an end. By the way, "togs" is short for the word for "gold," which covered Monico's front tooth.

In Sta. Rita, I became the Party's translation bureau, mostly translating into Filipino the English tracts written by Joma (alias Amado Guerrero), Mao's essays and *Peking Review* articles. It occurred to Joma one day that if I had my UP diploma, I could do more things for the movement.

And so, from the underground, I returned to Diliman in 1971 to remove a conditional grade of "4" and either make it a passing "3" or a failing "5." I passed. Now I was ready for bigger tasks.

Yes, years before the declaration of martial law in 1972, or even before the suspension of *habeas corpus* in 1971, Joma's organizations had been preparing for a revolution that would overthrow the Republic and establish a communist regime.

The Philippines was not an island insofar as the international situation was concerned. The late 1960s was a time of student activism in Europe and North America, mostly against the Vietnam War. It was also the time of the Cultural Revolution in China: a power struggle between forces within the communist party – that is, those aligned with Mao – and those supporting Liu Xiaoqi and Deng Xiaoping. At the same time, Chinese enmity toward the Russians manifested itself through heated China–Soviet polemics. The convoluted world situation was reflected in political alignments among concerned college students and young professionals.

Marcos was perceived to be a US puppet by activists who themselves suspected each other as stooges of either China, the Soviets or the US, as manifested in the quarrels of KM vs. Samahang Demokratikong Kabataan (SDK) vs. Movement for the Advancement of Nationalism (MAN) and Malayang Pagkakaisa ng Kabataang Pilipino (MPKP) vs. League of Filipino Students (LFS) vs. Bertrand Russell Peace Foundation (BRPF), and so on. These organizations would engage each other in political-cum-ideological polemics and at times in physical violence against each other to prove whose agenda was superior.

My wife Alma and I became part of the permanent CPP delegation that Joma sent to Beijing in 1971. The delegation's main mission was to smuggle Chinese arms to the Philippines, and coincidentally take care of Joma's three children, who went there with us for their education and personal safety. We were housed in an exclusive mansion, one of eighteen in a secret suburban compound.

Joma criticized the Lava brothers for not winning the revolution more than two decades after World War II (note that the revolution he supposedly led had now been going on for half a century). His reason was that the Lavas followed the Soviet model instead of China's Mao Tse-tung thought. To capture power, Joma thought that we needed arms, which China could very well provide just as it was doing in Vietnam. How could we convince Mao that the NPA had enough people to use the weapons? A revolutionary situation could be created.

The scheme was evil as it was idiotic: bomb a major political rally by the opposition Liberal Party, and blame it on Marcos, a Nacionalista. Kumander Pusa, an NPA operative loyal to Sen. Aquino, warned the senator not to attend the rally. He did not, and was spared the agony of his colleagues who were maimed by the grenade explosions.

Marcos suspended *habeas corpus*. On its heel followed Joma's MV *Karagatan* project in July 1972, which carried from Hainan Island in China arms and ammunition modeled on US-made ones but of an inferior quality. The cargo ship floundered at Digoyo Point in Isabela along the Philippine Sea near Benham Rise. The incident, aside from an alleged assassination attempt against defense secretary Juan Ponce Enrile, was used by Marcos as reason to declare martial law.

Joma made a follow-up proposal to China to smuggle arms into the country once again in 1974. Deng Xiaoping opposed it, but Mao prevailed. But the MV *Doña Andrea*, which was supposed to carry the arms cargo, floundered in the South China Sea (along the West Philippine Sea). Its crew were saved by China and were eventually integrated with our group.

Most people involved in the project are still alive and kicking. Several of us meet at least once a year to remember the past even as sinister forces want us to forget.

Plagiarized Class Analysis

China's rhetoric on worldwide revolution became a mere play of words as Beijing took away from Taipei China's United Nations seat in October 1971. Mao came up with a new version of the "three worlds." He lumped the US and the Soviet Union together as the first world of two superpowers, Europe and other advanced capitalist countries as the second world, and the underdeveloped countries that included China as the third world. With such revisionist theory, he had insinuated China into the third world, instead of the traditional second world of socialism. China's somersault in its worldview and Mao's death in 1976 left us – Joma's Beijing delegation – in complete disarray.

"Joma was severely tortured," Fe Mangahas says, referring to his imprisonment in a martial law torture chamber of the Marcos regime. But today? He is now in his netherworld in the Netherlands, while we Filipinos seek for the truth.

Two basic questions in order for a revolution to succeed, according to Mao, are: "Who is our enemy? Who is our friend?" The Maoist definition of revolution is "an act of violence by which one class overthrows another." Revolutionaries need to make a "concrete analysis of concrete conditions" or an actual study of the real situation. Joma did not do that. In *Philippine Society and Revolution*, which he wrote under the pseudonym Amado Guerrero, he just copied Mao Tse-tung's class analysis of Chinese society.

Mao wrote: "First, the rich peasants. They form about 5 per cent of the rural population (or about 10 per cent together with the landlords) and constitute the rural bourgeoisie."[2] Guerrero wrote: "a. *The Rich Peasants*: They are otherwise called the rural bourgeoisie and comprise about five per cent of the rural population."[3] When Guerrero wrote, "b. *The Middle Peasants*: They may be called the rural petty bourgeoisie and they comprise about 15 to 20 percent of the rural population,"[4] he was only mimicking Mao who wrote, "Second, the middle peasants. They form about 20 per cent of China's rural population."[5]

Again, Mao wrote: "Third, the poor peasants. The poor peasants in China, together with the farm labourers, form about 70 per cent of the rural population."[6] And again, Guerrero copied him almost verbatim: "c. *The Poor Peasants*. Together with the farm workers, the poor peasants are about 75 to 80 percent of the rural population."

When I pointed this out to him as he was revising its draft, then entitled "The Philippine Crisis," Joma reasoned that the movement did not believe in the bourgeois law on copyright, skirting the more substantial issue of him not doing an actual analysis of classes in Philippine rural areas, and that our society might not be the same as China's.

Apong Mon, Apong Nacio, Milan, Wufeng, Fengbin – NPAs who all served as crew to the MV *Doña Andrea* tasked to smuggle arms from China – would come out as rich peasants, tilling with their own carabaos and implements at least three hectares of land that they got from President Diosdado Macapagal's land reform code of 1963. And Apong Nacio was a barrio captain, too. A Chinese landlord was lucky if he had that much land. If we followed the Maoist

---

2. See "The Chinese Revolution and the Chinese Communist Party," *Selected Works of Mao Tse-tung*, Vol. 2 (Peking: Foreign Languages Press, 1965), 323.

3. See Amado Guerrero, *Philippine Society and Revolution* (Hong Kong: Ta Kung Pao, 1971), 250.

4. Guerrero, *Philippine Society and Revolution*, 250.

5. Mao, "Chinese Revolution," 323.

6. Mao, 324.

formulation, they would constitute the rural bourgeoisie. But they all joined the armed struggle in Central Luzon.

Joma and his followers insist that the basic class situation in the country since his plagiarized class analysis in the late 1960s has not changed. Statistics since the mid-1980s, however, reveal that our industrial production has surpassed that of agriculture. Please don't be bored if I refer to National Economic and Development Authority (NEDA) statistics showing that our industry surpasses agriculture as a source of national income.

Our major industries, in order of their contribution to the gross domestic product (GDP), are as follows: food processing; mining and smelting; automotive, mostly vehicle assembly and spare parts manufacturing; cement; chemicals; construction materials manufacturing; footwear, leatherwear and leather materials; marine products; engineering and metal works; garments; and wood products. We produce a limited amount of oil and natural gas. We are the second most advanced in generating geothermal power.

Meanwhile, agriculture, including forestry and fishing, contributes only 25 percent to our GDP, producing rice, corn, sweet potato, coffee, fruits and vegetables, rubber and ramie for the local market. We export banana, pineapple, tobacco and sugarcane. Government infrastructure projects and private construction activities for housing and business units lead the economic growth, mostly concentrated in cities like Baguio, Cagayan de Oro, Cebu, Davao and Metro Manila.

From both sectors, the top-dollar earners are electronics, including semiconductor devices and microchips; garments; crude coconut oil; chemicals; fresh and canned fish; and copper bars, rods and slabs. These are produced in the export processing zones of Baguio, Bataan, Cavite, Clark, Mactan and Subic.

Despite all this economic activity, we perennially suffer from an unfavorable balance of trade. Blame Marcos's foreign debt that President Cory Aquino preferred to pay fully and that we still pay today. But also blame our love of imported goods, aside from the much-needed oil, machinery, as well as raw materials and intermediate goods. These days, we face stiff competition with our ASEAN neighbors, too. Well, it's the economy, stupid!

Togs's smart alecky line then was: "Why is the Philippines a banana republic? Because its economy is sagging" (a play on words since "banana" in Filipino is "saging").

Still today, Joma insists that Philippine society is semifeudal and semicolonial, just as he wrote half a century ago, despite the fact that more or less 50 percent of our population now live in urban areas.

Yes, our country needs fundamental changes in order to develop faster and meet our people's basic needs. In this new millennium, however, do we need to stick to a Maoistic analysis? Do our people's main enemies remain the US imperialists and their so-called social base, the feudal lords? Our beloved Philippines was liberated from Marcos dictatorship more than a quarter of a century ago, but we are still gripped by poverty, corruption, backwardness, lack of vision and a national inferiority complex.

China on My Mind

After fifteen years in China, my family was able to come home on the heels of the 1986 EDSA revolution. A leading comrade from the International Liaison Department of the Chinese Communist Party reminded me of Mao's advice to foreign "comrades" to forget all their memories of China. One may interpret it as advice to do their revolutions their own way.

Be that as it may, how does one forget seeing the Great Wall that extended to infinity, feeling the snow that had melted on one's eyelids as soon as one entered the warm foyer, savoring Peking duck at Quanjude, smelling night soil in Hengyang, or hearing the miraculous chirping of a solitary bird in the dead of winter?

In the dead of winter a bird chirped and the telephone rang. The voice at the other end announced that the request of the comrades from Central Luzon mentioned above, including Francisco "Picio" Nava Cura and their political officer Salvador "Buddy" Pineda, was at last granted. They were now allowed to have their own home away from the Party delegation whose new heads had just been appointed by Joma from a student delegation stranded in Beijing following Marcos's suspension of *habeas corpus*. They, the *Doña Andrea* crew, did not recognize such leadership; they believed they were following Joma's ultra-Left adventurism and wrong analysis of Philippine society. An ILD officer, who at that time had just come back from an extended tour of duty in Manila following the establishment of RP–China diplomatic relations, commented that, to his mind, the Philippines was no doubt a capitalist country.

Returning in 1986, I taught at the Asian Center. It's UP Diliman's graduate school for Asian and Philippine Studies, although I only had a bachelor's diploma. It was UP President Edgardo Angara who gave me the teaching post. When he had visited Beijing a few months earlier, he came to know about me and my wife having no Philippine passport (we had left the Philippines illegally; how we did it is yet another story). Our two children, Maningning and Banaue, did not have proper citizenship documentation, either. China, like most countries, subscribes to the principle of *jus sanguinis* (citizenship by blood, i.e. the same citizenship as one's parents), rather than the American *jus soli* (citizenship by place of birth). Through President Angara's help, I got my Philippine passport. Alma and the children got theirs through Bataan Congressman Tony Roman. I could not thank them enough. President Angara gave me a faculty position in the Asian Center, even before I had obtained my graduate degrees. I'd say I did him proud by teaching diligently and well, and by finishing my MA and PhD, while doing whatever administrative duties were assigned me by the university, until I became dean before I retired.

Handling multidisciplinary graduate courses on modern and contemporary Chinese society, culture, economy, politics, the military situation and foreign relations did not make me a religious man, even as I no longer subscribed to communism. I expanded the courses I taught to include Korea and Japan, which together with China were classified as Confucian (and therefore agnostic) societies.

I also taught the course entitled Philippine Institution 100, on the life and works of Rizal, who fought against the medieval practices and beliefs of the Spanish regime. Readings and papers in my classes about East–West encounters and on primary sources about the early Hispanic conquest of our archipelago revealed a pre-Hispanic culture quite different from what we have now, with its Catholic overlay.

I joined the Asian Center faculty at a time when its dean was a Sikh. Next to him was a "non-practicing" Catholic, followed by an agnostic and a corrupt atheist. My best friends there were a Muslim and a former communist. We never talked about our respective religions. My Friday nights were invariably spent with Writers' Union friends who talked about literature, politics and girls, never religion.

But I still had nightmares of my China experience, the cries of revolt, revulsion and unending revenge during the Cultural Revolution made by people conspiring against one another.

"Let's do our own analysis of our social classes then," Fe suggested.

"What for?" I asked myself. Marx wrote in his Manifesto of the Communist Party, "The history of all hitherto existing society is the history of class struggles." But from what I have seen in China and other communist countries I have visited – North Korea, Albania, Vietnam – I no longer believe that class struggle is the only way for a people to live. I have read volumes of Marx, Engels, Lenin and Stalin, only to arrive at the conclusion that their explications about truth are simply untrue.

There are struggles and struggles throughout history – national, ethnic, gender, scientific, intellectual, moral, spiritual, religious – which cannot be categorized as class war. In the complicated world we are in, who are the exploiters and who are the exploited, the oppressors and the oppressed?

Recently, the building administrator of our condominium was removed from office. He asked my wife, "What will happen to my family now, to my children's education?" She asked the homeowners' president the reason for his dismissal. Apparently, residents on the eighth floor had complained about his incompetence. Their proof? The janitor's mop was too wet. Along their corridor, mushrooms had sprouted. Where was the class struggle here?

The Mystery of Truth and Faith

I had a heart attack and accidentally discovered that the hospital could be not only a microcosm of life, humanity and love, but also of greed and inhumanity. The insurance doctor packed four patients for angioplasty procedure within the two hours that he rented the hospital room. Instead of personally applying thumb pressure on my groin to prevent bleeding, he paid a high school graduate to assist him to do it. Meanwhile, the hospital bills for the "only available room" in the high-class hospital kept coming. My college dean heard about it and introduced me to another doctor in another hospital. My wife promptly paid our bills, exhausting all my medical insurance. I left without informing the insurance doctor.

The doctor in the other first-class hospital introduced himself as a born-again Christian. When he saw a rosary around my arm, he asked me to throw it away. If I didn't, the angioplasty might fail. I had already not been praying the rosary for years, but held it as a gift from my brother. I cried, refusing to be converted in such a manner. It was almost midnight and Alma reminded him about the procedure scheduled early the next morning.

One gold stent and two balloons that I needed cost half a million pesos. Alma had to source funds from various sources. Six months later, however, I suffered another heart attack that needed a quintuple bypass operation and, again, a big amount of money. Oh, there was a charity ward for the poor, while the rich could easily afford it. Those of the middle class like me had to look for our own resources. I had to ask for financial help from my five siblings, all professionals, in the US. It turned out that my brother, a plastic surgeon, had a classmate at medical school who was now a senior physician at the Philippine Heart Center – Dr Edna Garayblas-Monzon. She was heaven-sent.

I suffered from profuse bleeding after the operation and needed several bags of blood. Friends and former students from UP, Ateneo, Maryknoll/Miriam and the National Defense College asked their students for donations. The hospital staff were amazed that bags and bags of blood were registered under my name. Those that were not of the same blood type as mine were swiftly dispatched to victims of the ongoing dengue epidemic.

"Have you prayed?" my surgeon asked me.

"No," I replied.

"Why not?" he asked with a dejected mien.

"Because I know that many people have prayed for me."

And God took care of me.

I have a secret. When I pray, I give thanks to the Lord for the day that just passed and to have a good night's sleep, a nice dream. I thank him for the wonderful food that Nanay prepares, for my grandson Raj's creative drawings, for the smile from daughter Banaue's lips, and for her husband Dom's safe ride home. I don't pray for bigger things.

This practice started with a foolish game when I was little, and turned into a curse. When I didn't win an interscholastic oratorical contest, I blamed God. The next time I joined, I prayed to the devil. I won first prize, in a bittersweet victory. I learned from my coach that it was actually a tie. To break it, the judges had opened the gift prizes for the top two. The second would get a formal pair of pants. They thought the other guy, a poor orphan, deserved it more. The first got a pocket dictionary. Since then, I have become afraid to pray. Not to the devil. Not to God. In college, Marx became my opium.

Not that God did not come knocking. Oh yes, he did. And he has guided every step I have taken.

Alone in Beijing, when Alma and our two kids had been given the chance to visit the Philippines in 1984, I lit a candle upon learning that Mamma was in the hospital, having suffered from a stroke. Hours later, the candle fell for no apparent reason. Then the phone rang. Mamma had died.

I have mentioned our shipwrecked comrades in China and their request to the Chinese authorities to live separately from the Philippine communists in Liuyang. A chirping bird in the dead of winter announced the good news that their request had been granted.

Swimming in Davao, a strong undercurrent brought me deeper and deeper, and further away from shore. Then a voice reminded me to relax. As my hosts were getting frantic, they saw me swimming safely back to shore.

I felt a strange calm as the plane took off from the Washington DC airport when Alma and I had to cut short our US visit. A Korean lady seated next to me on the plane lovingly talked about her departed son who, like our daughter Maningning, was a poet/artist teaching in a university. Her story calmed me somehow. Due to my heart condition, nobody had told me that we were coming home for Maningning's wake. Dr Monzon was there at the airport. She has saved me through angioplasty four times, not to mention my recent stroke. She says it's not she who saves me, but the Lord.

Repeatedly, God sends me friends to guide me into his fold. A student once asked me to be his dissertation adviser when his professor retired. His name is Fr Sid Marinay and he became a family friend and spiritual adviser when I retired.

After a stroke which paralyzed me, Fe and Roger Mangahas introduced me to an Oriental therapeutic bed which helped me a great deal to regain my strength. They also brought me and Alma to a Bible study group.

Do I pray only for my family's daily bread? Not quite. Despite Jesus's admonition in Matthew to not use vain repetitions in prayer, I pray the rosary. And not only once have I prayed for the deaths of friends.

Jorge, an activist friend since college, was suffering from cancer. Colleagues, comrades and friends came to pray for his healing, conversion and salvation. He whispered to me that he could no longer bear the pain and he wanted to die. I prayed to God to take him, and he breathed his last.

Auntie Cion had been sick in bed for quite some time. She was greatly worried for her grandchildren, whose parents had no proper means of livelihood. "Who will take care of them?" she asked me before she fell into a coma. The last time I visited her, she was mumbling something. I put my ears to her lips. Then it was my turn to whisper to her: "Auntie, you have already done a lot for your grandchildren. You can rest now." And I prayed to the Lord to take her. I had not gone far when her grandchild called me back to say that Auntie was dead.

We visited Alma's hometown. Her old Uncle Ben was very sick in bed. I prayed to the Lord, and he took him away before I could go down the stairs.

How afraid I am now to experience another encounter with such mysteries.

"There are more things in heaven and earth, Horatio, than are dreamt of in your philosophy," says Shakespeare in *Hamlet*.

As a professor in the national university handling courses in multidisciplinal area studies, I tried as much as possible to be nonpartisan and nonsectarian in looking at the national, regional and international situation. I believe, however, that our country's history since the 1960s has not only been about Marcos and anti-Marcos forces, Maoist and pro-Moscow communists, class struggle between exploiters and exploited, imperialism or anti-colonialism. Rather, it has always been a history of individual dreams merging into something greater – a history of nation-building, economic pursuits, pride of place and trying to grasp life's meaning.

Now that I have retired and take care of a grandson, I pray that newfound Bible study friends might help me find God's truth.

5

A Peek from behind the Bamboo Curtain

Alma Cruz Miclat

Experience is the most brutal of teachers, but you learn, my God, do you learn! (C. S. Lewis)

Winter is Beijing's longest season. It is drab, dreary and desolate most times. The biting wind makes it worse, so that you ought to fully cover yourself, exposing your eyes only. Snow is the saving grace. The moisture it brings makes the air fresh and raises the subzero temperature a bit. And, of course, its white purity is a miracle to behold. Snow seldom comes to Beijing, even in winter.

Our first Christmas in Beijing in 1971 was the loneliest that my husband Mario and I ever had. We heard no Christmas carols, saw no Christmas decor, smelled no Christmas in the air. It was our fifth month in China. We had transferred from one secret house to another in Manila, flown to Hong Kong, taken a ferry to Macau and a coaster to Guangzhou where we stayed for a few nights, and then flown to Beijing. I had vomited a lot so my first day in the Chinese capital was spent in a hospital, where a doctor announced that I was pregnant.

"Do you want to keep the baby?" the doctor asked.

"But of course!" I replied.

How did a young girl from the fishing town of Orani in the province of Bataan, less than a hundred kilometers northwest of Manila, end up hundreds of miles away and staying in Beijing for fifteen long years?

My Big Provincial Family

My province is well known in Philippine history for the Battle of Bataan which started on 7 January 1942 and culminated in the US surrender of the peninsula on 9 April 1942. This represented the most intense phase of imperial Japan's invasion of our country during World War II and the last stand of the US Armed Forces in the Far East (USAFFE) in the country. Approximately 75,000 Filipino and American troops were forced to make the most excruciating and deadly 100-kilometer march to prison camps in Tarlac province, which is referred to as the infamous "Death March."

My father, who was from the island of Negros in the central Philippines, served as a USAFFE medical attendant in Bataan and survived the Death March by escaping, together with some other comrades.

I remember Father relating his story of escape from the cruel Japanese forces only to meet another scourge: starvation. They subsisted on anything that could alleviate their hunger, like coconut during good times, or, during bad, worms they gathered from the bark of trees in the forest.

When the war ended in 1945, he married my mother, whom he had met at the war front while helping her sister who was a USAFFE nurse. Father used his USAFFE back pay to open a bicycle rental business in Orani, Bataan. It failed. He decided to bring his young wife back to his hometown, Ilog. Life on Negros Island was not easy either. When they received news that my grandmother was gravely ill, they decided to go back to Orani. The ship they took back to the main island of Luzon was tossed up and down on the high seas during a strong typhoon. The young couple lost all their earthly belongings. My mother was traumatized. She wouldn't venture on another sea voyage after that.

They stayed put in Bataan. Father became a fisherman, like most men in Orani did. Mother sold his catch in the public market. Their children, all eight of us, came one after another at two-year intervals. Father then ventured into another business: making fish nets which he rented out to fishpond owners. To meet demand, he hired two men to help him.

It was not an easy life. Yes, we had a roof over our heads, which my widower grandfather had left to us after he remarried and moved with his new wife to another barrio. But we didn't always have enough to eat. Our municipality had no electric supply back then in the early 1950s. My eldest sister, Delia, had to read by a gas lamp and damaged her eyesight. Public toilets were built in the marketplace years later. We had to wait a few more years before we had our own toilet at home.

My mother was a strong-willed woman. She took after her father, who was a devout Christian. He was a pillar of the United Methodist Church in Bataan and she continued the tradition. She brought her children and grandchildren into its fold. One of my brothers chose to be a pastor upon early retirement as an engineer.

My parents' ingenuity and resourcefulness knew no bounds. Mother would find opportunities to earn and help add to my father's income. She opened a small *carinderia* (food stall) in front of our house. The pork came from hogs Father raised in our backyard. They were not only hardworking, but thrifty, too. They vowed to send us, their children, to college, which was the only inheritance they could leave us: the only way we could improve our lot.

Living in the small barrio of Masantol, the coming home of my mother's brother David from Guam, where he worked for some time, became a big cause for celebration.

Uncle David, who must have been the very first OFW (overseas foreign worker) in our neck of the woods, brought back a transistor radio for Mother. The whole barrio descended on our house to listen to this novelty. It was a welcome distraction from the humdrum existence of the barrio folk, whose entertainment fare consisted only of a puppet show called *"Kikong Baterya,"* which peddled some kind of panacea ointment, and a yearly fiesta that featured zarzuelas of a roving theater group.

My father was very much respected by everybody in the barrio. Here was a World War II veteran who was a good family man, an honest and hardworking guy who never lorded it over anyone. He would join them over bottles of the poor man's brew called *sioktong* like their old pal. They would go to him to intercede in a neighbors' quarrel, a revelry-cum-brawl or a spat between husband and wife. Knowing my father's qualities, our village voted him *kapitan del baryo* (barrio captain) for many terms without him campaigning or spending for it.

Activism at the State University

In high school at the Jose Rizal Institute in Orani, our history teacher, ex-seminarian Juan Rivera, engaged our class in debates about current events, like the presence of US bases in the Philippines. Bataan is adjacent to Subic Bay and many of my townmates worked on the US naval base there. In fact, I got to join our school *rondalla*[1] to play Filipino music on a US navy ship

---

1. An orchestra of stringed instruments that are our version of the Spanish guitar.

carrying wounded soldiers from the Vietnam War. I noted that there were Filipinos among them.

I entered the University of the Philippines Diliman in the Philippine capital when the Vietnam War was at its height. The campus was in ferment. At Kamia Residence Hall where I was staying, activist dormers were calling for meetings to discuss the issue. I got to join once and listened. Then I listened some more. The argument that the country was under US imperialism made sense to me. The presence of the US bases in the country – the Subic Bay Naval Base and Clark Air Base, which were the largest overseas military installations of the United Stated Armed Forces, both near my hometown – seemed proof enough.

I felt the dissonance between my anti-bases position in our high school debate and my participation in the *rondalla* for US forces fighting the Vietnamese. I welcomed the lectures organized by the *Progresibong Samahan sa Inhinyeriya at Agham*[2] as well as the Student Cultural Association of UP (SCAUP) and Kabataang Makabayan (KM). It was in a discussion group (DG) at the Sunken Garden that I met Mario Miclat, who was our guest lecturer. I would later join a special DG of five people facilitated by Mario, where topics ranged from the so-called people's democratic struggle against the Marcos regime, to socialism and even communism. Meanwhile, Mario would also invite me to watch films which tackled other people's struggles, like *Battle of Algiers*, *Cromwell* and *Burn*.

It was just a matter of time before we got married in a secret communist ceremony. It was an unconventional wedding on all counts. I did not know that I was to be married on that fateful day of Karl Marx's birthday, 5 May 1971. Mario brought me to his UG house in Quezon City. The "wedding" was celebrated by Fernando Tayag, known as Pandong, brother of Nilo Tayag, who co-founded Kabataang Makabayan with Jose Maria Sison. Nilo Tayag became KM's general secretary and then national chairman before his arrest as a subversive on 12 June 1970. (He would, upon release, become a bishop in the Philippine Independent Catholic Church.) Instead of a Bible, we swore on Mao's Red Book, choosing communist quotations as our wedding vows. Instead of wedding rings, we exchanged bullets, presumably to be used by one against the other if ever one betrayed the cause.

During my activist days, my relationship with my father took a bad turn. Whenever I went home to Orani, I would meet fellow activists in the nearby town of Samal which would later become a hotbed of anti-government actions and skirmishes between the communist New People's Army (NPA) and the

---

2. PSIA: Progressive Society in Engineering and Science.

military. I knew my father was not happy about my association with the activists. One casual discussion about my aversion to Marcos and his rule broke out in a shouting match. He was a staunch supporter of Marcos, who he believed was a World War II hero who had fought in Bataan against the Japanese.

Not long after, Mario and I secretly left for China. I just disappeared, and all my family's efforts to locate me failed. An urban legend arose about me: that I was in the fastnesses of the Bataan peninsula, coming down incognito as an old woman to see our house and my family from a distance. It was also said that government troops were watching our house to arrest me if ever I came for a visit.

One day, my family received sad news that a certain "Kumander Alma" had been killed in an encounter with government troops. Her body was brought to the municipal hall of nearby Dinalupihan town. My mother was inconsolable, so it was Father, together with some of my siblings, who went to claim the dead. He did not know whether to cry or laugh when he saw that the body was not mine.

Father was born a Catholic, although he did not go to hear Mass. Mother tried to convert him to the Methodist fold but failed. In the end, she told him to hear the Catholic Mass. He replied that he was a good person with no vices, something that could not be said about some devout churchgoers.

Once, some Catholics persuaded him to join the *De Colores* retreat. The devotees fasted and prayed without letup in a room whose curtains were drawn all day, preventing them from knowing the time of day (they were not allowed to bring any timepieces with them). Not knowing whether it was night or day, my father hallucinated and claimed to see me. He cried and cried unashamedly.

I believe that it was then that he not only forgave me for my activism and for disappearing from their lives, but also became proud of me for my courage that he now equated with his going to the World War II front.

My family would finally hear from me in 1979, when China's ultra-Leftist leadership fell. China, hitherto closed to foreigners, started opening to the outside world. We were able to find a way to communicate, first by way of a circuitous route, through letters sent via our friend from Hong Kong to the US, then to the Philippines. Then, in 1982, my mother and my sister Edna had a chance to visit us in Beijing. My mother said that Father was now actually proud of me.

We came back to the Philippines from China in 1986 when Marcos was overthrown by the People Power revolution. At home in Bataan, no words were said between Father and me. We just held each other tight while tears streamed down our cheeks.

Radio Peking

From 1971 to 1986, Mario and I lived in Beijing and worked at the Filipino Section of Radio Peking under the Chinese Ministry of Radio, Film and Television.

At the beginning, we lived in Shibasuo, a compound of the Eighteen Mansions located in the wooded area where the ancient Wanshoulu Road wound along the Yongdinghe Canal in the suburban western district of Beijing. The compound was exclusively for exiles from communist parties of countries like Thailand, Indonesia and (the former) Malaya. It was run by the International Liaison Department (ILD) of the Communist Party of China. We had English interpreters from ILD who took care of us, accompanying us to the hospital and to the department store, especially during our first autumn when we had to buy winter clothing. ILD leaders also visited us for briefings since our group was supposed to be the representative of the Communist Party of the Philippines and they had to liaise with us.

We worked from Monday to Friday and half day on Saturday at Radio Peking, staying at noon for lunch and afternoon naps at Zhuanjialou, the Foreign Experts Building, a stone's throw from China Radio International which housed the Radio Peking sections broadcasting in different languages beamed to countries all over the world.

We had many encounters with language experts from different countries living in Zhuanjialou at the cavernous canteen where our Chinese cooks served Chinese dishes predictably on a day-to-day basis. For example, *Tan tan mian*, the sesame sauce noodles, would be served, say, on Monday, and only on Monday. The residents therefore knew what day to go to the canteen for their favorite dishes.

Mainstays of the canteen were a Japanese couple, Mr and Mrs Soeda, with their children Minzi and Xiao Wu; a Brazilian couple with their two daughters; and Victor, a sulky old man from Bolivia. Every now and then, the Laotian expert married to a Chinese woman would bring his urinal-like container to buy rice. Malaysian Madin would pick up his wife Mary's ordered dishes. Other experts we met later and who invited us to their homes were Sri Lankans Thamby and Rani Sinnathamby from the Tamil section; Bhadra Gunatilaka from the Sinhala section; and Nita from the Thai section. They all became very dear to us.

Among other experts was the septuagenarian Paraguayan Arsenio Ibañez, who, after the Cultural Revolution, married a young Chinese girl who, skeptics said, was just after a passport to a foreign land. We got to be friends with and liked the food of the Pakistani couple Barakat and Atiya, Afghans Massoud and Mo, Bangladeshis Zahidul and Jamila Huq, and Indians Joshi and Punam.

Foreign experts who arrived after the Cultural Revolution had initial contracts for only two years, renewable for another two years. They included Americans Beverly Polokoff, Rachel Singh, who married an English-speaking Chinese man from China Central TV, Jonathan Wong, who married a Chinese officemate from the English section of Radio Peking, and Steve Miller; and Frenchwoman Barbara Brechet.

But there were those like us who stayed a long time for political reasons, like Thamby Sinnathamby and wife Rani, whose father was a leader of the Ceylon Communist Party. They met in China and got married there. There was also the Turkish expert Maci (we would later learn his real name, Ahmet Turkistanli; he had been imprisoned as an activist and studied in London, and was an artist and author of *Turkish Phrase Book*), who was married to the English expert from London, Yvonne Steward; and the German expert from Berlin, Jochen Noth, and his wife, Evi. We forged deep and lasting friendship with these "old China hands."

Double Lives

For nine years, Mario and I led double lives in Beijing. We lived at Mansion No. 3 at Shibasuo with the Communist Party of the Philippines delegation and went to work at Radio Peking, where we were provided with our own flat at Zhuanjialou together with foreign language experts from different countries. To keep our Shibasuo identity secret, we were introduced as Indonesians Harri and Tini. It was not a well-thought-out ploy as Malaysian Madin once asked us at the canteen what "rice" was in our language, and I answered *kanin* (in Tagalog). "Rice" in Malay and Indonesian was *nasi* (same as in Pampango). Our Indonesian cover was exposed!

When I became pregnant with my first baby, everybody was solicitous and even sympathetic toward me, young as I was. Our Chinese colleagues in the Filipino section were particularly attentive to me, advising me on what to eat, how to keep myself warm at the onset of winter and to be extra careful when walking on the slippery icy road. It was a difficult transition period for me, having moved from a tropical clime to a temperate country, now with a baby growing in my tummy – not to speak of the gnawing feeling of homesickness.

At the time we arrived in China, the Cultural Revolution was in full swing. It was a purge spearheaded by Mao Tse-tung against those who veered away from his dictum, the so-called "counter-revolutionaries," as well as "bourgeois" ideas, old customs, habits, practices, traditions and philosophies. It was a massive crackdown on the bureaucracy and the taking over by ultra-Leftist militants of all government institutions, units and establishments. Intellectuals became a prime target, with doctors, professors, scientists and experts being sent to the countryside to be "reeducated" by the masses of farmers and workers. Schools were shut down and under Mao's wife, Jiang Qing, the arts espoused only one style, dubbed the "proletarian." Artistic creativity was stifled and the arts in general became stagnant.

Six Peking operas and two full-length ballets became the staple theater fare repeatedly shown to the then 800 million Chinese used to hundreds of years of theatrical performances. *Shachiapang* was the very first opera I saw and would repeatedly see, alternating with *The Red Lantern* and *Taking Tiger Mountain by Strategy*. The ballets *The Red Detachment of Women* and *White-Haired Girl* were also regular theater fare, not to mention their film versions. One other sanctioned entertainment was acrobatics which, if exciting at first, ultimately became a bore. Acrobatic troupes like that of Beijing, Shenyang and Chungking (which eventually became globally known) performed the same politically sanctioned routines.

Later, we would be treated to films which were not shown publicly, some of which were from Albania, Romania, Yugoslavia and North Korea, and some old Soviet films of Leninist and Stalinist periods (1920s–1950s). We would learn later that Jiang Qing, who was a B movie actress in Shanghai before she became Mao's wife, enjoyed watching Hollywood films, her favorite being *Gone with the Wind*. The dissonance between her "bourgeois" lifestyle and the "proletarian" lifestyle she imposed on the Chinese people was appalling.

We arrived in Beijing in August 1971, and the following month, Mao's so-called closest comrade-in-arms and successor, Lin Piao, died in an airplane crash in Ulan Bator, Mongolia, fleeing after his failed putsch against the former. The news was divulged only months later and only in underground communication lines by the Chinese Communist Party. As we were ILD's special guests, we got a briefing from the Chinese earlier than most, in time for the movement against Lin Piao and Confucius ("Pi Lin, Pi Kong").

Earlier, we were invited to attend China's 22nd National Day on 1 October 1971, the first since the Cultural Revolution started in 1966, held in the Summer Palace grounds. I thought I would see Mao there, since old photos showed him at such celebrations. But he did not come. He never attended any such events that followed. We saw Cambodia's Prince Norodom Sihanouk and Princess Monique, though.

A most exciting event for me was attending our first New Year dinner for foreign "comrades" hosted by no less than the charismatic Prime Minister Zhou Enlai and his wife Deng Yingchao. Speaking in English, Zhou told me to take care of my health as he noticed that I was pregnant. Our ILD interpreter said it was the first such high-level Communist Party banquet since the Cultural Revolution. Other hosts who personally toasted their wine glasses with us included those who were later denounced as the "Gang of Four" (Mao's wife Jiang Qing, theoreticians Yao Wenyuan and Zhang Chunqiao, and Shanghai stalwart Wang Hongwen).

Martial Law and Its Ideological Fallout

We were already in China when Marcos suspended *habeas corpus* following the bombing of the Liberal Party rally at Plaza Miranda in Quiapo, Manila, on 21 August 1971. A number of key LP figures, as well as part of the audience, were killed, maimed or wounded.

The CPP delegation in Beijing, under the leadership of Politburo member Ibarra Tubianosa, started to negotiate with the Chinese Communist Party the sending of firearms to the Philippines.

MV *Karagatan* disembarked at Digoyo Point, Palanan, Isabela, with 1,200 M-14 rifles, grenade launchers and communication equipment. These were to be received by guerrilla forces headed by Philippine Military Academy lieutenant-turned-rebel Victor Corpus. The vessel was spotted by a logger in his helicopter, who reported it to the military, which then undertook operations by land, air and water. Fighting ensued and the guerrilla forces withdrew, salvaging only 200 pieces of the smuggled arms that fateful month of July 1972.

When Marcos declared martial law on 21 September 1972, another arms shipment was negotiated by the delegation. It took two more years and approval by Mao himself before MV *Andrea* set off.

That ship, however, did not even reach Hainan naval base, where it was supposed to pick up armaments. MV *Andrea*, manned by inexperienced and seasick NPA fighters and cadres, floundered in the South China Sea and got shipwrecked at Pratas Islands, about 340 kilometers southeast of Hong Kong.

The stranded crew of twelve were bombarded by naval forces from the Taiwan territory but were eventually saved by a Panamanian ship and brought to Hong Kong, where they asked for asylum from China.[3]

---

3. A detailed account of this can be found in Mario I. Miclat, *Secrets of the Eighteen Mansions* (Mandaluyong City: Anvil Press, 2010; repr. 2011).

At Shibasuo, the delegation, which included Tubianosa and his wife Estrella, Ricardo Malay and wife Rosario Ramirez, Mario and myself, Roger Arcilla and France de Lima, who was the governess of Joma and Juliet Sison's children Jana, Jayson and Jemima, started to become restless and disillusioned. The failed missions to smuggle arms to the comrades at home and the increasing reports of arrests of high-ranking communist cadres and NPA operatives, coupled with ennui and homesickness, brought dissatisfaction and conflicts in the group.

However, the group was one in its criticisms of the CPP leadership for the many mistakes it had made, not least of which was the bombing of Plaza Miranda. When a Party courier from Manila came one time, we decided that each of us would write a letter of criticism to express what we felt. All the letters we sent via a circuitous route ended up at the US–Canadian border, where the bearer was apprehended with the letters and a sizable amount of US dollars.

When Deng Xiaoping rose again to power and the ultra-Leftist gang of four of Jiang Qing was overthrown, the ideological and military support by the Chinese Communist Party of the Communist Party of the Philippines in particular, and of the "world revolution" in general, took a 180-degree turn. This was sealed by the establishment of diplomatic relations between the Philippines and China in 1975 following the visit of Imelda Marcos, which came after the "ping-pong diplomacy" between China and the United States initiated by US Secretary of State Henry Kissinger in 1971. Apparently, the "export of revolution" was starting to become a thing of the past.

The CPP delegation was relocated from Shibasuo in Beijing to a Chinese state farm in Hunan province. They would later be joined by the "Dirty Dozen," the moniker of the MV *Andrea* crew of twelve who were granted asylum by the Chinese government.

Mario and I, with our daughter Maningning, were left behind at Shibasuo as we continued working at Radio Peking. We made a visit to the state farm to be with the delegation and the Dirty Dozen every so often and to participate in farming and "reform through labor." On one such visit Mario stayed longer but I had to return to Radio Peking to continue my work. Maningning stayed behind with her father.

I became miserable without my husband and daughter, so I had Maningning brought back to me in Beijing. What was happening at the state farm – the political feuds, endless debates, wranglings, even personal quarrels leading to fisticuffs – was just a microcosm of what was happening inside the Party in our own country. And I didn't want Maningning to internalize what she was witnessing. I did not realize how deeply it had affected her until I read her account in the Postscript of her trilingual book of poetry, *Voice from the Underworld*,[4] when she was already twenty-eight. It read:

> One day, my mother asked me where I would want to stay, and I told her, with my father. She had to part with me tearfully. When I arrived at the countryside, my father was being held in a room after he was accused of "serious political mistakes" by a few of his compatriots[5] in the special compound in the countryside. Nobody was allowed to see him and he was not allowed to see the sun. Everyone pitied me and treated me like an orphan. So I roamed around in the most carefree way. There was a condensed milk factory in the village and I was allowed to take my cup near the pool where milk and sugar were being boiled and mixed. A Chinese auntie with rubber boots would fetch me a warm cup of condensed milk that made me feel fortunate.

Maningning further wrote: "That was more than twenty years ago . . . Fragments of memories tiptoe into the vignettes of here and now. For all that was heard, for all that has been, we become the keepers of our voice."

Change Is Coming!

I was finally able to get Maningning back to Beijing when a member of the delegation came to Beijing and brought my baby with him. And I got Mario back much later, when our Chinese colleagues in the Philippine section requested that the ILD let Mario return to Beijing to help in the translation of Party documents for China's national congress.

The intervention of the Chinese comrades enabled Mario to return to Beijing. By that time, Ibarra Tubianosa had already resigned as head of the Philippine delegation, which was in complete disarray. A new officer-in-charge took over and the verdict to expel Ibarra and Mario from the Party due to so-called "political mistakes" and "factionalism" came out. Ibarra asked the ILD to let him leave the state farm and be transferred to another place with his family. Some from the Dirty Dozen asked to leave the delegation too, with some returning to the Philippines, while others went to the Netherlands.

When Mario came back to resume his work at Radio Peking, he was gaunt and sick. He was diagnosed with primary complex TB, which he transmitted

---

4. Maningning Miclat, *Voice from the Underworld* (Mandaluyong: Anvil Publishing, 2000).
5. Some in the CPP delegation.

to me in no time. The ILD arranged a vacation for us and Maningning at Badaguan seaside resort of Qingdao (Tsingtao), Shandong province in East China. Although the city had become famous for its beer, which was a legacy of the German occupation (1897–1914), at that time, the tail-end of the Cultural Revolution, Qingdao beer was not served to us. However, the peace and quiet we found after the tumultuous events we'd experienced, coupled with the balmy sea breeze and fresh seafood, gave us new strength and energy when we returned to Beijing after a few weeks. It was also then that our daughter Banaue was conceived.

Changes had been transforming China. By 1978, Deng Xiaoping made another comeback. He was twice purged during the period of the People's Republic: first, during the Cultural Revolution as "capitalist roader," together with then president Liu Shaoqi in 1967; then in 1976, after a remarkable comeback in 1973 aided by Premier Zhou Enlai, during a power struggle after the death of Mao Tse-tung. He was in his seventies at the time of his second comeback, when he encouraged the creation of a market economy and capitalist enterprises. His contribution was monumental and changed China's stature for good, ushering in a modernized, industrialized country.

By 1979, we requested to move from Shibasuo to Radio Peking's Zhuanjialou. We thought a more normal life with the other foreign experts and their families would be good for Maningning and Banaue, who would be born in July that year. And since we would not be under the International Liaison Department anymore, we were asked by the Radio Peking's Foreign Experts Bureau to accept salaries which we had refused when we started working at the Radio in 1971.

Our transfer to Zhuanjialou heralded the many changes, mostly welcome, that would come our way. The opening up of China did not only mean political and economic change, but cultural change as well. The once barren and desolate cultural life in Beijing suddenly breathed new life.

We saw China Philharmonic Orchestra onstage performing Beethoven's Symphony No. 5 for the first time after the Cultural Revolution. We were also invited to watch Western operas in the Chinese language, such as *La traviata* and *Madame Butterfly*.

Foreign acts also were shown, such as the Old Vic Theatre from London performing *Hamlet*. Arthur Miller, meanwhile, directed *Death of a Salesman*. It was a delight to watch Luciano Pavarotti on a Chinese stage, and Herbert von Karajan and Seiji Ozawa with his Boston Symphony Orchestra charmed the culture-hungry Beijing community.

It was a wintry night in 1979 when we went to a Protestant church in Beijing. The choir sang Handel's *Messiah*. We had not heard a single church song in the previous eight years, and hearing the *Messiah* once again was overwhelming and overpowering.

As mentioned earlier, I had been brought up a Methodist by a mother whose father, Anastacio Capuli, was one of the pillars of the United Methodist Church in the province of Bataan. Growing up, my Catholic friends and I could not enter each other's churches. I didn't quite get it. Only when I studied in UP and was introduced to liberal, albeit radical, ideas did I embrace religious tolerance and ecumenism.

That year, 1979, saw the official opening of some churches not only in Beijing but also in Shanghai. We had the privilege of attending a Latin Mass at the Church of the Immaculate Conception in Xianwumen, Beijing. This was the cathedral which consecrated Bishop Michael Fu Tieshan, the first major event in the life of the Catholic Church in China after the Cultural Revolution.

Our life in Zhuanjialou took on some semblance of normalcy as we started to become friends with the other foreigners living in the building and our children played with their children. We had now done away with the limousine earlier provided for us while we were living in Shibasuo. We learned to ride the metro, the underground train. And we squeezed ourselves onto the crowded buses just like the regular Chinese.

Even though the Radio Peking Foreign Experts Bureau arranged entertainment fare for us, like a weekly film at Youyi Bingguan/Friendship Hotel where other foreign experts from other Chinese institutions like Foreign Languages Press were staying, we also ventured out on our own. We rode bikes exploring *hutong* (narrow lanes) with our Turkish and British friends and found places of interest and quaint restaurants offering delicious food.

With the salaries that we now had, we first invited my mother and sister Edna to visit us in 1982. They were followed by Mario's mother and brother Manny the following year. Our Maningning and Banaue finally met their grandmothers on both sides.

Our opening up, if obliquely, presented an opportunity to meet Consul Nona Zaldivar of the Philippine embassy in Beijing. Daughter of Supreme Court Justice Calixto Zaldivar, Nona was a career diplomat. She invited UP Cherubims and Seraphims to perform in Beijing and met up with the China Central Radio Children's Chorus of which Maningning was a member. Nona was delighted to meet a Filipina member of the Chinese choir. But at that time, we were still supposed to be incognito and Maningning held back, afraid that she was revealing her parents' cover. I felt sad that my ten-year-old daughter could be so affected and feel distraught over her parents' political situation.

When my mother-in-law came to visit one time and we encountered Nona again at the Friendship Store exclusively for foreigners, we were ready to befriend her. We met again later and exchanged visits between our Zhuanjialou and her embassy flat. Through her, we got to meet the other Filipinos who went to Beijing to teach, like Mrs Nieves Epistola, whom we fondly called Mrs E., and students like Sunny Benitez and Connie Ladrido, among others. Through her also we got to meet and watch Gilopez and Corazon Kabayao perform in Beijing, as well as Lucrecia Kasilag and Carmencita Lozada. We also got to meet and interview the Unyon ng mga Manunulat ng Pilipinas (Writers' Union of the Philippines) delegation, headed by its chair, Virgilio S. Almario, right at the embassy.

Our visit to the Philippine embassy emboldened us to apply for a passport for myself and our two daughters. With the help of our Congressman in Bataan, Tony Roman, who was close to my parents, we were granted passports. Prior to that, we met his wife, Mrs Herminia Roman, who visited us at Radio Peking when she went to China.

With the newly acquired passports, I flew to Manila with Maningning and Banaue in 1984. It was a very emotional reunion with my family after thirteen years, and their first time meeting my daughters. Our happy visit, though, was marred by sadness when Mario's mother passed away in New York and her remains were brought back to Manila.

In Beijing, Nona Zaldivar, who was then the officer-in-charge in the absence of the ambassador, prepared all the documents to grant Mario a passport to be with his departed mother before she was buried. She tried her best to get the approval of the Department of Foreign Affairs home office, but to no avail. Mario Ignacio Miclat, whose name was listed as one of the subversives wanted by the government, was refused a passport to travel to see his mother for the last time.

The Journey Home

The year 1986 ended our exile in the erstwhile communist country when President Ferdinand E. Marcos, the Philippine dictator who had ruled the country for twenty-one years, hastily fled Malacañang Palace after the EDSA People Power Revolution. The confluence of events – a series of mass demonstrations which started in 1983 after Ninoy Aquino was assassinated and culminated in February 1986; the breaking away from the Marcos regime by Defense Minister Juan Ponce Enrile and Armed Forces of the Philippines Vice Chief of Staff Fidel Ramos; and the support of Jaime Cardinal Sin who rallied thousands of people to EDSA in a peaceful revolt – had heralded the downfall of Marcos and the return of democracy in the land.

Mario and I listened intently to the shortwave broadcasts – Voice of America, the BBC, Radio Australia – on 22–25 February 1986, the last few days of martial rule in the Philippines. Our own Radio Peking was reporting news culled from the communist-approved Hsinhua News Agency, which was eons away from what was happening on the Philippine streets, saying that Marcos had won the elections. And, obviously, the events during those four days in February 1986 shook the Philippines, if not the world.

We were ecstatic at the turn of events after our fifteen-year stay in China. Our friends at Zhuanjialou were also happy. The Japanese experts came to our office and our home to toast the success of EDSA People Power. The wife of Mr Junichiro Ide, Kazuko, who was vacationing in Japan at that time, sent by express mail hours of Betamax footage of the EDSA revolution.

The euphoria brought about by the success of the struggle against dictatorship ignited our desire to come home. Mario went first to see if the call by President Cory Aquino to Filipinos abroad to come home to participate in rebuilding the nation was true. He visited UP and its president, Edgardo Angara, whom we had met in Beijing when he visited prior to the EDSA revolution. His invitation made to Mario during his Beijing visit to teach at UP was reiterated. He wanted Mario to report to the dean of UP Asian Center, Ajit Singh Rye, and start teaching the following day.

Mario returned to Beijing and our family prepared for our journey back home. In a *despedida*[6] hosted by the Chinese comrades, our host spoke about leaving China and leaving its memory behind. He said that once we had left, we must make sure to forget what we had seen in China.

With hindsight, I feel that this was an admonition not to copy China's revolution, not to import revolution. It meant *Jili gengsheng*, "depending on your own (strength)," fighting your own revolution.

In 2002, I had a chance to visit Beijing again, sixteen years since I had left China. My husband, my daughter Banaue and I went to Shibasuo, the Eighteen Mansions, and found that the monumental changes that had catapulted China into becoming a world power had also reached this hidden enclave of communists from different countries. Only three out of the eighteen mansions were left and had become offices of trade companies. Meanwhile, our five-story

---

6. A farewell banquet.

Zhuanjialou, the Foreign Experts Building, was soon to be demolished, to give way to a high-rise condominium building.

Before we left Beijing, we were feted by our Chinese colleagues at Radio Peking. It was an emotional dinner where we exchanged not only pleasantries but also their revelations of what they had gone through while we were working with them but which they had kept secret from us all this time. For example, when we visited them unannounced during those days, they would afterwards be visited by the militia, trying to find out what we had done or said or what they had divulged to us. They could laugh about it now, as when one quipped, "You know, you don't have to pilfer eggs from your pantry to give to us anymore!" They were remembering those survival times in the 1970s when China was so poor after the disastrous "Great Leap Forward" and "Great Proletarian Cultural Revolution."

Three decades after we left China for good, we were able to contact some of our old foreign friends from Zhuanjialou, thanks to the wonder of the Internet. In 2015, Mario and I visited London, stayed with Yvonne Steward and visited her daughter Ceren. Rani Sinnathamby also visited London from Sri Lanka. Sadly, both she and Yvonne are widows now. We also got to visit widower Jochen Noth and his daughter Jule in Berlin.

Earlier in 2010, Mario met Yvonne in Istanbul on his visit there with a UP delegation headed by President Emerlinda Roman. It was a very touching visit as Yvonne brought Mario to the tomb of his bosom friend Ahmet Turkistanli. That visit gave birth to a poem written by Mario expressing the friendship that had been forged decades before in China:

> To AHMET MAÇI
>
> I cannot find you in Istanbul,
> > my Turkish friend.
> The music they play in Hagia Sofia is soft and mellow
> > compared to the marching songs of our revolutions.
>
> The Virgin's house in Izmir is too holy
> > for Christians and Muslims,
> And the ruins of Ephesus too ancient
> > when seen from our promises of a new world.
>
> The baclavas of Gaziantep
> > melt in the mouth
> Unlike the bullets spewed
> > by the barrels of the guns of our armed struggles.

The ice cream of Kahramanmaraş
is smooth and sweet and cold.

Ah, the ice cream
of Kahramanmaraş.
Abraham's Balik Ligöl in Sanliurfa
reminds people of love among humankind.

No, I do not find you in all of Anatolia,
my Turkish friend.
Its highways now
are too straight and wide
Against our Maoist thought
of twists and turns, our ups and downs.

You left this earth too young. And I
am too old to see the paradigms unfold –
Your Turkey, riding the tide
of globalization;
My Philippines, slashed by typhoons
of our intellectual poverty, arrogance and neglect.

Our journey has been long. And our country's journey even longer.

6

Uncle Sam behind the Scenes

A View from the Corridors of Power

Willie Buyson Villarama

My story begins on Friday, 21 February 1986, at 3 a.m. in Cambridge, Massachusetts. I was in my last semester at Harvard's Kennedy School, finishing my master's in Public Administration. It was 4 p.m. in Manila when Mila Cruz, the executive assistant of Minister of Labor Blas F. Ople (BFO) called me in my Harvard dorm known as Peabody Terraces.

Her trembling voice ordered me to fly to Washington DC as soon as possible to meet my boss, BFO. I was BFO's assistant minister for Legislative Affairs after my stint as vice governor of Bulacan from 1972 to 1980, and I was currently on study leave. He was also my wedding godfather[1] when I got married in 1983.

I was rattled. When I asked Mila why, she replied: "There is a problem here. I cannot explain." She dictated the flight number, United Airlines 54, arriving at Dulles Airport, and hung up the phone.

Busy with my studies, I did not know what had been happening in the Philippines. I took the first plane out of Boston to Washington DC and waited for the arrival of Minister Ople and party.

He arrived with Ambassador to Russia Alex Melchor, Ambassador to the United States Kokoy Romualdez and POEA Deputy Administrator Manuel Imson, his regular traveling companion and my wedding godson. He was the

---

1. This is a practice at weddings, having godparents watch over the couple about to be wed.

one who helped me recall these historical events because he kept a diary and had an album of photographs.

NEDA Deputy Minister Ramon "Eki" Cardenas, an Ateneo classmate, was on another flight bringing luggage containing papers and documents. When I interviewed him for this article, he told me that the instruction given to him by Malacañang was just to take a plane to Washington where somebody would pick up the luggage. He had to surrender the baggage claim tags to whoever approached him. He did not know what the documents inside were, nor did he know the person who would approach him to pick up the luggage. I was with BFO almost twenty-four hours a day and I can say with 101 percent accuracy that we never got the documents he was supposed to show the US authorities. Up to now, Eki had been with the Marcos family. He was the chief-of-staff of Sen. Bongbong Marcos, and now the chief of staff of Congresswoman Imelda Marcos.

Mystery?

I greeted Minister Ople and Ambassador Melchor. I heard Minister Ople tell Melchor, "See you tomorrow for breakfast."

I found out that Melchor's assignment was to introduce Ople to the State Department, where he would explain the political situation in the Philippines and deny the black propaganda being spread by political opponents of President Marcos who were contesting the results of the elections of 7 February which Marcos had supposedly won.

He was also going to explain the strength of the NPA because the US Congress was going to cut US military aid to the Philippine Armed Forces by half.

The snap elections had been announced by President Marcos on 4 November 1985 on the American Broadcasting Company TV show *This Week with David Brinkley*. Hosts Sam Donaldson and George Will "asked [President Marcos] about his policies and support when, without warning he announced that he would hold Snap Elections on February 7, 1986, a year earlier than the supposed 1987 elections."[2]

During the counting of votes, thirty-five computer programmers walked out of the COMELEC's electronic counting held at the Philippine International Convention Center (PICC), claiming massive cheating. To complete the drama, they went to the nearby Baclaran Catholic Church to seek sanctuary. This was covered by national TV and radio, which led Cardinal Ricardo Vidal,

---

2. "Philippine Presidential Election, 1986," Wikipedia, https://en.m.wikipedia.org/wiki/Philippine_presidential_election,_1986.

President of the Catholic Bishop's Conference of the Philippines, to release a declaration stating, among other things, that if "a government does not of itself freely correct the evil it has inflicted on the people, then it is our serious moral obligation as a people to make it do so."[3]

Reports later showed that some of the programmers who had walked out were related to participants of the military coup.

The problems of President Marcos and his cronies had started when the *Mercury News* published a series of articles from 23 to 25 June 1985 revealing "a list of names, showing how the Filipino elite had illegally invested millions in the U.S., why real estate conditions made California a prime investment territory, and how capital flight fueled Philippine insurgency."[4]

These stories were reprinted in Philippine newspapers and caused protests in the streets. The stories were later printed in major American newspapers, such as the *New York Times*, *Washington Post*, *Boston Globe*, *Los Angeles Times*, and in *Newsweek* and *Time* magazine. America has a track record of showing its strength in destroying rulers it does not like. Unfortunately, in almost all cases of leaders it has deposed, the situation has led to more problems for the citizens.

The official election results whereby Marcos had won were the basis of his proclamation by Congress. The results were not accepted by the opposition. Instead, they went out onto the streets, orchestrated by both local Filipinos and sympathizers from other countries. Candidate Cory Aquino was proclaimed President by a revolutionary government backed up by the military, led by Minister of Defense Juan Ponce Enrile and AFP Vice Chief of Staff Fidel V. Ramos, both once avid followers and students of President Marcos.

Minister Enrile, during the coup, admitted that he had cheated Aquino of 350,000 votes in his province of Cagayan.[5] In real life, the winner is always forgiven for the sins he or she has committed in the past. The loser is sent to Hawaii, killed like Sen. Ninoy Aquino or jailed like former president Gloria Macapagal Arroyo, a good friend and boss whom I served for twelve years.

The Singapore icon Lee Kuan Yew was a strong, tough leader : "Lee's rule was criticized for curtailing civil liberties (media control and limits on public protests) and bringing libel suits against political opponents. He argued that such disciplinary measures were necessary for political stability which, together with rule of law, were essential for economic progress."[6]

---

3. "Philippine Presidential Election, 1986."
4. "Philippine Presidential Election, 1986."
5. As reported by *Mr and Ms Magazine*, 28 February 1986.
6. "Lee Kuan Yew," Wikipedia, https://en.wikipedia.org/wiki/Lee_Kuan_Yew.

His tough anti-corruption stance led to the suicide of Teh Cheang Wan, Minister for National Development, when Lee ordered an investigation into complaints of his corruption. He limited families to two children, introduced caning, and prohibited chewing gum and long hair. He was the idol of Filipino politicians who wanted change. Really?

Back to Washington. BFO, Manny Imson and I checked in at the Mayflower Hotel, room 858, where one incident worried me a lot. When I had introduced Minister Ople as the visitor, I was immediately given the key without having to register. This led me to think later that the notorious CIA – Central Intelligence Agency – might have taken over our group.

A few days later I was proven correct.

Upon checking out of the hotel, I discovered that the room had been registered under my name, Willie Villarama. Manny Imson, our historian, was able to keep the bills, including those for all telephone calls made under my name. I found out only recently that the luggage from Malacañang had got lost on its way to the Mayflower Hotel. This will be explained later.

We had a comfortable room with an adjoining small room for me. Administrator Imson had his own room.

At around 3 a.m. on Saturday 22 February (4 p.m. in Manila), I received another call from Mila Cruz, Minister Ople's Girl Friday. I had disengaged Minister Ople's phone so as not to disturb his sleep after his long journey from Manila. I was acting as the telephone operator.

Mila wanted me to wake up the minister. I told her he was very tired from his hectic trip from the Philippines, but she insisted. When I asked why, she said, "Mrs Ponce Enrile was on the radio, crying, looking for her husband Defense Secretary Juan Ponce Enrile, who is missing. There is something happening here in Manila."

I woke up the minister and heard him say, "What, Enrile is staging a revolt? That is impossible! Is he that brave to go against Marcos?"

I agreed with my boss, but there are sometimes incidents in one's life that force one to be brave – especially when one is about to be caught by one's superiors trying to unseat them from power through a military coup. One of the soldiers involved in the coup had had a change of heart and squealed on them.

Fear of death or imprisonment creates heroes. People have reasons for all their actions, right or wrong, lawful or unlawful. Rationalization has been a terrible fad, even among those who interpret the Bible. The Natural Law is twisted for convenience and to justify one's actions.

Since BFO was now awake, he asked me to order coffee for us and to turn on the television to CNN. We were both surprised that Camp Aguinaldo was shown with a CNN reporter announcing that something was brewing.

When the faces of Secretary Juan Ponce Enrile and General Fidel Ramos appeared on the screen in a press conference, Minister Ople remarked: "Life is really unfair. We should be the ones in Camp Crame." He was referring to his role as the "conscience" of the ruling party, as at times he had expressed disagreement with government policies. The most publicized of these was his statement which had made the headlines of most newspapers on 4 March 1985: "Government is in INTERREGNUM, OPLE." All of us had had to borrow or buy a dictionary to find the meaning: "INTERREGNUM: Noun. A period when normal government is suspended, especially between successive reigns or regimes."

After Minister Ople's death, *Time* magazine came out with a story by Anthony Spaeth dated 20 December 2003 with the heading: "Eulogy: Blas Ople":

> In 1986, BLAS OPLE was the guy Ferdinand Marcos dispatched to Washington just before he ordered tanks to try to quell Manila's People Power revolution. In a starched *barong tagalog* and with an extraordinary baritone, Blas vainly lobbied Capitol Hill that Marcos wasn't all that bad. One day he admitted to the press what he shouldn't have: that the Philippines under Marcos was in an "interregnum." Blas, a big talker and determined erudite, loved that word.
>
> He was a Marcos Cabinet member for 18 years, but he wasn't corrupt, and that anomaly plus the widely admired interregnum comment . . .[7]

I could not download the whole story, but I guess what the minister had meant with his comment that the Marcos government was in an "interregnum" gave the opponents of Marcos from within and outside the ruling party a glimpse of the president's health, which in turn emboldened them to put him down. This is just my guess.

The day after the "interregnum" headlines, BFO called me to his office to prepare his IBM electric typewriter, because he was going to write the president his letter of resignation. Marcos had not liked his remark that the government was in a state of interregnum. "Preparing" meant that, apart from his typewriter, there was a pack of Winston cigarettes, a lighter, an ashtray and a cup of *barako* black coffee.

---

7. Anthony Spaeth, "Eulogy: Blas Ople," 20 December 2003, *Time*, http://content.time.com/time/magazine/article/0,9171,565986,00.html.

That date, 5 March 1985, was historic for me because it was that morning I received a telex from Harvard Kennedy School admissions office that I had been accepted on the Master's in Public Administration program for the school year 1985–1986.

When Minister Ople sat on his chair to start typing his letter, he said: "I am going to type my letter of resignation. The president wants to see me. He was very displeased with my interregnum remark."

That was a blow to my dream of studying at Harvard, but I told him: "Sir, that is bad news – your resignation. But there is good news: I was accepted by Harvard."

To this he replied, "We will be out of a job after we go to Malacañang. Sorry about you losing your scholarship."

I replied, "Sir, that is no problem. I will join you wherever you go after today."

Marcos never asked for his resignation, but instead he reminded BFO how they had first met and of the political battle they had gone through. Before leaving, BFO told Marcos, "Mr President, I hope we can meet often" – to which Marcos replied, "Sure, Blas, just be careful with the words you use."

So I went to Harvard on a scholarship.

Secretary Blas Ople was like a second father to me. I learned the meaning of integrity in public service from him. My bragging right is that I was one of the few he hired twice in his career: first, as his assistant minister of Labor and Employment from 1982 to 1986, and second, as his chief of staff when he was a senator from 1992 to 1998. And in 1998 he "loaned" me to Vice President Gloria Macapagal Arroyo and I became her first chief of staff. In 2001 I ran for Congress in my home province of Bulacan, and won.

Going back to that morning when Ambassador Melchor apparently lost his way to the Mayflower Hotel coffee shop where we were waiting for him, I thought I would never "discover" what had happened to Minister Ople's "special guide" (Melchor) who was supposed to accompany him to the State Department.

Recently, when I attended the wake of a friend, I happened to meet the military officer assigned to the office of the then Philippine Military Attaché, who was Melchor. I had been telling a friend who was with me when Ople had arrived in Washington about this book on EDSA 1. I asked her if she knew where Ambassador Melchor had gone when he disappeared. She pointed to one of the visitors seated behind me and said: "Talk with him. He was the one who fetched Ambassador Melchor."

She was referring to then Navy Attaché Fernandez "Jun" Tucay, Jr. He was very cooperative and agreed to email me his recollections of those days. They bolstered my conclusion that the EDSA 1 "miracle" was made not altogether in heaven but also somewhere on earth.

The following are excerpts from his email to me:

Day 1. Friday, 21 February 1986

Arrival at the Dulles International Airport (Washington National Airport) of Former Executive Secretary Alejandro Melchor Jr. and Foreign Affairs Secretary Blas F. Ople.

Upon securing Melchor's luggage, we proceeded to Hotel One Washington where he was booked for the duration of his stay in Washington.

From what I understood, the two officials were sent by the president to explain to the US government officials about the political, economic, public works infrastructure, security, and other programs of the government aimed toward improving the lot of the Filipino and for national progress.

Day 2. Saturday, 22 February 1986

At 8 a.m., I escorted Melchor to the Pentagon for his scheduled rounds of calls and meetings.

[Note: Melchor was supposed to meet with Minister Ople for breakfast but did not show up. Even President Marcos was looking for him that morning. – WBV]

At noon, he asked that he be left alone with no escort, but that he would call if he needed me. I did not receive any call from him. At the end of the workday at 5 p.m., still no word from him if my services were needed.

At 9 p.m., I called front desk of the hotel, identified myself, and asked to be connected to his room. The attendant obliged, but I received no answer.

Day 3. Sunday, 23 February 1986

I left my house early the next day and went straight to the hotel, arriving at around 7 a.m. Front desk told me that a "Do not disturb" sign was seen hanging on Melchor's room door.

I learned later that the secretary had returned to the hotel at around 3 o'clock in the morning. He appeared later at the embassy and talked to me. He talked about the grave situation in the country and had urged me to switch sides.

"This Ponce Enrile jumped out[8] from the Marcos bandwagon because of his displeasure that he did not get the blessings of Marcos to become the country's prime minister instead of Cesar Virata."

On Ramos's case, Melchor expressed the former's disgruntlement on why Gen. Ver continued to hold on to his position as chief of staff, AFP, despite the fact that orders had been signed and published designating him chief of staff, Vice Gen. Fabian C. Ver.

I replied that I was staying put because Marcos was still the duly constituted leader. His parting word was that when I came home, I must see him and he would give a good word about me to General Ramos. That was the last meeting I had with Melchor.

I found out that Melchor stayed most of the night of Monday with the National Security Adviser John Poindexter, a co-alumnus of his at the US Naval Academy.

The reader can draw his or her own conclusions as to whether there was treachery or double-crossing here.

To continue my own story, on Saturday, 22 February, at 9 a.m. (10 p.m. in Manila), President Marcos called and asked me if I had seen Ambassador Melchor. I told him that I had seen the ambassador the previous day when he arrived with Minister Ople.

"Tell him to call me when he arrives there."

BFO asked me, "Who called?"

"It was President Marcos, sir," I replied. "Why did you not let me talk with him?"

"He was not looking for you."

This was the time when, according to the email account of the Navy officer assigned to Ambassador Melchor, Jun Tucay, he was escorting Melchor to the Pentagon "for his scheduled rounds of calls and meetings."

From the very start Melchor was against Marcos. Classic Trojan horse story. But I do not condemn him. He must have had his reasons. May he rest in peace.

After the call of President Marcos, I got nervous because Ambassador Melchor was supposed to have breakfast with BFO. Marcos knew they were due to meet. My sixth sense was accurate. The super speed of our check-in

---

8. Itong si Ponce naman, nag-bailout siya.

confirmed that people outside and inside the Philippines were doing things that threatened the independence of our land. And after many years, finding out about the lost documents that were brought by Eki Cardenas proves that there was a conspiracy from the very start to depose Marcos. There were traitors around him. The visit of Minister Ople to the US was just a ploy to make the events dramatic. We spent the day meeting with Philippine Embassy officials like Boots Anson Roa Rodrigo, Fred de la Rosa, who was the Philippine Labor Attaché, and others.

On Sunday, 23 February 1986, around 4 p.m., BFO and I were having *merienda*[9] in the coffee shop of the hotel. "Don't you know anybody here in Washington DC?" he asked.

I panicked and realized that my suspicion was correct. Ambassador Melchor had abandoned my boss, with nobody to bring him to the State Department. And worse, the luggage full of documents had also got lost on its way to the Mayflower Hotel. Minister Ople did not have a single page to show the US authorities to answer the issues brought against President Marcos.

As his assistant minister I never asked him questions unless he asked me for my views. I did not even know what his assignment was in coming to the US. I could sense what was happening, but I kept it to myself. As a subordinate, I was never in the habit of opening my mouth unless asked or unless it was a situation that would affect his physical safety or his career as a public official.

I replied, "My professors fly here on weekends, but they cannot be disturbed on weekends, which are sacred to Americans."

His question was asked out of frustration. Melchor, his guide to the corridors of power, had disappeared without trace or even a call.

This to me was a strong indication that the Americans had a hand in our historic "EDSA miracle." It was a miracle made in Washington DC, but also a genuine miracle in that few were killed in Manila, unlike in some countries where hundreds were killed. When the US meddled, such as in Hawaii, Iran, Iraq, Kuwait, Afghanistan, Libya, Syria, Vietnam and Korea, many died for democracy, American style.

As an example, the first territory that the US took over outside the mainland was Hawaii. The US military arrested Queen Liliuokalani upon the behest of American businessmen who controlled the pineapple plantations and used the natives as slaves. Sanford B. Dole was appointed the territorial governor and Castle and Cooke were among the big five pineapple plantation owners. On 16 January 1893, the queen and her cabinet ministers were forced to surrender

---

9. An afternoon snack.

when they found out that an American gunboat was in the harbor with 162 American soldiers on board.[10]

The strategy that the opponents of Marcos implemented was to withhold from BFO the information he could use to explain the political situation in the Philippines to American authorities. He was given the feeling that he could save President Marcos with all the papers he had with him. However, without his knowledge he went to Washington with a "Trojan horse." How was BFO going to explain the political situation in the Philippines to Secretary George Schultz when his guide had disappeared as well as the documents brought by Minister Eki Cardenas?

As we were having our *merienda*, I noticed a tall American in a suit standing in a corner; when our eyes met, he signaled me to go near him. As I stood up BFO asked me, "Where are you going?"

"I think the hotel security wants to talk with me," I replied.

"OK," he said.

When I got near the big American, he asked, "Are you Assistant Minister Willie Villarama?"

"Yes, sir," I replied.

"Are you with Minister Blas Ople of the Philippines?"

"Yes, sir."

"Thank you!"

As I went back to our table, BFO asked me, "What did he want?"

"Hotel security checking on us. He just wanted to know our identities," I replied.

Less than five minutes later, the cashier answered a call and signaled that it was for me. We were seated near the cashier, with me in full view.

"Where are you going?"

"I have a phone call."

"You have phone pals even here?" he remarked with a smile.

I was a notorious telephone addict. I was one of the few then to have a portable phone as big as a shoe box, and one of the first to have an Apple computer. Being in public service, I had to have a perfect network, especially when my superiors were asking me to help others.

I answered the phone. The voice at the other end said, "Is this Willie?"

"Yes, sir."

"Are you with Blas?"

---

10. Stephen Kinzer, *Overthrow: America's Century of Regime Change from Hawaii to Iraq* (New York: Times Books/Henry Holt, 2007), 24–25.

"Yes, sir."

"Tell him this is Mike Armacost."

Mike Armacost was the former American ambassador to the Philippines. He had been transferred to Washington and became Undersecretary of State for Political Affairs.

I went back to our table and jokingly said to BFO, "Sir, our problem has been solved. The CIA found us already. Ambassador Armacost is on the phone."

BFO rushed to the phone. I was prepared to take notes, but all I could report was what I heard: "Yes, Mike, we will be there in one hour."

"Willie, get a hotel limousine. We will meet Secretary George Shultz. Let us prepare."

All the hotel cars were taken so I was instructed by BFO to call the Philippine Embassy for a vehicle. I reported that we had to take a cab because no one was answering the embassy phones.

We had to take a cab with Manny Imson and Fred de la Rosa.

I was so excited to be "walking in the corridors of power" – in the State Department of the most powerful nation on earth. But at the same time, I was very worried that my boss had been trapped into flying to Washington DC with a "guide" who had been supposed to bring him to Secretary Shultz but who had got lost on his way to the coffee shop of the Mayflower Hotel.

Knowing Ka Blas, he would not have flown to the US if he had known he could not get an audience with Secretary Shultz. He was supposed to present the side of President Marcos. I am certain he had been assured that he would be able to present to President Reagan and Secretary Schulz that his boss had won the election. And he knew all the documents were prepared not only about the snap elections, but also about the seriousness of the insurgency problem whereby the military could not afford a budget cut in aid from the US Congress. But the luggage containing these documents had disappeared. Was there a mole in Malacañang who had caused the hijacking of the papers brought by my dear Ateneo classmate Undersecretary Cardenas?

I know personally the Malacañang executive who prepared the documents that were supposed to be used by Minister Ople. When I told him over our weekly Saturday lunch that I was writing my memoir about EDSA 1, he smiled. He confessed that he was the lawyer who had put together the papers proving that Marcos had won the election and documenting the extent of the NPA problem. This lawyer stayed with Marcos until Marcos's dying days, and at the time of writing he is still the lawyer of the Marcos family. He was surprised when I told him we never received the documents. He is Minister for Legal

Affairs, Office of the President, Justice "Lolong" Lazaro, an outstanding and much-sought-after lawyer to this day.

Unfortunately for Marcos, the canvassing was stopped by the walkout of the NAMFREL (National Movement for Free Elections) pro-opposition volunteers. Was this a drama written by unseen hands? NAMFREL's head was appointed a Cabinet member by President Cory. I cannot say with certainty whether this was a reward for the walk-out. Secretary Jose Concepcion became my boss at the Department of Trade and Industry, where I was his assistant secretary. I never asked him about his role in EDSA 1.

That day was the most suspenseful day for me, but my gut feeling was that Marcos was a goner, as well as my scholarship at the Kennedy School. Together with other Filipinos, I was a scholar through the Philippine government. I was with an illustrious group of Filipinos: Patricia Sto. Tomas, who became Secretary of Labor; Emy Boncodin, who became Secretary of Budget; Antonio Basilio, who became Ambassador; Arthur Aguilar, who became the Head of the National Development Company and now Member of the Constitution Commission who would review the Philippine Constitution; and Jesuit Priest Fr Ed Martinez, who became President of the Ateneo De Davao.

Our taxicab was met at the entrance by Undersecretary Michael Armacost, who was the recent ambassador to the Philippines, and John Maesto, who had been assigned to the Manila US Embassy office and was a frequent visitor of BFO's in our office.

When I asked John what he was doing in Washington, his reply was: "Interesting times in the Philippines. I have to be here." His smile stretched from ear to ear.

We were led to a waiting room and served coffee and cookies. There was small talk, but one could feel the tension on both sides. Ambassador Richardson, who was a good friend, must have been feeling guilty that he was bringing his Filipino friend to the slaughter room, where BFO would be read the decree that Marcos had to step down.

For my part, I felt bad that BFO had been sent to Washington with Melchor, a trusted man of President Marcos, only to be abandoned after their airplane had landed in Washington DC. Melchor was a powerful former executive secretary of Marcos.

After an hour, Ambassador Mike entered the waiting room and announced that Secretary Shultz was ready to receive BFO. We all stood up, and being a camera freak, I had my mini-camera prepared. As BFO and Shultz shook hands, I clicked my camera, only to be warned by a security guard who shouted, "That is not allowed!"

I was able to rush to the side of BFO and was instructed to shake hands with the secretary and to leave them alone.

It was a long, long wait in the guest room. It felt like eternity. After more than an hour, BFO came out. He looked worried. He hurriedly told us we were leaving. As we left, I asked him if there was a problem. His reply was, "These Americans are meddling in our sovereignty."

He was quiet on our way to the hotel. After dinner, he asked me to borrow an IBM electric typewriter from the front desk. When I found that none was available, he asked me to take a cab and go to the Philippine Embassy.

It was late at night. When I entered the office, I saw most of the staff busily clearing their desks of their personal things. Abandon ship!

I brought the typewriter to our room and as usual prepared his pack of cigarettes, lighter, ashtray and a cup of coffee.

He had to make several corrections. When he was finished, he asked me to take his letter to the embassy to be sent by telex immediately to Marcos.

Of course I read the letter, which was brief. I had a photocopy made, but I lost it.

I recall that it went something like this:

> Dear Mr President,
>
> I had an audience with Secretary of State George Shultz, and his message to you is this.
>
> In the event you decide to visit the United States, you will be accorded the respect and honor of a visiting head of state.

The American definition of "respect and honor" is of course culturally different from our definition. When Marcos was brought to Hawaii, all his personal belongings and confidential papers were confiscated, including cash and valuables.

According to Imson's notes, in their meeting, Secretary Schultz asked Minister Blas Ople "to be a major channel to Malacañang for transmitting the final message of President Reagan."

The embassy operator called me around 2:45 a.m. to inform me that Malacañang had received the telex for Marcos. After around fifteen minutes our phone rang. It was Marcos asking to talk with BFO.

I arranged the phone in his room and woke BFO up.

It was a sad conversation from my end. BFO just kept listening to Marcos and kept on saying, "Yes, sir." I guess that Marcos was explaining something to him.

I will always remember what BFO said when it was his turn to say something: "Mr President, you ought to take your oath of office because you won the election. Let history judge you."

BFO hung up the phone. I was seated on the rug waiting for him to say something. He was quiet for a few seconds, holding his cheeks with both hands.

I asked him, "Sir, what happened?"

He replied, "I pity the president. He is really sick. He asked if any of his friends from abroad could help him. The United States want him out of the Philippines."

On my way back to the Philippines after graduating from Harvard, I went via San Francisco to meet a schoolmate who had been an insider in the palace. He confirmed that Marcos had been inside his room, incommunicado; nobody could talk with him during those crucial days.

BFO decided to go back to the Philippines when almost all the Cabinet members were leaving. I begged him to stay behind because he might be harmed by the incoming administration.

His classic reply in Tagalog was: "*Uuwi ako. Wala akong kasalanan sa taong bayan sa aking panunungkulan*" ("I will go home. I have not done any wrong to our people").

He came home and led what was left of the opposition. As a sign of respect from newly installed President Cory, he was asked to lead the five-member opposition contingent at the 1987 Constitutional Convention.

Part II

Days of People Power

7

Snap Elections 1986

Melba Padilla Maggay

It was a morning like any other morning. A drowsy summer haze drew a pallor over the soft yellow tones of a sun early risen. Yet somehow there was something else, something thick and sharp, a tenseness in the air.

The first telltale sign that something extra-ordinary was afoot was the sight of elegant matrons standing by coolly, peering over the shoulders of worn and weathered teachers commandeered to preside over the ritual motions of election procedures. It had been seventeen years since we last saw an election. Forced to once again have a semblance of a new mandate, Mr Marcos had called for a snap election. This time, citizens took the outside chance that something might yet happen that would overturn the iron hand that had long repressed and ruled over us.

As a volunteer poll watcher of the National Movement for Free Elections (NAMFREL), I had been assigned to head and organize the poll watchers who were to guard with their lives the ballot boxes and the integrity of what was to happen in the dozen or so election precincts stationed at Quezon City Hall.

It was six-thirty in the morning and already we were up and about, a ragtag band of citizen watchers. We looked like a scruffy, almost funny mix of an army drawn from a grab bag and hastily assembled: plump and droll housewives, eager students with stars in their eyes and fire in their bellies, quietly efficient professionals, grand ladies who now, by some twist of historical circumstances, had been roused from political indifference or middling militancy into a white-hot sense of outrage. "This is not just an election," whispered one matron to me as she fanned herself due to the growing crowd and heat, "this is a battle between good and evil, don't you think?"

For various reasons we had come together, embarked on a project that looked like a doubtful and, perhaps, deadly contest against those who would seek to thwart anew the long-suppressed will of the people. It was a wonder that we were there at all. Years of martial law had taught us futility, a sullen and stolid surrender to the hard and inexorable will of unrestrained power. Yet this election we were there, somehow aware that all hands were needed to grab the opportunity to turn the wheels of history and rescue us from permanent despair.

For we really had no great expectations, and, I surmised, neither had the people who streamed into the polling booths. Yet we all came, the few who were rich and the many who were poor, all lining up to do what we felt we had to do, even if we could not dare to hope for the change we longed for. The poor, especially, turned up in droves: women with babies on their hips and brown, brawny men who, unused perhaps to the labors of literacy, stayed long in the voting booths, sweating and their hands quivering before the awful blanks of ballot papers that needed to be filled in. It was, admittedly, the vast lack of sophistication that made us all present, hoping in our simplicity that something could still be done, as the poet T. S. Eliot put it, "on the margins of the impossible."

The day saw garden-variety irregularities, the usual anomalies that had accompanied our previous elections. Partisans coached the voters they had rounded up, peso bills tucked inside their folded ballots. There were reports of intimidation, names missing on the voters' lists, slapdash systems. But there was also, for once, an element of embarrassment in those caught committing these infractions, a sheepish recognition that something new was arising in our political life: rectitude, watchfulness, the diligent insistence on correct procedure and decency by a committed citizenry.

The society matrons stood prim and unmindful of the sweat and grime of the miscellaneous rabble. The harassed teachers performed their duties with a patient dedication freshly heartened by the moral support of the poll watchers. My activist friends, children of the 1960s and 1970s, applied talents that were once reserved for grand visions of social restructuring to the modest and painstaking work of ensuring due process. We did not know then that in the small act of guarding the sanctity of the ballot, we were being initiated once again into the strength of institutional democracy, and the possibility of a backhand success against forces of immense power.

By late afternoon, poll watchers and election officials from various parts of the city started to stream in, hugging the locked ballot boxes entrusted to their care. Seeing the coming crowds and anticipating the ensuing chaos, I asked someone to look for one of our key staff members who could bring order to the masses of people pouring in. "Amanda is already there," said Jun, one of our male staff, pointing to a diminutive figure above the heads of the crowd. A small but feisty woman I fondly call "Gabriela Silang," Amanda had unceremoniously climbed atop a table and was directing the snake-like traffic of people massing into City Hall, the nerve center for the counting of ballots from other districts.

From the counting that evening, the election returns from all over the city showed a clear trend that Mrs Corazon Aquino, widow of the slain Marcos rival Benigno Aquino Jr., had won with a resounding margin over Mr Marcos.

Something in our gut wanted to dance in the streets for the unexpected outcome. I thanked our people and we all went home with our hearts full. We were aware that the elections were a frail basis for hope, a narrow gate to a political normalcy that was yet far off. But our people took it, used it with a fierce decisiveness that left victor and vanquished stunned, shocked into the recognition that here were a people finally made angry and wise, patiently waiting for the time when they could throw off the yoke of a long, long season of suffering and discontent.

The experiences of this historic election have yet to be fully analyzed.

Over the ensuing years, the personal lessons I have gained from it have at least helped me to frame my responses when I have been groping in the dark for a way out of a world where there seems to be no exit from the hard and constant struggle for justice and insight.

Foremost among these lessons is the discovery that, while power is on the side of the oppressor, it is not so organized as to be absolutely monolithic. The stunning reversal in the fortunes of our political overlords during those events of February 1986 tell us this.

It is true that from time to time, we feel as if we have dropped down the abyss once again and we can smell the smoke from the bottomless pit. But the universe is wide open and by no means shut tight and windowless. We do not live in a closed system of merely mechanical causes, but in a world of infinite plasticity and creative energy, giving us a sense of both regularity and a wondrous intractability.

As with the world, so with power. Ecclesiastes tells us, "I saw the tears of the oppressed – and they have no comforter; power was on the side of their oppressors . . ." (Eccl 4:1). It is true that there is such a thing as organized injustice. Institutions can be hijacked by evil forces, and these can perpetuate oppression by using the apparatus of power. But there is always this margin of mystery which can thwart our usual expectations: "the race is not to the swift, or the battle to the strong . . ." (Eccl 9:11).

There is sometimes a wild card, an intractability, to human life which lends to the cause of the weak and the small the fighting possibility of an outside chance. People of the kingdom may look weak and unorganized, but we are not unaided. There is an unseen hand that works for the good of those who try to stand for God's original purposes for society and its institutions.

It is not altogether accurate to think of the party in power as fully in control. No government is, even in countries where the iron hand of authoritarianism grips people tightly. Somewhere in the vast machinery of what looks like overwhelming power there is a loose screw, a bolt out of place that could wrench the entire structure and send it reeling and tottering. I saw this firsthand in the aftermath of the snap elections.

The election returns that clearly showed Mrs Aquino to be winning were quickly reversed when the ballot boxes from all over the country were sent to *Batasang Pambansa*[1] for official canvassing by the Commission on Elections. Against the results of the counting at ground level, Marcos was declared winner. But then, quite unexpectedly, the volunteer techies who were manning the computers tabulating the results walked out en masse. They were witness to the gross attempts at manipulating the counting. This was followed by a series of street protests. For our part, we felt it was time for resistance, to oppose the continuance of an abusive power that had lost its mandate.

ISACC (Institute for Studies in Asian Church and Culture) and our new friends, the society matrons who had gravitated toward us – banded together under the banner of "*Konsiyensiya ng Febrero Siete*" (KONFES; "Concerned Christians for Truth and Justice"). The unusual mix of church people, activists and society ladies provided an opportunity to get creative.

On the day when Marcos was to be proclaimed winner, protesters trooped to the *Batasang Pambansa*. The massive crowds were stopped and ground to a halt while still at the turning along Commonwealth Street, barricaded by the police. Since we were in cars and not on foot, dressed in our best *barong* and *Filipiniana* attire to look like respectable and important citizens, we went past the guards and managed to get inside the grounds of the legislative building. We folded our banners that were made of cloth and stuffed them inside the big, fashionable bags of the society ladies. Since some of them had

---

1. The final large meetings organized in advance by contending parties just before the election.

the right connections, they escorted us, two at a time, past the tight security. We stationed ourselves in strategic places once inside the assembly hall.

When Marcos was formally proclaimed winner, we took out our banners and unfurled them before the startled legislators and the foreign press who eagerly took pictures. The guards were taken aback, and there was some hissing and rustling behind the side doors. They wondered how on earth we had managed to get in. But we sat there politely, and quietly made our scene. No one made a move.

The session over, we filed past the guards and smiled at them. Some smiled back on the sly, some did not know what to make of us, and still some hurriedly shoved us to the door, glum over the prospect of being taken to task for dereliction of duty. Once outside, we breathed an air that somehow seemed purer, and our unlikely band of protesters had a great laugh.

The incident taught me that the vigilant tenacity of a small minority can make a difference. A creative community of militant consciences can provide an environment necessary for the flourishing of workable alternatives to the terrible excesses of unchecked power and the dysfunctions of corrupt governance. There are no easy answers to the problem of effecting changes that are fresh, sharp and deep. Turgid monolithic thinking from the left and right sides of the ideological divide and the makeshift muddling of those in the center leaves us with very little to bite upon as inch by inch we work at long-term solutions to the hard fact of persistent poverty and injustice.

Seeing the rise of a quiescent people who finally said "*Tama na, Sobra na!*"[2] gave me confidence in the basic decency and undiscovered political strength of our people. There is too much written about the way we seem to have hooted out of the public square time-honored values that keep societies functioning. In this election and our subsequent "People Power" revolution, our people had shown that there is an unmined power in our more indigenous and primal longing for justice and righteousness. Citizens with nothing but conscience and the courage to stand by the authority of moral conviction have a nascent force whose full dimensions have yet to be understood and used.

My generation of social activists grew up believing in Mao Tse-tung's saying in the Red Book that "power grows out of the barrel of a gun." We must not forget that history ultimately does not turn by sheer force of arms. Moral pressure and the spirit of a people can shake empires and tire out the strongest of nations. See the witness of Mahatma Gandhi, whose nonviolent campaign for independence after the massacre at Amritsar showed up Britain to the

---

2. Roughly, "Enough is enough, it is too much, we won't take it anymore."

world as a brutish and hulking monster that had a soft underpaw. Likewise, the Vietnamese people fought a war against the strongest military force on earth and showed that it could be wounded fatally and retreat. Brute and brazen power is in the end a stick that can break before the invincibility of a genuinely just cause and the will of a people to be free.

Perhaps our best hope lies, not in endlessly tinkering with the social system, but in our own agency and will as a people to attend as watchful midwives over the birth pangs of truly significant changes that are happening quietly below the radar screen of the powers over us.

8

Seventy-Five Long Hours

Adrian Helleman

The seventy-five long hours began for me on Saturday, 22 February at 7 p.m., when I was monitoring Radio Australia. The news that Defense Minister Juan Ponce Enrile and then Acting Chief of Staff Gen. Fidel Ramos were holding a press conference at Camp Aguinaldo electrified me. The details were still unclear so I switched to Radio Veritas, the Catholic radio station, which was virtually the only source of reliable news other than the shortwave. Then came the announcement that the two men had withdrawn their support from President Marcos. This was a scenario that no one had anticipated.

The boycott movement had already gained popular support and was beginning to make an impact, but everyone realized that it would take many months. Also, it was common knowledge that there were dissidents within the military, but for these two men to take this step was unexpected. I remember thinking that citizens should go out to Camp Aguinaldo and offer these men their help; others, apparently, had the same thought. Jaime Cardinal Sin, the Archbishop of Manila, and Butz Aquino, the brother-in-law of Cory Aquino, went on the air on Radio Veritas with the request that people come out and help defend the camp. Little did I realize then that I would eventually join those Filipinos at the barricades.

The next few hours were full of suspense. Amid reports on Veritas of thousands of people flocking to Camp Aguinaldo, I also kept a watchful eye on Channel 4, which was the government station. They were still broadcasting *Faerie Tale Theatre*. Later that evening it was announced that President Marcos would soon be holding a press conference. People were urged to keep calm, but no explanation was offered. President Marcos later went on TV and informed the nation that a plot to assassinate him and the First Lady had been uncovered, and a witness was produced to testify to this supposed plot. Marcos's statement to the press seemed as unreal as the earlier program.

My wife, Wendy, and I went to bed very late. We were awakened at 6 a.m. by a phone call from a friend asking us to join their group at the camp. I am the chairman of a missionary taskforce which is part of this group called KONFES (*Konsiensya ng Febrero Siete*: "Concerned Christians for Truth and Justice"). Among other things, our taskforce had tried to set up an appointment with Philip Habib, the special envoy of President Reagan, but it had been unsuccessful. Seemingly the American Embassy did not place a high value on the emissaries of the kingdom of God.

Because of the tense situation, I went to church alone. I had to skirt the back of the camp, and when I reached EDSA I saw the barricades for the first time. The highway was blocked off so that no vehicles could enter. After church, I noticed that many more people had arrived in the meantime. It was more a festival than a revolution, judging by the honking of car horns and the flashing of the "L" (*Laban*, meaning "fight") sign.

Since I had to preach at our own service that evening, I stayed home that afternoon. When we arrived at the home which we use for worship, we discovered that some of our members had already joined the barricades; so we decided to hold a prayer meeting instead of our regular service. Afterwards, all the men decided to go to the camp. Armed only with flashlights, transistor radios and food, we joined KONFES at about 8 p.m. That afternoon, Enrile and Ramos had moved their headquarters to Camp Crame. By the evening, a sea of people covered the highway which divided the two military camps, Camp Crame and Camp Aguinaldo.

Only later did we learn that Enrile and Ramos had only three hundred men with them when they started their "rebellion," and that only half of Camp Aguinaldo was under their control at that time. Marcos could have wiped them out, if only he had struck then.

I left briefly at 1 a.m. for a few hours' rest. By that time, many side streets were barricaded with buses and trucks. Barbed wire was even stretched across one intersection not far from our house. At 5:30 a.m. I returned amid radio reports of an imminent attack. Tear gas had apparently been lobbed into the crowd at that one intersection with the barbed wire, but that had not yet been confirmed. After my return to the barricades at the break of dawn the situation was very tense.

The crucial moment came at 6:30 a.m. when Sikorsky helicopter gunships swooped in low over the highway while we stood locked arm-in-arm in front of the main gate of Camp Crame. We could all have died on the spot, but the

Lord decided otherwise. When the helicopters landed, I rushed into the camp together with some reporters. The pilots had defected and so the "rebels" now had the nucleus of an air force. These helicopters were used later that morning for an attack on Villamor Air Base, where many of the helicopters remaining under Marcos's control were destroyed on the ground.

Since I had a weekly Bible study with some prisoners inside the stockade, I, accompanied by the Protestant chaplain, then visited them and prayed with them. They were "sitting ducks" during these four days.

At 8:30 a.m. it was reported that Marcos had left for Guam. Enrile and Ramos came out for the celebration. An image of the Virgin Mary was raised by some of those present. This was not surprising since the Philippines is a predominantly Catholic country. Only later did I discover that someone who had not received permission to do this was responsible. However, no one had the courage to tell him not to do it either. Although Enrile was apparently a devout Roman Catholic, Ramos was a Protestant. In fact, I later saw another image of the Virgin in the helicopter of Enrile's wife.

Unfortunately, the celebration was premature. I had just gotten into my car in order to go home when I heard Marcos's voice over the radio. Once at home I discovered that this was a live broadcast from the palace and that Marcos had not left the country. Quickly, I showered and rushed back to Camp Crame. I was again allowed to enter the camp.

That morning the "rebels" had captured Channel 4 and now had access to the largest radio and TV network in the country. This was one of the most serious blows for Marcos, who had previously used TV for his own benefit. It was the beginning of his isolation.

I spent the rest of the afternoon in discussions with the Protestant chaplain, who was a friend, and others about the situation. It was relatively peaceful and at no time did we feel threatened, except during that early morning aborted attack. In the evening I went home again, since I did not want to burden the soldiers there with one extra person to accommodate for the night.

The next morning I had no further plans to return, but I did so when I heard about the loyalist defense of the tower of Channel 9, which was the only TV station left for Marcos. Yet in spite of this, even that station was put off the air just as Marcos's inauguration was about to begin. At that point Marcos had no access to radio and TV anymore.

When I arrived at the camp, Enrile and Ramos were leaving for the inauguration of the new president and vice president. The site of the inauguration was only a few hundred meters away, but we could only listen on the radio since there was no live TV coverage of this historic event. However, I could see the helicopters hovering over the site.

When Enrile and Ramos returned, I followed them into the headquarters building. There I had lunch with some prominent officials who were gathered in a room beside the "war room." I was asked who I was. "A missionary," I replied. "What are you doing here?" was the next question. "I am a citizen of the Kingdom," was my answer. Everyone understood what I meant, and during the rest of the afternoon we discussed such controversial issues as "the separation of church and state."

At 3:30 p.m. Enrile and Ramos left for Camp Aguinaldo, since that camp was now secure. At 5 p.m. I decided to go home. A major told me that he expected everything to be over in five or six hours' time. I did not realize at the time how accurate he was in his prediction.

After supper my wife and I went to visit the KONFES group for a worship service scheduled for 8 p.m. I attended an executive meeting of the group after the service in which we made further plans for the succeeding days. I was scheduled to give a message at the service the next day in front of the gate to Camp Aguinaldo. It was unnecessary.

At 9:30 p.m. we heard the fire crackers, but dismissed the rumors that Marcos had left the palace. Remember, we had been fooled once before. Wendy and I went home, and only then was it confirmed that Marcos had left for Clark Air Base. Finally he was gone; the people had won.

We let Filipinos celebrate out on the streets. This was their victory. However, we were as thankful as they were. It was 10 p.m., 25 February, seventy-five long hours after we had heard the initial reports of the "rebellion."

Was this a revolution? Perhaps not. If Groen van Prinsterer is right in characterizing unbelief as the spirit of revolution, then this certainly was not. I prefer to call it a political reformation because of the evident faith.

The picture of nuns sitting in front of tanks made the words of Jesus, "Blessed are the meek," a reality for me as never before, and those people who offered cigarettes and food to Marcos's soldiers gave new meaning to the command to "love your enemies."

The Philippine "Revolution" of 1986 was unique. It was fueled by prayer. Everyone, whether Catholic, Protestant, Muslim or Buddhist, prayed as never before. The secular press largely disregarded the phenomenon of "praying people power." The same press also exaggerated the violence, yet at the last count there were only thirteen deaths, with none directly attributable to the revolution!

Many people claim it was one "miracle" after another. God's hand was very evident at every moment. Never before have I so experienced the lifting of the veil which hides the kingdom of God. During those four days, many believers were able to see its present reality.

Cardinal Sin, the day before the election, described it as "a battle between the forces of good and evil, between the children of light and the children of darkness." To some this may have seemed a very superficial analysis, but as events unfolded over the next few weeks, it became apparent that he was right. This was a spiritual struggle.

This also explains my involvement. Normally, missionaries do not get involved in elections in the host country, except merely as spectators. However, this election was different. My intent was not to be partisan, which is contrary to Philippine law, but to be a witness, no matter how small, to evangelical participation in this struggle.

My wife and I had discussed the consequences carefully. We knew the dangers: possible death, deportation and dismissal from my job. We also realized the precarious position in which we were placing the mission, yet we were so certain of the final result that we went ahead anyway. We had to do something during the seventy-five long hours.

9

Onward, Soldiers of Faith

Rolando Villacorte

After lunch, Enrile and some of his men fell asleep from sheer exhaustion. They never had time to take off their shoes, and the men just slumped down whenever they could inside the minister's office for the badly needed shut-eye.

Then suddenly Enrile woke up with a start, awakened by his military aide who told him they must prepare to move out. For a moment he thought they were already under siege. Actually, they had just received reports about Gen. Tadiar's impending massive assault on the two rebel camps. Tadiar was coming in shortly with his dreaded Marines riding in tanks and other armored vehicles from Fort Bonifacio.

"It's better for us, sir, to move across to Camp Crame to consolidate our forces with those of Gen. Ramos," Enrile's aide explained, much to his relief.

As Enrile was reflecting on the matter, he could hardly believe they were in this kind of situation. It all seemed so unreal to him, just like a dream – a bad dream. His mind raced back to the days of his youth when he, as member of the resistance, had been captured by the Japanese military police and incarcerated for almost a hundred days.

"It was like *déjà vu* to me," he recalls of that Sunday moment.[1]

At about 2 p.m., Enrile and his men moved out in "a very disciplined formation." To reach Camp Crame they had to negotiate a distance of nearly a kilometer. They were accompanied by a group of nuns and other supporters who were praying audibly, and by a convoy of six trucks and four jeeps.

---

1. All the quotes and accounts shared in this chapter are from first-hand oral interviews between the author and the key players.

"We're moving out but we're not going to surrender," Enrile told the journalists with a wide grin, as he caressed his Uzi submachinegun slung around his neck. He was wearing the same denim pants and olive-green jacket he had on the previous day.

With its departure, the Enrile force had left behind Gen. Balbanero's military police brigade and Lt. Col. Jerry Albano's security escort contingent inside Camp Aguinaldo. These two men had been trying their best to prevent bloodshed between the contending forces, although Albano had committed himself to Enrile in case of an actual showdown.

Enrile marched on foot with only three hundred men. Wasn't this the same number of troops Gideon had had when he fought and vanquished more than a hundred thousand Midianites with the help of the Sovereign Lord?[2]

"God does not march with the big battalion," says Fr Francisco Araneta. "He loves to bring down the mighty and lift up the lowly." A handful is all God needs to carry out his purpose.

Upon emerging from Gate 2 on EDSA the rebels were astonished to see a huge mass of civilians shouting, clapping and cheering – and jamming the twelve-lane highway. Everyone had on something yellow. Car horns blared and people chanted: "John-nee! John-nee!" Banners and placards were waved energetically above the multitude. One of the big placards read: MINISTER ENRILE – YOU ARE HEAVEN SENT.

The yellow sea of people turned into a tidal wave as Enrile and his men began to cross EDSA toward Camp Crame's main gate about fifty meters away. Halfway up the tall steel lampposts, in the middle of the traffic island, some men, mostly in pairs, were comfortably perched and waving banners. They were the modern Zacchaeuses eager to gain a view of their "messiahs" who were passing through. There were no sycamore trees around as in Jericho, not even acacias, so they had to make do with the shadeless Meralco posts.

"My men had to surround me for security reasons," Enrile says. "With a crowd like that, somebody could stick a knife in your belly or back, and that's it."

But surprisingly, the tidal wave parted to give way to the marching rebels whose nerves were visibly taut. The space created, however, was just wide enough for them to wade through. The people instantly linked arms (*kapitbisig*) to form protective walls on both sides and thus clear the path for Enrile and the reformist troops.

It was a wondrous sight, reminiscent of the spectacular parting of the Red Sea which let Moses and his people escape from Pharaoh's thundering army

---

2. Judg 7:7, 22.

of chariots and cross over to freedom. This time, though, it was a yellow sea that was parting for freedom, and to the tune of "Onward, Christian Soldiers" sung fervidly by a Protestant flock.

"Oh my God," Enrile thought to himself as he forged ahead through the dense and jostling crowd. "With such people support, how can we fail?"

The bursts of shouts and claps and cheers grew louder when Enrile finally entered the gate where Gen. Ramos, contentedly puffing on a long cigar and unarmed, was waiting for him.

Of that great "yellow sea" experience, Honasan, who had been shielding Enrile all along, recounted: "I was very scared when we started out. But when we reached the first row of people, they started to wipe our brows, give us food and thank us. I knew then that we had won. All my fears disappeared."

"Inside Camp Crame," the mustachioed security officer went on, "some of us were crying. There was a lot of tears and emotions among the soldiers. The impact of the change which was about to take place was too tremendous to cope with."

Ramos took Enrile to his command post up on the third floor of the four-story PC headquarters building. This was the same building that had housed scores of political detainees during the fourteen years of martial law. Ramos and Enrile then went up to the balcony, or viewing deck, on the top floor, which commanded a panoramic view of the camp and its surroundings. From that vantage point, under the soft blue and glistening sky, the two "crusaders," their left hands holding on to the metal pipe railings, repeatedly waved and smiled at the inspirited military men, nuns, priests and civilians gathered below and at the motley crowds pressed against the gates. Some of the men and women outside were in wheelchairs.

"Don't be afraid, I'm with you, not against you!" Enrile yelled as he flashed the "L" sign amid louder hurrahs from the throngs.

Enrile and Ramos marveled at the spontaneous combustion of People Power, at the enormous human wall that stretched along EDSA from P. Tuazon street in Cubao to Ortigas Avenue in Pasig about two kilometers away, and along Santolan Road. From the air the overflowing arteries (EDSA and Santolan) looked like a monumental cross with Santolan Road forming the horizontal beam. From that moment on they both instinctively knew that victory was theirs; it was only a matter of time.

By this time, Camp Crame's defense plan was well in place. The planning and execution were being carried out by the PC Operations Center which was established by then Col. Alexander P. Aguirre. The Operations Center was housed in the same PC headquarters building where Gen. Ramos's command center was, although the two centers were physically apart from each other.

Aguirre had reported to Ramos for duty at about 4 a.m., shortly after arrival from Baguio City on an official mission at the Philippine Military Academy. Ramos's instructions to him were simple and brief: set up the camp defense, galvanize and make maximum use of People Power; and undertake no provocative military action against the loyalist troops. In other words, fight only in *self-defense.*

Only in self-defense? This revolution was "unique in the military annals," Aguirre thought, and definitely "contrary to the time-honored military principle that 'the best defense is offense'!"

With such guidance, Aguirre immediately buckled down to work. He organized his officers and men into two groups, one group to stay put in the office and serve as operations staff, and the other to venture outside and work as intelligence operatives. Aguirre says that the latter group, led by Majors Ding Reyes and Zondy Hizon, operated around the periphery of the Aguinaldo–Crame complex. The two majors were likewise directed to contact their classmates and other sympathizers for the Enrile–Ramos crusade.

"All throughout the operations," explains Aguirre, "these officers were feeding PC Operations Center with information on the loyalist troop movements toward Camp Crame, thus enabling me to make the necessary counter-moves to cause the blockade of pertinent strategic routes to the camp. Having my own source of tactical intelligence was very necessary to our operational decision-making process."

Aguirre then alerted all provincial commanders surrounding Metro Manila and the sectors under the PC Metrocom/Metro Police Force.

"But they were directed not to move into Crame unless ordered to do so," says Aguirre. "They were just instructed to maintain peace and order and stabilize the situation in their respective jurisdictions and send reinforcements only on call." He also contacted all the PC regional commanders and gave them similar instructions.

Soon enough Aguirre evolved a concept of defense called *defense in depth.* This strategy called for carefully avoiding any offensive action or hostility, delaying enemy action and preventing the loyalist troops from getting within artillery or shooting distance of Camp Crame. Because Crame was only a small camp and because it had just a handful of defenders (fewer than eight hundred, including Enrile's three hundred), the strategy, according to Aguirre, would work only with the "precise and organized employment of People Power."

Through the ever-growing People Power army, the camp's defense area "had extended its perimeter boundaries to the south along Ortigas Avenue, to Ortigas-Santolan-Mariposa streets in the west; to Libis in the east; and to P. Tuazon-EDSA in the north."

Since Sunday morning, the entire EDSA-Santolan area had given off a festive atmosphere with the conspicuous presence of hawkers of all sorts of snack items: ice cream, fried fish balls, boiled and roasted peanuts, banana-Q and boiled corn on the cob. There were also the ubiquitous vendors of balloons and of Ninoy and Cory Aquino souvenirs, especially T-shirts, headbands, fans and pins, all in bright yellow.

Transistor radios, hand-held or mounted on the roofs of parked motor vehicles, were constantly playing at a high volume in their owners' eagerness to share the running news broadcasts with everybody. Not a few had their pocket radios pressed to their ears – especially now that Radio Veritas, with only an emergency transmitter functioning, was starting to give a faltering signal.

Sure, two or three other stations (including DZAS of the Far East Broadcasting Company) were providing coverage of what was going on, but, as a screenwriter puts it, it was different. Markedly different. "They were merely observers of the revolution. Veritas was an active, vital participant."

In reality, FEBC broadcasting service was in a difficult situation. Its DZAS staff was of split loyalty; some were pro-Marcos and others pro-Cory. If they gave full coverage (particularly after Radio Veritas went off the air) and Marcos won, retribution would be dreadfully swift.

FEBC was performing an important Christian ministry in the Philippines. It was operating ten domestic stations and enjoying the rights to broadcast the gospel internationally, even to such countries as China and India. It was just too prudent, too cautious, to risk all these.

But though DZAS had unfortunately missed out as pinch hitter for the temporarily disabled Veritas, thank God that he quickly provided another station to carry on the battle of communication and information.

The EDSA-Santolan crowds seemed to be in a state of perpetual motion as the people, in pairs or in groups, kept walking to and fro in the fair sunshine and the comfort of the gentle breeze. Some, including family groups, appeared to be only promenading (a family of four even had their pedigree pet dog in tow). Others, especially the conspicuous assembly of college students, were chanting "Co-ree! Co-ree! Co-ree!" as they walked about and held banners aloft. Even the roof of the seven-foot-high guardhouse at Camp Crame's main gate was blooming with unfurled banners of cause-oriented organizations.

Only People Power could provide such color and spectacle, sounds and smells.

On seeing the throngs milling all around, a perplexed foreign correspondent was heard exclaiming: "I thought you were going to have a civil war! I didn't realize it was going to be a revolution by milling around!"

The foreign correspondent scratched his strawberry-blond beard, hitched his belt up over his ample tummy and departed in search of action, narrated writer Francoise Joaquin. "Milling around, indeed, seemed the order of the day at critical 'people power' (the day's timeliest cliché) points all over Metro Manila. Sporadic bouts of 'action' happened so swiftly and suddenly that harassed reporters, foreign and local, found themselves dashing from place to place in their disheveled, day-old clothes missing one or another bit of news. Milling around, however proved the success story of this revolution."

No doubt it was an extraordinary period of time. There was a pervading spirit of camaraderie, of genuine brotherhood. Strangers exchanged friendly smiles and "L" sign greetings; everyone was willing to share what he or she had with the next person. Everybody was a kindred soul.

A motorist hurrying to EDSA that afternoon accidentally bumped another car, denting its rear bumper and a fender. The two drivers got out to inspect the damage. The victim, also on his way to the barricades, just shook his head, smiled at the culprit and told the latter to forget about it. Ordinarily, that accident would have sparked off either a heated discussion or a lawsuit, or both.

At a food center, somebody holding a plate of saucy *caldereta* spilled a liberal dose of it on the newly pressed shirt of another waiting for his turn. Instead of igniting an altercation or a fistfight, the incident merely provoked laughter from everyone.

But why were these people here at EDSA? Did they come out of mere curiosity or out of ideological concern? It soon became clear that this flowing sea of humanity – except the tightly organized band of red-banner-waving extremists – was energized solely by a common desire to have the tyrant Marcos ousted and by their ineffable faith in the Sovereign One. They were all ready and willing to make a sacrifice, but a good many were totally unaware of the terrible risks that lurked ahead.

Few were the souls who were privy to the actual happenings behind the scenes that day as the demonstrators massed on EDSA, Santolan and Ortigas Avenue, to form a buffer zone. Varied events were rapidly taking place in different directions, but all formed part of the central plot of the divinely scripted play.

Had it at all been possible to monitor those concurrent events that afternoon, I imagine it would have been like sitting inside a master control room and simultaneously viewing the different images on a dozen or so video screens. But who, except the Master himself, who is in full control of human affairs, could have watched or seen those thrilling pictures all at once as a perfectly blended and unified whole?

Right in the center of the array of screens, for instance, would have been two large ones, one projecting the excitement at EDSA during the Enrile march, and the other the scene within the palace, where Marcos was then exhibiting the four arrested coup plotters in a televised press conference at the Ceremonial Hall.

It was an impressive press conference, to be sure. It was attended by foreign correspondents and representatives of international networks, as well as by Cabinet members, top bureaucrats and the Armed Forces of the Philippines brass hats led by General Ver. The presence of this large group of officials was meant to convey the idea that the Marcos government was still intact and potent.

"No, it's not true that the Armed Forces is divided into equal factions," Marcos was saying. "Barring those who are now with Enrile and Ramos, I don't believe there are other officers willing to be included in the list of the rebellion or identified with the coup."

In a sepulchral tone the *barong*-clad president was warning Enrile and Ramos that loyalist troops were set to pulverize Camp Crame. "Let the blood of those who will die be on your conscience."

Marcos aired the warning after saying that Tadiar's troops had surrounded the two camps and that some were around the Corinthian Gardens adjacent to Aguinaldo.

This was not exactly so, for another of our imaginary video screens would have shown that at that precise moment Tadiar's armored column had just rolled out of Fort Bonifacio toward Camp Aguinaldo, from where they intended to launch their deadly assault on Camp Crame.

"The options are with us," Marcos was bragging. "We could finish this in one hour, but it would be a bloody mess and I don't want that."

Marcos was apparently determined to bring the matter to a "non-bloody end." But Enrile, the man he wanted to negotiate with, was giving him a wide berth.

"I was willing to converse with [Enrile] on the telephone but he suddenly clammed up when I told him that [he and Ramos] would have to face trial, that they would have to confront witnesses against them in legal proceedings . . .

But I'm trying my best to get in touch with Johnny Ponce Enrile, so we can use intermediaries, one of whom they approved of – retired Lt. Gen. Rafael Ileto, ambassador to Thailand."

A reporter made Marcos's hackles rise when he asked the Chief Executive if he was about to resign. "Of course not! Of course not!" Marcos was heard to retort. "Certainly I will not resign on the mere say-so of those who criticize my administration."

Another image that could have simultaneously appeared on one of the monitor screens would have been that of the two choppers which had been reconnoitering above EDSA for nearly an hour by then. They had been sent up by Col. Antonio Sotelo, commander of the 15th Strike Wing who earlier had been alerted by the PAF chief to mobilize his helicopter gunships for a possible fatal strike that afternoon at Camp Crame.

Still another interesting picture would have been that of various concerned groups excitedly preparing to join the barricades. Among these were *Konsiensiya ng Febrero Siete* (KONFES) and Diliman Bible Church (DBC). As early as 4 September 1983, barely two weeks after the Aquino assassination, DBC had issued a "Call to Repentance" which exhorted the whole nation "to turn from our wicked ways, and to trust God who alone can forgive us and heal our land."

"While we are not partisan politicians," the evangelical church stated, "we realize that widespread poverty, social injustice, government graft and corruption, the lack of press freedom, unfair elections, increasing militarization, one-man rule, a spineless Supreme Court, a rubber-stamp parliament, and uncertainty over succession, are concerns that involve all of us. We share the guilt of allowing these things to happen, particularly without a whimper of protest from us. It took the death of Ninoy Aquino to awaken us from our long stupor."

DBC was also among the first evangelical churches, if not the first, to condemn the fraud-tainted snap elections which it said had "unmasked the pervasiveness of wickedness in low and high places" and "also unveiled the heroism of many."

And now that a rebellion had openly broken out against the man chiefly responsible for the nation's aforementioned ills, DBC, along with KONFES, was only too eager to stand up and be counted.

Early that afternoon, following their Sunday worship service, about a hundred DBC volunteers, led by Pastor Isabelo F. Magalit, hied off to EDSA to help man the barricades day and night on a shift basis until the flight of the benighted ruler. Food for the barricaders was provided by the church. KONFES, with about thirty people at its core, issued a call over Radio Veritas to all evangelical churches in Metro Manila and in the neighboring provinces to come to EDSA and join the revolution. Fortunately, an appreciable number responded positively, with some of the delegations coming from as far as Batangas and Laguna provinces.

Inside the Camp Crame command centers, Ramos and Enrile continued their "psywar" broadcasts which were particularly beamed to various military commanders throughout the country. Every so often, Ramos would announce the individual defections that undoubtedly demoralized the ranks of the loyalist forces and conversely buoyed up the legions of sympathizers, so that before the night was through he was crowing that the level of Armed Forces support for the uprising had risen to 90 percent of PC command in the field.

This claim could have been a bit exaggerated, but it was all part of the psywar game (for bandwagon effect) that Ramos was skillfully playing in partnership with June Keithley, the heroine of the airwaves. Marcos, of course, pooh-poohed the Ramos "propaganda" out of hand, saying the Armed Forces were fully behind the government.

Ramos said sixty-one provincial commanders and seven Metropolitan District Command chiefs nationwide had informed him by radio of their support. Among the provincial commands he cited were those from the so-called Ilocano bloc of Marcos.

The four Metro Manila police superintendents – Brig. Gen. Narciso Cabrera, Brig. Gen. Ruben Escarcha, Brig. Gen. Alfredo Yson and Brig. Gen. Alfredo Lim – had likewise signified their change of heart.

Near midnight, thirty crack troopers of the Presidential Security Command, the elite military unit in charge of the Marcos family's security, also defected. Two of the defectors were to seek refuge at Camp Crame while the twenty-eight others went into hiding for fear of liquidation, "after being forced by their superiors to obey what they termed 'illegal orders.'"

The big switch was on, but the most crucial defections were yet to come.

10

Diary from the Barricades[1]

Melba Padilla Maggay

Saturday, 22 February 1986

It has happened. Now, in the gathering darkness, the stray bullet, the outside chance, the quirky twist that jars and turns awry the best-laid plans of mice and men, has happened.

Fidel Ramos and Juan Ponce Enrile, pillars of the regime's armed support, have declared insurrection. Butch Aquino on the radio has called for a human buffer to stay the hand of bloodshed between the partisan troops. Meanwhile, the voices of Ramos and Enrile hogged the airwaves, tough and resolute voices steeled by despair and maybe the sense that somehow, somewhere, help will come like lightning from a clear sky.

"So be it," said the fast-talking minister of defense, asked by the press corps about the prospect of fighting to the last man the formidable forces he had helped assemble for many years. The tone of fatalism, of desperate surrender to the all-powerful and inscrutable hand of God, was something new. What is he really like? we thought. Of all the king's men he was there – at the center of the terror of having soldiers come in the dead of night for a brother or a sister who at crack of dawn would be found hogtied, brutally salvaged. Is he merely frightened, a hare on the run wanting to go down with a bang and not a whimper? Or is he part of an elaborate plot, stage-managed from somewhere, meant to steal the thunder from underground elements waiting in the wings and secure a historical opportunity for some interested friends?

---

1. Originally published in the 1985–1986 Philippines Yearbook of the *Fookien Times*.

But the voice, surprisingly, had the ring of truth in it, and in places where it faltered because hope was nil it was moving. One sensed that something quite out of our usual reckoning had taken place – a man's fitful struggle with conscience and the Power before whom all are accountable; a coming to grips with the costly demands of principle, without which life is cheap and not worth the air we breathe.

Where does it start, this inner movement toward integrity of being? What is it that makes us grope for light, for the searing heat that burns the lie and makes us pure and entire? The two men have made a wild shot at mutiny; the boldness of the bid perhaps could only come from a bracing experience of the singular force of being, for once, on the side of principle. Righteousness makes any man a lion.

I turned off the radio and looked out the window. The stars were few. For many years we have lived in a vast universe of silence. The country is like the land of Kafka: one gets jailed for reasons no one knows, and there is no one to turn to for redress, no one to give an answer for the howl of grief one hears in the dark of night. Here, under the starless sky, we are asked to believe that an unseen hand has come down in mercy and has wrought a transformation only slightly less dramatic than St Paul's vision on the road to Damascus, striking him blind and getting him down on his knees.

While in many ways suspect, this military defection to the cause of the people is nevertheless a marvel worth falling off our seats.

Sunday, 23 February

It had been a sleepless night. Morning came by stealth, soft and uncertain. I and a number of friends who had banded together under the name KONFES (*Konsiyensiya ng Febrero Siete*) sat huddled together in the shadows – quiet before the Presence, awed and sobered by what we had done. It must have been like this, I thought. Those old warriors must have felt dull and grim, dumb before the perils that lay ahead as resolutely they grasped a spear cold to the touch in the early morning light. The quiver and the fear were there, but so was something else, the sense that what needed to be done must be done. Lighten our darkness, Lord, we prayed; by the mercies of your dear Son, defend us from the powers and dangers of this night.

Thus we went in faith, our own great weakness feeling. We were ordinary people; we had no massive organization behind us, nor were we the sort who would normally run around in the streets with a placard. There were some among us who had had experience storming the gates of Malacañang or some such things, but we were young then; life was green and we had not known the greying wars of innocence besieged and precariously unsurrendered. We could not tell then the lie from the dream, the dream merchant from the visionary. We chanted and raved under the impulse of feeling that all things were possible. Now, many years after the disillusionment of seeing friends die under the cruel and overbearing strength of monocratic power, we did not know if we were being brave or simply being foolhardy.

But we went, and there we were: a small band of people wanting like the rest to put an end to the monstrous power that had gone haywire. The scene was like the many things we do as a people: bright and chaotic and irrepressibly festive. The air reeked with sweat and broiled squid, streaks of yellow assaulted the eyes pleasantly, and all around were grimy monuments to the Filipino's entrepreneurial spirit, long used to wresting opportunity from the marginal side of things.

It was no way to conduct a revolution, but perhaps it was truer than the stone-cold stringency of the usual uprising. Great upheavals of the spirit, like suffering, take place in the most casual of circumstances, as when "someone else is eating or opening a window or just walking dully along," as the poet W. H. Auden puts it. Something big and deep was growing inside us as a people, and how else was it to come to birth but in the merry and familiar sights and sounds of the marketplace?

Casual grit. That was what it was the afternoon the tanks came charging. The engines began to roar, but the people refused to move, a defenseless but determined wall of restraint against the tidal lust for bloodshed. It was a war of nerves, but perhaps, more deeply, a trial of faith: faith in the rightness of standing there, quaking yet fortified by an instinctive sense that the doing of that which is right will pay off somehow. Like much of the serious business of life, it had its light moments. Besides the tanks moving toward us, carabaos had wandered on the road, and someone held up a cross as if to ward off evil – gestures of instinct and ritual that come to our aid when all else fails.

A group of priests and nuns ringed themselves round some troops, sprinkling holy water. It was as if the demons of violence, brutish and palpable, could be exorcised by the steady and relentless application of timeless appurtenances to the sacred.

With the tanks held at bay, there was the problem of maintaining attentive vigil all through the night. We were assigned to guard Gate 2 of Camp Aguinaldo, along with some Muslims, some of whom were former Moro National Liberation Front warriors. It was a peculiar show of solidarity – Catholics, Protestants and Muslims all ranged together for a war against war.

Seated back to back, we barricaded far into the night, fighting off sleep and resting on each other's shoulders.

Morning would find us aching from the ingenious contortions our bodies had to resort to. But the watchers remained in formation, faithful to the end to the calling to keep watch.

Monday, 24 February

The moon was full though pale and wan when I woke up at three. It shone like a stage prop just above the rooftops. EDSA looked forlorn and deserted except for pockets of vigilantes. Radio Veritas, shut down and silenced for hours the previous night, was holed up somewhere and once again was beating the drums, this time on another frequency. June Keithley, flurried and distraught, appealed to nearby citizens to spill out of their houses onto the streets and reinforce the sorely depleted columns valiantly staying the troops that were then determinedly advancing.

Being neophytes in the art of surviving military violence, we were told to wet handkerchiefs as added protection from tear gas. Somebody distributed *kalamansi*, the juice of which we were to rub on our faces to keep the skin from burning. We closed ranks and once again stood in formation, a frail chain against the impending rush of soldiers approaching EDSA.

Radio pleas for more people sounded more and more shrill and frantic. The troops had broken through the first line of columns. Sikorsky gunships could be heard rumbling in the distance. Since the rebel forces were all in Camp Crame, we were told to forsake the Aguinaldo gate and fortify the pitiful remnant left at the Crame gate. Once again we stood there, shoulder to shoulder. Then the helicopters came, blotting the sky.

It was but a moment, but the waiting seemed to last forever. Are these the enemy? we asked. We shall die, then, not by sharp and swift bayonet thrusts, but by fire dropped from the sky. "Oh, this is the end! This is it!" cried some of our people. I looked up to the sky and prayed.

I thought of home, of failing to say goodbye. Is it worth it? I asked myself. This is romantic, a gesture of youth. There is more important work to be done than standing here like sheep to the slaughter. "Give us guns," said our comrades, the ex-MNLF. I could understand. Nonviolent resistance is against our very human blood. And yet, really, when all the options are taken into account, there is really no other way to keep blood from flowing than to stand there, helpless but resistant. For this belief we stood together, locked in communal defense of whatever it was that had brought us there, to serve as proof that there is power in powerlessness.

The helicopters hovered, then landed straight into the Crame compound. For a while there was tense silence. Then the news swept through us: the air force had defected! We were stunned – then very wide grins broke out on our faces. We felt happy and stupid at the same time. The joy of it was hardly getting in when reports of defections among the advancing troops tingled in our ears.

And then the unbelievable news circulated: Mrs Marcos had left the afternoon before, and Mr Marcos left early this morning. The news was unconfirmed, but soon things broke loose and seemed to make it true: Ramos and Enrile came out of the gate and cheered. We sang and jumped and embraced one another in tears. Bags of *pan de sal* started to be passed round, then someone took it into his head to playfully throw some to the people up on the ledges of the gate. The crowd joined in, and all of a sudden the air was full of a jolly traffic of *pan de sal* being thrown back and forth by the people up and below. The gesture was more than fun; it was an unwitting sign of what we were about. Other struggles had bullets and stones; we had bread, and joy thrown along with it.

It was an utter privilege to be part of the occasion. We wept, perhaps for the years of suffering and silence, perhaps for the experience of solidarity in a country whose revolutions had always remained unfinished for failing to get its act together. And maybe we wept even for ourselves, for having been touched by something bigger, humbled by the sense of being caught up into the larger and surer ways of the One whose nature is always to have mercy. We felt part of a great sacrament, the "sacrament of the brother" – of the wonder that had been performed before our eyes, and that we were witnesses to its awe and stunning power.

Like all good Filipinos, we took pictures of ourselves for posterity's sake, to show to our children's children the pride and joy unspeakable of so great a liberation. We walked home along EDSA as in a dream, pleasantly dazed by a sky that had never seemed so glorious and warmed by the faces we met in the streets. We hailed each other with the *Laban* sign, now fast becoming a more universal symbol of a people's will to be free.

But when we got home, the puffy, sleep-deprived face of Mr Marcos stared at us. He was on TV, proclaiming to all and sundry the inescapable fact of his presence. We blinked and dropped our weary selves onto a seat. Was it a last-minute piece of propaganda, or should we take to the streets again? Telephones rang to confirm that, yes, the man was still around. We sat in silence. There is a tenacity, a hardness, to evil we would all do well to always take into account.

"Very well then," I said, "we shall go back to the barricades and slug it out for many more nights. But first let me get some sleep." So off I went, tracking down dragons in sleep; it was at least a way of keeping the monster at bay.

Afternoon found us regrouping. We prayed and asked for strength, aware of the ache and weariness in our bones and of the prospect of a protracted struggle of millions teeming along EDSA. Once again we felt our faces changed by an inward glow kindled by God's presence.

There was talk of strafing during the night. In spite of this, our ranks swelled. The fiesta atmosphere intensified with the primeval drums of the Ati-Atihan and the periodic noise barrage. There was much singing among us, as well as rosaries and novenas among the brown-clad Nazarene women beside us, a brass band going up and down the length of EDSA, and stars from the movies and other arts on parade. This is not a revolution, some said as they shook their heads.

Well, perhaps not; it was perhaps more ancient, more inveterate and romantic than the atavistic desire to tear things down and make them altogether new. In the pomp and folksy pageantry, in the ritual call to the gods, we see resurfaced perhaps a people's collective mechanism for the expelling of a hideous spirit, not quite unlike the banging of pots and pans in the old days to frighten away the dragon that was thought to be swallowing the sun.

Refusing to forget the danger, we asked everyone to make a conscious decision whether or not to stay for the night. Most elected to stay, spreading newspapers on the sidewalk and every space that could be colonized for some stretching and sleeping. The pavement was a very hard bed indeed. Packed side by side and lying supine, we looked at the stars together and wondered what a blitz looked like. A blaze of fireworks, perhaps; a pity we might not be there to see it.

Late in the night I shook off sleep and surveyed the hundreds of bodies lying around me. One or two of our men sat glued to the radio; some were out reconnoitering. The silence was strange after the boisterous singing just a few hours before. Just then, I felt the weight of having to make an answer for the loss of each life spread out and breathing there before me. But then, perhaps, no one can be made to answer. Every one must do what he or she needs to do. There is really no other way to live; some things are of more value than life itself.

Tuesday, 25 February

At half-past four almost everyone had roused themselves from sleep. There was some mist, which made the morning gray and pale. Smoke rose from piles of garbage being burnt, as the enormous amount of litter in the streets threatened sanitation. Unlike the morning before, there were lots more people who had camped out.

We gathered to praise and worship God together for the relative safety of the night before. The day was expected to be tense, as both Mrs Aquino and Mr Marcos had indicated their intention to get proclaimed as newly elected president at noon. We braced ourselves and got more organized.

Mrs Aquino's swearing-in was a brave, confident vote for a liberated future. Things still hung in the balance; while on her side were the people and a marginal collection of armed defectors, on the side of the incumbent was an immense firepower, a monolith of wayward armipotence. But perhaps power could take alternative shapes. Mr Marcos's inauguration was cut off in mid-air, rebel troops having taken over the TV channels. Radio Veritas continued its media siege, a uniquely novel use of information as handmaid to revolution. And of course there were the people, swarms of them – a throbbing, busy, bustling swirl that for many years had been thought to be docile and inconsequential in the mathematics of power.

The people at the barricades were not the dreamed-of masses rising in arms, sufficiently primed and programmed to wage class conflict. It was a miscellaneous rabble of regal matrons and scruffy riffraff, priests and nuns and bedraggled vendors, middle-class adventurers, quiet dissenters and gristly veterans of the parliament of the streets. There were babies, old women, portly housewives on garden chairs. It was a revolution incredibly supplied with accoutrements to a pleasant survival: a flow of food and drinks, tents, quilted mats, beach umbrellas, even a snap toilet brigade for those who suffered discomfiting calls of nature.

Revolution is not a picnic, Mao Tse-tung said. This one is, and perhaps, rightly so. It is always a joyful act to participate in the toils of freedom. Besides, the Filipino people being what they are, it is only apposite that their rites of passage toward political maturity and power be singularly recalcitrant, irrepressibly happy improvisations that defy the usual iron rules of power struggles.

Toward evening there were rumors that negotiations between Enrile and the beleaguered president were going on, the nature of which we could only infer from the helicopters flying overhead to somewhere. Violent streetfighting was going on in Mendiola, we were told; would we like to go and serve as a tempering presence in the conflict? We discussed the issue together and decided to stay put, feeling a certain inevitability of vehemence in the surfacing of long-repressed feelings of rage. Malacañang was being stormed by an angry mob; we prayed for restraint, for the gift of decency and dignity on an occasion of great though understandable temptations to violence and excess.

The news traveled fast and loose: Mr Marcos and company have left Malacañang, and are quartered in Clark Air Base for an early morning journey to Hawaii. This time we were wary and wanted verification, feeling like horses who had had the experience of being led to water without being allowed to drink.

"It's true!" shouted some in glee. I merely stared, stumped by the fact that the wounded tiger who had seemed so dangerous and deadly, threatening a comeback strike, had turned its tail for a run. Quietly, without the flush and flare of triumph, we embraced one another and mulled over in our secret places the meaning of the boon that had come to us.

The Ati-Atihan sounded its drums. Cars honked and people began to shout and dance in the streets. We lustily sang hymns of praise, and saluted marching passersby with a final and rousing rendition of "Bayan Ko." Once again there were tears, triggered by memories of abject humiliation, of a nation once cowed and quiescent, conditioned into a self-protective subjection by centuries of colonization. This revolt has surprised us, has made us aware of what we are capable of doing and of becoming as a people. Pride in ourselves, in our future as a nation, swelled our hearts and dimmed the eyes that beheld each other in newfound wonder. Shortly after midnight I was walking along EDSA headed for home, arm-in-arm with friends. Streams of people walked with us, shouting and stomping and making a din and a noise that was pleasant to the ear.

Tonight we had frightened away the dragon that had long swallowed the sun. Tomorrow, for sure, we shall wake up to a morning with a stream of yellow sunlight bursting through the window.

11

The Darkest Moment

Rolando Villacorte[1]

The cool Monday dawn found most of the barricaders up on their feet. Many of them were moving about, apparently to shake a leg. The radios were still playing and June Keithley, though obviously tired, was gamely hanging on in her clandestine radio station. She had resumed broadcasting shortly after midnight with the help of a group of volunteers, including brothers Paolo and Gabe Mercado, both teenaged sons of writer Monina Mercado.

Gen. Ramos's now very familiar voice also kept reverberating all around with his psywar broadcasts. He announced the defection of the thirty crack troopers of the Presidential Security Command who had deserted their posts in Malacañang near midnight the previous night. Two of the defectors had reportedly fled to seek refuge in Camp Crame, while the twenty-eight others had gone into hiding for fear of liquidation.

The general likewise announced the defection of retired Brig. Gen. Guillermo Pecache, chief of the National Pollution Control Commission. The reason given was that there was too much pollution in the Marcos government. Pecache accused the dictator's regime of having destroyed the credibility of the government and the military.

Brig. Gen. Eduardo Ermita, commanding general of the joint staff of the Civil Relations Service and a Ver loyalist, had earlier joined the rebel camp according to Ramos. Ermita, in fact, was already with Ramos and Enrile at the command center that morning.

---

1. All the quotes and accounts shared in this chapter are from first-hand oral interviews between the author and the key players.

I was up as early as two-thirty, and what a cold morning it was! I couldn't sleep well because of the offensive urine smell, and because of my extremely uncomfortable sleeping position, not to mention the constant blare of radios around me and the chill weather. Besides, the tension and excitement really made it impossible for me to snatch more than forty winks. From vigilance, so they say, comes but little sleep. How true!

To stretch my legs and keep myself warm, I walked up to the front of Treffpunkt Jedermann, a German restaurant at the street corner two blocks away, and did some calisthenics there. It was already closed at the time.

EDSA was relatively quiet, for many of the barricaders, now looking weary, were enjoying their shut-eye. Their ranks had noticeably thinned. I could see them curled up everywhere: on the wide avenue itself and on the pavements, on the traffic island, against the four-layer sandbags at the corner of EDSA and Santolan Road, and in parked motor vehicles (Pastor Magalit was snoozing inside a car belonging to a deacon). In fact, they occupied every available space.

Over near Camp Crame's main gate I noticed some merrymaking going on. A batch of barricaders was gathered around a bonfire and singing lively tunes to the accompaniment of a guitar. Occasionally they would interrupt their songs with peals of laughter and banter.

Suddenly the merrymakers burst into applause and cheers as they stood up to greet Ramos. The general, a physical fitness buff, had stepped out to go on a jogging tour around the camp. Actually, it was a combined jogging tour and patrol sortie.

Wearing a pair of sneakers, a dark blue shirt and a matching pair of denim pants, the bespectacled general was accompanied by a handful of security men. As he jogged along, he held a Tabacalera cigar with his left hand and smilingly waved to the cheering crowd with his right.

Soon after he rejoined Enrile at the command center, beads of perspiration rolling down his cheeks, Ramos received three unsettling reports at roughly half-hour intervals. The first was about the sighting at Santolan Road near Horseshoe Village of "three tanks" getting ready to break Camp Crame's back door nearly half a kilometer away. Quickly Ramos dispatched plainclothesmen to verify the information.

The same report caused a civilian leader to sound a call for volunteers to man the camp's rear gate.

From EDSA a group of around two hundred men responded. Some rode in a military vehicle through the camp, while others merely walked, unmindful of the slight drizzle that had started minutes before. After more than half an hour of watchful waiting, the volunteers, whose ranks had just doubled, began to feel the gnawing pangs of hunger and the discomfort of the cold and damp weather.

One of the vigilantes espied a lighted store ahead across the street. He pointed it out to several companions of his and in seconds the small group briskly walked over to see what they could buy. They found the owner, a middle-aged housewife, tending the store by herself. She was listening intently to June Keithley's non-stop radio broadcasts.

The storeowner's eyes lit up when she learned that her customers, looking cold and famished, were volunteers manning the Camp Crame gate. One of the men fished out a ten-peso bill from his wallet and politely asked the woman for cigarettes.

She scooped up from the shelf three cartons of cigarettes, each of a different brand, and handed them over to the man with the money. "Here," she said with a maternal smile as she placed a tiny box of matches on top of the merchandise, "take all of these to keep you warm. And keep your money because we may never have anymore use for it tomorrow." She was harboring fear of a possible outbreak of hostilities, or full-blown revolution.

Just then the aroma of freshly baked *pan de sal* reached the men's nostrils, and their hungry look became more evident. It emanated from right behind the store, which, the surprised men found out, doubled as a bakery.

"Ah yes!" the woman exclaimed. "We already have some *pan de sal*, fresh from the oven." She disappeared behind the shelves and came out moments later with a big cardboard box full of hot *pan de sal*. The starving men's eyes bulged.

"For all of you revolutionaries," she said banteringly, as she deposited the ample box on the counter. Again she waved off any offer of payment, saying it was her modest contribution to the People Power Revolution. "The old fiend's days are numbered, aren't they?" she gleefully remarked, referring to the dictator.

The grateful vigilantes took leave of the kindly woman and hurried back to rejoin their comrades. By then there were already around a thousand people massed at the rear gate. There just wasn't enough bread and cigarettes to pass around, not even for everyone to receive just a piece.

If they could have multiplied the stuff they had in the same way the five loaves of bead were multiplied to feed the five thousand gathered on a lonely hill in Galilee early one evening, the vigilantes would have quickly done so. But possessing no such divine power they multiplied the bread and cigarettes in the only way they knew: they broke each *pan de sal* into two, while two men took the same number of puffs from a single cigarette.

"Share and share alike," they happily said. What a heartwarming display of unity and brotherhood!

Meanwhile, Philippine Navy 2nd Lt. Sylvia Yanga, detailed at the office of the deputy chief of staff at the General Headquarters, announced her defection over Radio Veritas.

"It's high time for the elements of the AFP to speak out," said the young navy officer, the first female officer to cross over to the reformists' camp. According to her, officers and men at the GHQ shared her sentiments but were still hesitant to make a stand.

At 4:30 a.m., Ramos received a note and he looked amused as he read it. "Good news!" he proclaimed on the air. "The three tanks sighted at Santolan are no tanks at all. They are all garbage trucks." He quickly added with a chortle: "But that's symbolic. After all, we have been getting nothing but garbage all these years!"

Everybody laughed. The tension in the room was instantly relieved. But hardly had the laughter died away when June Keithley's voice came on excitedly, relaying a caller's information (second report) that soldiers had massed at Fort Bonifacio and were already leaving for Camp Crame.

Those were Tadiar's battle-tested Marines – two battalions of them. Led by Col. Balbas, they were on their way to annihilate the rebel bastion with the combined brute force of three LVT-H6 tanks, three V-150 commando armored vehicles, three 105 howitzers and more than a dozen mortars. To provide them air support were the 15th Strike Wing's two heli gunships.

The cigar fell from Ramos's mouth. He grabbed the phone which was the hotline to Radio Veritas and earnestly sounded off: "Now it is clear. It is Mr Marcos who is massing troops, not us. This is blood of our people on his hands. We pray that he will not resort to this. We know this is not the real Mr Marcos that we knew. We knew him as a true guerrilla leader. He has now degenerated into an irrational individual."

Gen. Ermita followed up Ramos's speech with an impassioned appeal to the Filipino soldiers.

Enrile, in the meantime, was blissfully dozing off in his chair, an Uzi machine pistol nestling in his lap.

At this juncture, Col. Romeo Zulueta, Metrocom deputy commander, rushed in with three aides to confirm Keithley's information. He said there were other opposing forces set to besiege Camp Crame.

"I have verified reports, sir, that the enemy forces will attack at five," Zulueta told Ramos. That was the third report.

Ramos glanced at his watch. "It's past five already. Where are they?"

"Sir, there are two battalions in our rear, Horseshoe Village area, and two battalions led by Col. Rolando Abadilla, deployed at Annapolis Street, Greenhills."

By that time, Balbas and his men had reached the intersection of White Plains Avenue and Santolan Road barely a kilometer to the east. Actually, they were beginning to disperse the thin flank of the still sleepy vigilantes there with tear gas.

Ramos hastily called to a conference all the civilians at the headquarters. Most of them were media people. He apprised them of the critical situation. "Gentlemen," he said in a grave tone as he flicked the ashes off his cigar, "you are now free to make your own individual decision as to what you will do from here on. You may stay or may not. Whatever your decision may be, we shall not hold it against you. We shall consider you still to be friends and heroes of the revolution."

But the reporters chose to stay. Ramos took note of their nationalities: American, British, Japanese, Swiss, French and others. He then immediately announced their presence at the headquarters to their respective embassies in Metro Manila.

"There is some danger about to come upon us, and because of this danger they are free to go," the general stressed. "But should anything happen to them here, please take care of them." He urged the embassies to exert their influence on Marcos to call off the attack.

Then he aired a last-minute emotional appeal: "All Filipino soldiers out there: Don't inflict harm on people who have no arms. The blood spilled today will be on Marcos's hands. We offer nothing but friendship. Mr Marcos has assembled an overwhelming force against us. Mr Marcos has done nothing constructive. We are ready, but please tell the world it is Mr Marcos who is about to inflict violence and terror, not us."

Turning to the newshounds, Ramos said that should the hostile forces ignore their "friendly overtures," then the rebels had no other choice but to fight. "We have to defend this movement in order to survive, in order to keep this movement going. They're obviously overwhelming forces, and we don't have enough force to counter them."

Enrile, who minutes before had been roused from his sleep by an aide, was now talking with Ambassador Bosworth on the phone. "Just for the record," he said, "we would like to inform you that Marcos's troops will attack us any moment now. We are going to fight to the last man to save freedom in our land." The conversation over, he turned to the eager reporters: "Ambassador Bosworth said he would inform his government right away."

Ramos shook hands with everybody and said goodbye. Everybody's spirits were at their lowest ebb. "This may be the last time we will see each other," Ramos said solemnly. He advised the civilians to go down to the ground floor where it was safer for them. No one seemed willing to move, although a soldier was persuasively showing them the door. Finally, only about twenty remained.

Overhead, a pair of low-flying jet bombers kept circling, their thunderous roar striking fear in the hearts of the people below.

Marcos, meanwhile, pressed his counter-offensive on the airwaves. In an early morning broadcast, he overconfidently said: "I have the power to destroy this rebellion if I feel enough is enough. I am not sick, I am strong. I will not resign. I will even lead troops against Enrile and Ramos. I smell gunpowder like an old war horse."

At about 6 a.m., while a group of reporters huddled around a small radio set outside the war room, Cardinal Sin came on the air. "May we come to a peaceful solution to our crisis," he intoned. "I will bless the men in uniforms, but only those who are for peace."

"Huh, how's that for final absolution?" quipped Col. Luis San Andres, Gen. Ramos's public information officer.

Inside the command center, in Gen. Ramos's office, the atmosphere became more oppressively solemn as the seconds ticked away. Everyone was just waiting for the final moment when death would bring its sting. It would come in a heavy barrage of artillery and rocket explosion.

Indeed, what else was there to do but wait? The rebels had no artillery, no armored vehicles and no planes or helicopter gunships with which to retaliate. All they had were around eight hundred soldiers inside the camp and an unarmed mass of praying people out there on the highway. Of course, they had hundreds of Molotov cocktails, produced through the efforts of Col. Imperial, the chief of logistics, but what good were they against an aerial attack?

Camp Crame was a sitting duck from the start, and now it was teetering on the brink of disaster.

But once you accept your own death, says Saul S. Haskins, all of a sudden you are free to live. You no longer care about your reputation . . . you no longer care except so far as your life can be used tactically – to promote a cause you believe in.

This indeed was the rebels' cause and that of the Filipino people too: to dethrone a leadership that was "inhuman and retrograde" so that "justice may flow like a stream, and righteousness like a river that never goes dry," and that freedom, democracy and prosperity might become a tangible reality, not just an evanescent or a pipe dream.

Col. Honesto Isleta, who was among those present in the command post, remembered his little compact Bible (Today's English Version) which was on his desk at the corner just outside Gen. Ramos's inner office. Since there was nothing else to do but wait, he sat down at his desk, opened the Bible to Psalm 91 and began meditating on its every line. He knew from personal experience how powerful a psalm it was. It proclaims God's unfailing protection of those who seek him and trust in him. It is a most appropriate Scripture reading for one's darkest moment such as they were facing now.

Isleta ended his meditation with a prayer: "Father, if you decide that those by the Pasig river should continue to rule, then your will be done. Otherwise, I now claim your promise as contained in this psalm, that anyone who calls on you for protection will surely be delivered. This I pray in Jesus's name. Amen."

Isleta then thought of sharing the wondrous promise with the men inside the war room. He would ask Ramos to let him read it aloud to them.

Meanwhile, the funereal gloom that pervaded the command center had descended upon the entire ranks of the EDSA blockaders who were already all up on their feet. Although they were not aware of the drama taking place within the command center, they were kept posted on the movement of the hostile troops via the airwaves and through scouts or couriers.

In truth, a number of tear-gas victims themselves managed to alert the blockaders about the incident. They came on board screeching vehicles and screamed that black-shirted (I thought I heard "blackhearted") anti-riot troops had teargased the crowds at Libis and Col. Balbas's fearsome infantry and armor had already entered the Logistics Command compound which occupied a corner of Camp Aguinaldo. The report sent a ripple of fear among the barricaders.

The civilian organizers quickly instructed the barricaders to bring out their face towels or handkerchiefs or any piece of cloth which they had brought with them precisely for such a type of emergency. Hastily they soaked all these in water containers placed in strategic areas. We soaked ours in a big plastic pail waiting beside Gate 2, very close to our assigned area.

Each of us picked up a *kalamansi* (lemon) from the containers that were being passed around by the organizers. We were supposed to cover our faces with the wet cloths or face towels in case of a tear-gas assault and squeeze the *kalamansi* on the affected parts of our bodies to relieve the itchy or painful effect of tear gas.

On instruction we faced the Camp Aguinaldo wall and linked arms to form a human chain. We were going to halt the advancing Marines with our frail bodies and brave the suffocating tear gas and, who knows, maybe even a hail of Armalite bullets! They mustn't be allowed by any means to break through and reach Camp Crame!

I was a bit more concerned that we – my wife and I – along with some fifty people from KONFES and Diliman Bible Church led by Pastor Magalit himself, were directly facing the gate. It was through this gate that the heavily armed Marines were expected to break out. Not only were we in the line of fire, we were also in the first line of defense. Oh, what a bind! I thought.

That certainly was the darkest moment of the People Power Revolution. For once, the armies of barricaders were strangely quiet. The pall of gloom hung heavily over us. But like the rebel leaders up at the command post, we were prepared for the worst – or rather, we were resigned to our fate.

My wife and I were naturally both apprehensive, but the apprehension stayed deep down. We just stared at each other and we understood. Together with the DBC folk we were praying in our hearts. No need to be in dark despair, really. Only the Good Shepherd knew what was going to happen next; only he by his grace could lead us through this "valley of the shadow of death." And we could feel his strong presence in our midst.

In such a situation, there is also much confidence and courage to be derived from the following passage of Scripture: "For we know that if the earthly tent we live in is destroyed, we have a building from God, an eternal house in heaven, not built by human hands" (2 Cor 5:1 NIV).

Cardinal Sin somehow eased the gripping tension. He exhorted the people to be calm and pray. "God is with us," he reminded them.

This was really a time for ardent prayer. Only a while before June Keithley herself had been praying emotionally on the air (she said she was terribly upset and felt helpless when she heard the cries of those being tear-gassed):

> Lord, you know that there are many people out there. You know what we are going through. There are many of us and we are going to do our duty. We ask you to please guide us, Lord. You teach us to always turn the other cheek. We ask you to show us in many concrete ways that truly nothing can come from evil. Show us, Lord, that only good will work in this world. Please take care of all who are out there. Protect them and save them from harm. There are children out there, young girls and boys, parents, brothers and sisters, husbands and wives. Who knows what they may have to face this morning? We add our prayers to the prayers of the people in our country. Lord, I am not very good at this, but I just ask you, please, in Jesus's name, please save our people. Amen.

By 6 a.m. Col. Balbas and his force had made a stop at the Logistics Command to assess the situation and to plan their next moves. How Balbas came to be chosen for the terribly difficult assignment and what had happened afterward were a striking revelation themselves: a revelation of God's continuing intervention in the People Power Revolution. Following the embarrassing fiasco at Ortigas Avenue, General Fabian Ver and Josephus Ramas determined to launch a full-scale assault on the rebel camp. They would mobilize not only a composite anti-riot force using tear gas, but also Marine troops and artillery, helicopter gunships and low-level bombers.

Shortly after 3 a.m. on Monday, Ramas gave Tadiar the "go" signal for two Marine battalions to mount a "fresh attack." For the job, according to the McCoy-Robinsons-Wilkinson report, Tadiar said he had "a choice of two commanders: the level-headed Colonel Balbas or the more gung-ho Colonel Reyes. (Reyes, it will be recalled, was with Balbas at Ortigas).

However, Balbas had then just arrived at Fort Bonifacio from Ortigas and White Plains-Santolan Road, exhausted and hungry. So the choice inevitably fell on the "well-rested Colonel Reyes."

Miraculously, when it came time for Tadiar to give the order to lead the attack all of a sudden, he "blurted out" the name of Col. Balbas. "It was probably an act of God," Tadiar says of his "bizarre" decision. He also believes that Ver's and Ramas's planned attack on the two rebel camps (which culminated in the Ortigas fiasco) was "sabotaged by an act of God."

It was around 4 a.m. when the assault troops and the armored transports set out. Balbas recalls the episode:

> By this time, I was in command of almost 950 soldiers. We also had with us three tanks and three armored vehicles, the ones you might have seen on TV. In addition, we brought along some cannons and mortars. Escorted by the anti-riot units from the Army, the Philippine Constabulary, the Philippine Air Force and the Philippine Navy, we arrived again at the intersection of White Plains and Santolan Road. It was around five o'clock in the morning, and we hadn't slept for almost twenty-four hours.
>
> When we were again barricaded by the people, the anti-riot units dispersed the crowds with tear gas. While people were scampering away, we removed the barriers in the areas. They had put several vehicles across the road, trying to prevent us from moving forward.

"Everything really happened so fast that I did not have time to scream," says Maria Fe P. Paller who was there at the scene. "We just scrambled for safety and started running. My eyes were burning and my lips were smarting. Someone fired into the air and I could hear guns being cocked.

"My left eye felt really sore. Would I become blind in the left eye? I asked myself. Oh, God, please . . . how can I become an actress if I go blind.

"We continued to run. A woman came out of her house and offered us water. I washed my face. The burning sensation spread all over my face. Somehow, with a little fresh air, I felt better. I was so grateful I could still see with both eyes."

Soon cries of "Tanks!" and "Tear gas!" were reverberating in the darkness as a number of people ran in a wild helter-skelter. Half-blind, some were stumbling, while others were gasping for breath. Still others (mostly women), too stubborn to break away from the barricade, just lay down on the ground, weeping and wailing.

A man lost a tooth when a captain elbowed him while he was stopping the anti-riot troops from breaking into their ranks on Katipunan Avenue.

The priests, nuns and seminarians, who were in the frontline of the barricade "to soften the hearts of the attacking troops," tried to talk with the soldiers, but the soldiers shoved them away with their recoil-less rifles. They tried to pacify some of the blockaders who were arming themselves with stones and shouting insults at the uniformed men. One of the priests went around the chain with a cup filled with *kalamansi* juice. "Here," he said, "wet your handkerchiefs with this. Put some on your faces."

"Get out of the way!" one of the truncheon-wielding anti-riot troopers shouted before pressing their advance. "You will just get hurt."

The vigilantes, forming a seven-row defense beside the Caltex gas station, ignored the warning; instead, they braced themselves for the attack by locking their arms tighter and kept praying. They couldn't see the soldiers because the headlights of their trucks were blinding them.

Above the uproar suddenly rose the voice of a priest chanting the Lord's Prayer, and soon everybody joined in. One of the black-uniformed men then hurled tear gas canisters in quick succession in front of the blockaders as the troopers, with fixed bayonets but without gas masks, rushed forward. The human chain backed up a few feet but it did not break.

"Suddenly a gust of wind blew the gas away from us into the line of the soldiers," recounts Lito Bantayan who was in the second line. "Their line broke! I told the priest beside me: 'Father, the breeze is blowing toward them!'"

Luis D. Beltran, in his column "Straight from the Shoulder,"[2] wrote that one of the officers who led the tear-gas attack became a "born-again Christian" after that dramatic incident. He ascribed the instant conversion to divine intervention.

The unidentified officer was reportedly flabbergasted when he saw the wind abruptly shifting and enveloping his unit instead. Some soldiers, it was said, had to be rushed to a clinic for treatment.

"That's the time I decided God was on their side, and I wasn't going to be left behind," the officer was quoted to have told reporters.

Here's the rest of Lito Bantayan's interesting account:

> We stood there until the soldiers were able to form a line again. The sergeant had a hard time convincing the soldiers to line up. They were reluctant. Nobody wanted to be in front to form a solid line and they moved ever so slowly. I knew we had won. Even after they drove us away during their last rush forward, I knew we had won. The soldiers were with us and I felt it.
>
> I could see that from under their helmets they were smiling, they were hitting their shields instead of hitting the people. Even when I stopped running, they went past me. Nobody raised his stick to hit anybody, they were mocking it. Even some of the priests stopped running.
>
> I walked towards Camp Crame, past the lines of soldiers, and nobody bothered me. I was so far back that the tanks were already behind me . . . When I reached EDSA and joined in the singing of the National Anthem, I was close to tears. It was all over, I said to myself. Suddenly I was very tired and weary. I was wet and dirty, but I was very, very happy.

Having thus cleared the way, Balbas and his column entered the Logistics Command premises through Camp Aguinaldo's east wall, about three hundred meters away. They were now practically within shouting distance from the defense ministry building and the ISAFP headquarters where a small contingent left behind by Enrile the day before was staying. This contingent was led by Col. Rodolfo Estrellado of ISAFP.

In a short while Balbas and his 950 tough Marines would push deeper inside the camp to occupy a more strategic position from where, according to the Ver-Ramas plan, they were to pulverize the rebels' stronghold at Camp

---

2. *Philippine Daily Inquirer*, 13 March 1986.

Crame. Remember that aside from 950 assault rifles, Balbas and his men were equipped with three tanks, three armored vehicles and over a dozen 105 mm. guns and mortars.

Moreover, a trigger-happy Ver had ordered PAF Chief Vicente Piccio to send at least two helicopter gunships from the 15th Strike Wing based at Villamor Air Base and another two jet bombers from the 5th Fighter Wing based at Basa Air Base in Floridablanca, Pampanga, to provide tactical support to the early morning ground operations against the recalcitrant mutineers.

That was the situation the defenseless EDSA barricaders were in at about six o'clock that foggy Monday morning as they stood between the two camps with linked arms and thumping hearts. On the basis of the radio report, the convoy of Marines should have attacked by now. "Where are they?" the anxious barricaders asked. "Where are the trucks and tanks?"

Pastor Magalit led the DBC–KONFES group in prayer ("Lord, we have no courage of our own; we entrust our lives into your loving and mighty arms . . . Amen"). Then we all sang, most solemnly, the national anthem. When we came to the last line, *Aming ligaya na pag may mang-aapi ang mamatay nang dahil sa iyo!* ("But it is glory ever when thou art wronged for us thy sons to suffer and die!"), not a few choked up. The pastor was one of them.

Minutes later we were instructed to move over to the other lane in front of Camp Crame's main gate, where we continued our anxious waiting. Suddenly from afar, from the direction of Ortigas, came the whirring sounds of helicopters. They looked like tiny dots against the hazy sky, but as they came closer and closer they began to look like giant dragonflies. There were seven or eight of them. Initially, we could make out only three, and they seemed to be in a triangle formation.

After a few seconds the other dragonflies emerged, to form a single line with the rest as they loomed larger and larger.

"Sikorsky!" someone yelled. "Airwolf!" countered another.

But what were they – friends or foes? everybody was nervously asking. With bated breath and with craned necks we helplessly watched as the rotor flying machines started to circle over Camp Crame. We feared they were now preparing for the mortal stroke, or what the French call the *coup de grâce*. But we enthusiastically waved at them nonetheless, earnestly hoping and praying they would hold back.

And look at those two low-flying jet bombers! They kept "reconnoitering," as if trying to decide where to drop the first bomb. But the sky was cloudy with haze, in effect obscuring the pilots' view of the target.

My God, I mumbled to myself, those aircraft could easily make us mincemeat just as Marcos had boasted on the air! Those snarling helicopter gunships alone could accomplish the ghastly job in one minute flat. With lethal accuracy their guns could shoot two thousand rounds of ammunition per minute. What carnage and what a blood river EDSA would turn out to be, I thought. The prospect was ghastly, enough to make one's blood run cold.

Providentially, the eight hundred soldiers manning the camp's defenses had orders not to fire unless fired upon. And so they, like us civilians, just waited watchfully, their guns at the ready.

The choppers, having completed a circle, appeared to be maneuvering away, but within the wink of an eye they were coming back in a diving formation. *"Ayan na!"*[3] some people shouted, with no little alarm. We thought they were circling in on their target.

To our great surprise, they gradually descended and landed one by one on the parade ground before the grandstand facing EDSA. The pilots were waving white flags and were flashing the "L" sign with their fingers. They had defected! People shouted, cheered and wildly applauded.

The helicopters disgorged Col. Sotelo and his sixteen pilots. With the helicopter rotor blades still turning, civilians and soldiers inside the camp rushed toward the airmen and jubilantly welcomed them with hugs, kisses and handshakes. Those on EDSA had to content themselves by watching from a distance. Some overeager ones, though, managed to climb over the concrete fence topped with sharp-pointed iron bars, while others merely peeked over the six-foot-high concrete wall.

Journalists armed with handy tape recorders immediately surrounded the colonel for an interview, while cameras merrily clicked away.

After answering a few questions Sotelo begged off, saying he wanted to see Minister Enrile and Gen. Ramos first. At this very moment, Col. Isleta was asking permission from Ramos to read Psalm 91 aloud to his colleagues around.

"Why not?" the Protestant general said, his face lighting up. "Here, use my Bible." It was a standard-size Bible lying covered with papers on his desk.

As Ramos handed the book to Isleta, it somehow opened to Psalm 91! As the colonel was calling the men's attention so he could start reading the psalm, the door suddenly opened and in came Col. Sotelo and his pilots accompanied by a security officer. The rebels – who only a few minutes before were bidding each other a tearful goodbye – were simply dumbfounded.

---

3. "This is it!"

Meanwhile, the two jet bombers zoomed by again and made one or two more passes. Seeing perhaps what the helicopters had done, they finally tilted their wings as if in salute and roared away back to their home, there to sit out the revolution.

Part III

The Morning After:
Views from the Margins

12

Thoughts on the Aftermath

Willie Buyson Villarama

EDSA 1 was a double cross by people close to Ferdinand Marcos. Some of them became wealthy, some very rich. The leaders of the EDSA picnic had their own private army, courtesy of the government. The soldiers they handpicked as their security were sent to schools like the Asian Institute of Management for master's degrees. It was greed for power, and not love for the poor, that made them turn their backs against Marcos when they did not get the positions they were lusting for and when they saw that he was sickly and being viciously attacked by the American media.

They were the super turncoats.

With EDSA 1 they got into power but the poor remained poor or even poorer. Vote-buying became rampant. Corruption continued. Killings of farmers never stopped. Injustice was committed against the urban poor, the underpaid workers, the *lumads*,[1] women and many more.

A genuine EDSA miracle would have created a society with fewer poor, fewer uneducated, fewer overseas Filipino workers (OFWs) because there were jobs here, capital for aspiring small entrepreneurs, fewer extra-judicial killings (EJK) and much more. As leaders of a revolution, we expected a complete change from what Marcos had been accused of.

It was the same with EDSA 2: nothing was different from the previous EDSA. The same corruption existed but with new names.[2]

---

1. The indigenous mountain peoples of various tribes in Mindanao.

2. The first EDSA was the highway known as Epifanio de los Santos, named after one of our heroes, where people massed together for People Power against Marcos; EDSA 2 is the People Power against President Joseph Estrada, who was derelict of his duties, in drunken binges with

149

Allow me to briefly narrate my experiences when martial law was proclaimed on 21 September 1972.

EDSA 1 Happened because of Martial Law

Martial law was a bad dream.

I was elected the youngest vice governor of Bulacan (at twenty-seven years old) under the Liberal Party. My mentor was Sen. Benigno "Ninoy" Aquino who convinced me to run. I wanted to run for councilor in my hometown in Bulacan. But Senator Ninoy insisted that I run for vice governor. I nearly lost my life in Plaza Miranda when two hand grenades were thrown onto the stage. My younger brother and I were lucky we were six rows behind.

The start of our term was 1 January and I was always with Ninoy, being mentored. After less than eight months he was arrested and martial law was declared. The evening he was arrested, I was supposed to have fetched him at the Hilton Hotel where they were having a joint meeting with members of the Senate and the House of Representatives. I had to cancel my meeting with him because of a family dinner I forgot I had organized. I passed by the hotel and wrote a note of apology for not being able to join him. A few hours after I left, he was arrested and all his staff with him. I would have been arrested for a few days too if I had been there.

The saddest part of the politics of the period was that nobody from the Liberal Party (LP) then had the courage to continue leading the party. This again happened recently when most members of the LP joined PDP-LABAN which is associated with President Rodrigo Roa Duterte. It may be a coincidence that Sen. Mar Roxas is leader of the LP at the time of writing, losing almost 95 percent of its members to PDP.

This reminds me of a sad encounter I had with Sen. Gerry Roxas, who was the then LP president. It was 8 December 1972, sixty-eight days after martial law had been declared, the anniversary of the death of the political giant Senate President Eulogio "Amang" Rodriguez. I saw Sen. Gerry Roxas standing by the window and approached him.

"Mr President," I said, "in Bulacan I am still leading the fight against the Nacionalista governor of Marcos."

---

his "midnight cabinet," and spent extravagantly for his family and mistresses, apparently with extorted money from gambling lords, etc.

His reply nearly caused me to jump out the window in disappointment: "Willie, you are still very young. It would be a pity if you ended up in jail like Ninoy."

I immediately called a meeting of my thirteen Liberal Party mayors (out of twenty-four). As Chairman of the LP in Bulacan, being the highest elected official of the province, I told them they were free to join another party. Most of them left me and joined the Marcos party – the KBL: Kilusang Bagong Lipunan.

It seems that history is repeating itself. We have martial law in Mindanao and the LPs are again not in fighting form.

My birthday, 8 October, was celebrated for the first time inside the provincial jail in Malolos as a sign of protest for Senator Aquino's arrest and detention. This practice was continued for decades until the jail became too crowded for any celebration inside the premises. I now just distribute Bibles every 8 October.

Martial law cannot be discussed without taking into account EDSA 1, and vice versa.

The EDSA events did not create real change. They only changed the faces of the corrupt, of the *trapos*,[3] of the greedy businessmen from the martial law period. They were not really "miracles" because if they had been, we would have fewer beggars on the streets, fewer slums, fewer jobless people, and fewer OFWs who are separated from their children and are favorite targets of drug pushers.

The removal of Marcos and ERAP did not improve the living conditions of our poor. It created taipans and tycoons instead. Some jokingly say that our grandchildren will grow up with ten families controlling all businesses, the water they drink, the electricity they use, the communications system, the banks, the expressways and all basic services. Pretty soon the few rich will control everything, including politics.

Is this democracy? Is this God's will?

Martial law brought us to EDSA 1 and continued to EDSA 2. Rulers learned how to abuse the power of the gun, the military. He who has the guns *rules*. This sounds like the statement of Mao Tse-tung: "Political power grows out of the barrel of the gun."

Up to this day, it is the soldiers and policemen who are pampered, rather than the teachers and low-paid government employees. This was the effect of martial law, and EDSA 1 and 2.

---

3. Short for "traditional politicians."

I personally view these two historical events as a "political war" between two families: the Marcoses and the Aquinos. President Marcos and Senator Aquino were fraternity brothers from the University of the Philippines. Both had the same passion to be the leader of the Philippines until they died. Marcos saw Aquino as one who would cut short his term as a strong ruler, and Aquino also saw Marcos as one who would stop his dream of becoming president.

Knowing both of them, they were scared of each other because both had the same capability to use out-of-the-box strategies to stay in power, similar to the rulers of our neighboring countries. After both leaders died, the fight continued among their children: Noynoy vs. Bongbong. The mutual hatred is unbelievable. The "victims" of martial law have closed their eyes also to the corruption and abuses of the regimes after Marcos.

I had a rare opportunity to listen to Sen. Ninoy Aquino telling me of his dreams. We were coming from a speaking engagement and I brought him home to Times Street. We were standing outside his house from 11:00 p.m. to 5:00 a.m., immersed in our conversation until the sun started to show her glory. When I asked him what he would do to clean up the Bureau of Customs and the Bureau of Internal Revenue, two notorious, corruption-ridden agencies, he replied: "I will get a dozen each from both agencies and line them up against the wall and have them shot. This will be shown on lTV."

When he saw I was shocked, he added: "But of course, they will be tried. Due process shall be observed."

I am narrating this because I believe Marcos knew the capability of Sen. Ninoy to use violence. The senator had been friendly with the NPAs whose major hideout was in Hacienda Luisita in Tarlac, a 7,000-hectare sugar plantation owned by his in-laws, the Cojuangcos.

Marcos, in declaring martial law, ended the political career of Sen. Ninoy Aquino. An unknown killer ended Ninoy's life on the tarmac. Still today, the mastermind behind the killing is not known. Many ask why, after six years of President Cory, six years of her anointed successor President Fidel V. Ramos, and another six years of President Benigno Aquino III – a total of eighteen years – no serious attempt has been made to find out the mastermind behind the killing of Ninoy. Some quarters are asking if there were people close to Senator Ninoy who wanted the killing unsolved. The findings might show that not Marcos but somebody else or a group of power players was the mastermind.

This would be a blow to the memory of Ninoy, who is known as a martyr for freedom and democracy.[4] Eighteen years in power failed to solve his killing. Why?

From my EDSA 1 experience and limited participation in accompanying Minister Ople in Washington DC during the last days of Marcos, I cannot believe that EDSA 1 was not planned many years before President Marcos was finally ousted.

There was an international group that believed that Marcos had his gold bullion and was scared that he might dump his gold on the market and drive down the price of gold. He had started to act as a leader independent of the United States. The strategic geographical location of the Philippines and our rich mineral resources became the target of superpowers.

The Americans started destroying President Marcos by showing his investments in real estate located in the US. It was a slow death. Our peso was forced to devalue, which led to the bankruptcy of many businessmen. Foreign lending institutions offered us funds to embark on white elephant projects we were not prepared to undertake and manage. We could not digest the funds that they forced us to borrow, and they drove us to an economic crisis that made it easier to depose Marcos.

To close this section, I quote from one of the greatest politicians in my opinion, Senate President Blas F. Ople, on how he perceived EDSA 1 from Washington. The following are extracts from an article Ka Blas wrote one year after EDSA 1:

> . . . There followed a call from Melchor, who gave his address as 1 Washington Square, but Alex spent most of the five minutes on the phone describing his intimate association with General Fidel Ramos. I told Alex he was released from any further obligation to me . . .
>
> I was the official representative of a government in the throes of death, against the backdrop of a revolutionary drama and national rebirth being played out on the TV screens of most

---

4. Narratives like that of Charles Colson, a Nixon cabinet member jailed for his involvement in the Watergate scandal and subsequently founder of Prison Fellowship, spoke of a spiritual deepening, possibly even the conversion, of Ninoy during his incarceration. In a personal interview, the late statesman and Senate President Jovito Salonga said that Ninoy visited him in California on the way to his fatal trip home. Ninoy seemed to be determined at that point to meet his destiny, whatever it might be, and had already foreseen the possibility of what eventually happened to him on the tarmac (Editor).

homes in America. I would have to command some appeal and excite some curiosity if not compassion.

When Congressman Solarz in a TV show told me, "Blas, why don't you do something historic? . . . The whole world is tuned in," I said, "What are you suggesting?" He said, "Declare for Aquino now!"

[Ka Blas replied,] "My loyalties were more stable than that. I saw my role in the United States now as one of conducting my President to the gates of history, from where he can exit with some dignity and grace."[5]

Ka Blas perceived his mission to be as follows: "I was asked by State Secretary George Shultz to be a major channel to Malacañang for transmitting the final message of President Reagan."

On Ka Blas's role in the US, here is a tribute from Mrs Katherine Graham, publisher of the *Washington Post*: "You conducted yourself with great dignity in an unbelievably difficult time."

A noted Washington columnist, George F. Will of *The Washington Post*, wrote Minister Ople a note saying, "I could not imagine anyone doing better in such a difficult task."

And after a few months, Secretary Shultz met Minister Ople in a reception at Manila Hotel, where he said: "Blas, we meet now in entirely different circumstances. Good luck to you." Ka Blas winked at him to indicate he understood.

And Ka Blas ended his story with: "For one who never thought he would be the last ambassador of a dying regime in the United States, these words gave a not inconsiderable comfort."

In his note of thanks to his traveling companion, POEA Deputy Administrator Imson, Minister Ople wrote: "We would not have succeeded in converting an incongruous mission into an opportunity for meaningful communication to the American people, their media and their Government. . . . We compelled America to listen. We earned the trust of the US Government. That trust allowed us to play a role in facilitating the decision of President Marcos to step down and save many Filipino lives . . ."

He continued, "We were embraced – actually fought over – by US media because they believe us to be sincere, courageous and respectful of the truth. We gained a whole constituency in the United States." Moreover, BFO wrote

---

5. This is not an exact quote. Part of it is from an article by Blas Ople of which the original cannot be found, and part is personal reminiscences from an acquaintance of mine.

to Manny Imson, "I did not want to miss this opportunity to say, in a letter, that that incredible week in Washington should also be a prized memory for you since you were so much a part of it and a crucial element in our success."

He ended his letter by saying, "Today, we bring home the trophy of that personal triumph. The cause was incidental – we brought off a process that did credit to our country, enriched the meaning of loyalty and helped save the lives of many of our countrymen that should have been lost in a civil war."

Moving Forward in Our Politics

All these sad and happy events in our history will hopefully lead to a cleansing of our society. It is a journey, just like all nations have gone through, but this time of the Filipino people.

It has been a history of exploitation. We were "discovered" by foreigners when we already had our own alphabet and *barangay* government.[6] We were robbed of our lands when Spain created the Torrens title. We were forced to follow the American system of government when we had our own system of leadership that kept peace and order among the tribes.

Martial law created a vacuum of young leaders because a one-party system – the KBL – dominated the political scene, similar to the PDP-LABAN today.

The old two-party system – Liberal Party and Nacionalista Party – had a mechanism called Party Convention similar to the primary system in the USA. The two parties were responsible for choosing their candidates from municipal/city councilors up to their presidential candidates.

Martial law rule created hand-picked new politicians and promoted political dynasties close to the president. Unfortunately, this was not corrected afterwards.

This discouraged those without connections from entering politics. It gave rise to the "weather-weather"[7] remark of President Joseph "Erap" Estrada, meaning that a politician has to be with the current president at all times to survive politically.

There is no place for meritocracy or genuine party platforms in our present political system.

This reality has turned our millennials (those born in the 1980s or 1990s) off the idea of entering politics. As of today, they number 25 million, a powerful

---

6. The basic unit of government; from the boat "balangay" used by our ancestors in going to the islands, capable of loading a whole clan or cluster of families, hence its use as a political unit.

7. Slang for riding the tide or bending to the political winds of the time.

force to change society. They can act as policemen against grafters through social media. They can make or unmake politicians if they wake up.

Leadership needs seasoned wisdom, having learned from mistakes committed. There is no school for politics except the streets, where would-be politicians should be walking around, talking with people about their problems.

Faith-based groups and social action civic clubs should promote public service, which includes entering politics as a career. Win or lose, they have to think of how to help the poor through specific projects, laws, ordinances and programs.

I say to the young generation: let us all be active in politics, in choosing our leaders based on the teachings of Christ in the Bible. Let us ask these questions of candidates:

- What is the lifestyle of the candidate?
- What were his or her past actions before running for office?
- Are his or her supporters people of God or people of the devil?
- Are his or her election practices within the legal framework?
- Does he or she have a reputation among his or her peers to be proud of?

To all our fellow Filipinos: NEVER AGAIN TO MARTIAL LAW!

13

A Nonviolent Revolution

Adrian Helleman

My experience at EDSA in February 1986 is without a doubt the most revolutionary event of my life. I had never participated in a revolution before, nor have I since. The effects were enormous. The People Power Revolution has left an indelible mark on the Philippines, and on the rest of the world, but it also marked my own life and that of my family in a dramatic and life-changing way. Even now, some thirty years after the event, those heady days are still fresh in my memory. But what exactly did that "revolution" mean – for me and for the Philippines immediately afterward and now, all these decades later?

Within weeks of the People Power Revolution, I wrote a short article, "Seventy-Five Long Hours," documenting EDSA from my own perspective. This article, without any subsequent revision, can be found elsewhere in this collection.[1] When I was asked for this article, I could only find a copy printed on an antiquated dot matrix printer; I did not have a digital version. That alone illustrates the passage of time. As that document makes clear, I was present on EDSA for most of those seventy-five hours. You may ask right away: What was I doing there? To help explain my presence, I will begin by providing some background information. This will be followed by some thoughts on revolution in general, as well as some reflections on the People Power Revolution. I will conclude with several theological remarks.

---

1. It was submitted to some Christian journals in North America, but for various reasons was never published. Our understanding of the significance of what happened in the Philippines at that time was published by the Canadian weekly, *Christian Courier*, when somehow they received a letter we had sent to friends, a letter that was never intended for publication.

My Motivation for Joining the Revolution

From mid-1977 until the end of 1986, I served as a missionary with Christian Reformed World Missions in the Philippines. Upon arrival, I was first stationed in Bacolod City, where I taught at the Christian Reformed Seminary and Bible College, and I was also involved in church planting in the nearby barangay of Sum-ag. In 1984, I was transferred to Manila, where, among other things, I initiated a worship group near the University of the Philippines. In response to contacts through the Back to God Hour broadcasting in the Philippines, I also started a Bible study group with some political prisoners in Camp Crame. Both of these ministries were important factors contributing to my involvement with EDSA.

My work of teaching, leading Bible studies and worship groups did not exclude an interest in political developments in the Philippines. Being politically inclined by nature and motivated to pursue justice issues by upbringing, I soon tried to understand the role of President Ferdinand Marcos, whose declaration of martial law had given him control of nearly every aspect of the government of the Philippines. Some of my colleagues at the time described him as a "benign" dictator, but I rejected that qualification. As I witnessed the enormous social and economic inequality in the Philippines, I started discussing the need for justice all over the country with Filipinos. They welcomed such discussions. Throughout the Philippines the cry of injustice grew louder every year. The stench of graft and corruption was plain for all to notice. And heaven also heard their cry.

Even during his dictatorial rule, Marcos maintained a semblance of democracy. When Marcos called a snap election for 7 February, I, along with many others, immediately suspected significant dishonesty and massive corruption during the election. The results confirmed this. I was personally present in the Batasang Pambansa when the votes were scrutinized, and many ballots had to be rejected. The situation, especially in Manila, was tense. Together with many other believers, my UP Diliman worship group held intense prayer sessions, as we foresaw the possibility of a bloodbath. The defection of Juan Ponce Enrile and Fidel Ramos was a surprising development. It was also a necessary catalyst for change: something had to give. Within hours of their defection, our friends at ISACC (Institute for Studies in Asian Church and Culture), some of whom attended my worship group, invited me to join them on EDSA. It did not take me long to make up my mind to do so.

I knew that there would be consequences for myself and my family. Missionaries were not supposed to involve themselves in the politics of a foreign country, but that is precisely what I was doing. I had discussed the alternatives with my wife, and she agreed to my joining our Filipino friends, even knowing the risk. This revolution might fail, and we would be asked to leave the Philippines by the Marcos regime. It might also succeed, and then I might be asked to leave by my fellow missionaries. Both of us knew that death was also a possibility, but we did not discuss that. Somehow, I was not worried about that consequence; I trusted in Cardinal Sin's diagnosis of EDSA as a struggle between good and evil. Since I saw myself on the side of the angels, what bad thing could possibly happen to me? With this thought, I (somewhat naively) joined my friends.

The only time during those many hours that I felt my life was at risk was early on Monday morning when Sikorsky helicopters circled the highway and then landed inside Camp Crame. Because of my work with the political prisoners, the guards there knew me and let me in to visit with them. At that point I learned about the latest defection. Immediately, I suspected that with the loss of a major part of his air force Marcos would soon be finished. I realized that I did not need to be worried any longer about my personal safety or that of the rest of the crowd assembled on EDSA.

But there were serious consequences for myself and for our work serving with Christian Reformed World Missions. Soon after the defection of Enrile and Ramos, at a time when the future of their rebellion was anything but certain, our mission board had contacted the families of the missionaries in the country to check that they were all safe in their homes. Of course, I was not home. My immediate missionary colleagues later took it ill of me that I had not stayed home as we had all been expected to do, and as had been reported. Their message was clear: as far as they were concerned, my missionary career in the Philippines was finished. And by the end of the year, I did leave the country. My departure came at a good time, however, coinciding with our children's educational needs and my own desire to work on a doctorate. My life and that of my family were changed irrevocably by EDSA.

Our dreams and anticipation of working in the Philippines for the rest of our lives were dashed, but it was soon clear that God had other plans. We spent several years in Toronto, where our children attended high school. By the early nineties, I had acquired a doctorate in Reformation studies and ecumenism. Our next destination was Russia, where my wife and I taught for seven years at Moscow State University. When our work there came to an end (the Russians demanded our departure), we transferred to the University of Jos in Nigeria, and subsequently also taught in Tanzania and the Gambia. We did not return to visit the Philippines until 2005.

Reflections on Revolution and Active Nonviolence

During EDSA, it became clear that prayer had played an important role in preparing for this revolution. Large sections of the country had participated in seminars on active nonviolence, typically led by priests and nuns. Prayer had sustained Filipinos throughout the long period of martial law leading up to EDSA. During the final days before Marcos left, they discovered that God had been busy answering the prayers of Filipinos, both Christian and Muslim, for a peaceful transition. Marcos's departure was achieved in a nonviolent way.

Permit me to make a digression about prayer. Prayer and nonviolence are very closely connected. Not that nonviolence is impossible without prayer; after all, even atheists can practice nonviolence. Rather the reverse: prayer should lead to nonviolence. Prayer is too often misused; it is understood to mean that God will give us everything we ask for. However, God never gives us evil things, but only what is good for us, such as nonviolence. Prayer is not a phone call to heaven informing God of whatever our hearts desire; instead, it is his way of telling us what his will for us is. Thus we need to listen carefully. In the period leading up to EDSA people had prayed earnestly for change, and God told them to use nonviolent means. It was not that Filipinos were more religious than other people, but God used nuns and others to prepare them for the revolution.

Since that event, I have had numerous occasions to reflect on the role of active nonviolence in effecting political change. As a Reformed Christian, I had long accepted the classic view, held by many Catholics and Protestants alike, of a "just war": that there are situations and conditions in the life of the state or governing body which gives it the right to declare war, and citizens the right to pursue their just demands even if that involves violent confrontation. The state and its citizens must also wage that war using appropriate means. My experience of EDSA had a significant role in causing me to exchange the classic view for another view of political engagement, namely active nonviolence, which is typically associated with the Anabaptists, but has now been adopted by many Christians, myself included.

There had been many revolutions before EDSA. So what made the People Power Revolution different? For one thing, EDSA was clearly an answer to the many fervent prayers of the Filipino people. What else accounted for the difference? I suggest that nonviolence did. Indeed, this revolution got rid of Marcos, and achieved that goal through nonviolent means. In contrast to many revolutions, it was almost completely bloodless; the few deaths that occurred at the time were incidental.

There are many views on revolution, but for me, the following two are most important. The transition from one to the other has fundamentally changed my stance on war and peace, as well as on the nature of revolution itself.

The Anabaptist or nonviolent view of revolution runs counter to the Dutch Reformed tradition in which I had been raised – that of Abraham Kuyper (1837–1920) and, before him, Guillaume Groen van Prinsterer (1801–1876), in the Netherlands. Kuyper was a theologian, newspaper editor, founder of a university, and for a few years prime minister of the Netherlands. Groen van Prinsterer was a Dutch politician and historian whose views influenced Kuyper to found the Anti-Revolutionary Party (ARP).

Kuyper rejected "the Revolution," by which he meant the French Revolution, because of the political and social system embodied in it. He dismissed it as advocating the very opposite of what Christians had always believed, cherished and confessed. He wrote that it led to a complete emancipation from the sovereign claims of Almighty God – indeed, to the complete rejection of God. The French Revolution was godless. It was also violent.

Historians agree that the French Revolution was extremely violent. Unlike the earlier American Revolution, with which it has often been compared, it was a bloodbath. Its symbol was the guillotine, not the liberty bell. Thus these two revolutions should not be confused. The spirit of godlessness in the French Revolution was unacceptable to Kuyper and the ARP. This party was called Anti-Revolutionary because of its opposition to the godless French Revolution. They did not recognize such godlessness in its American counterpart. Yet their analysis is useful if only to expose the true nature of the French Revolution, which is generally assumed to have been beneficial. It may have rid France of the *ancien régime*, but it led to many decades of political unrest and further revolutions. That is why I have elaborated on the view of the ARP so extensively: I wanted to refute the common misapprehension concerning the goodness of the French Revolution. It was evil, violent and extremely bloody.

The ARP should not be understood as opposed to all revolutions as such, but rather to the revolutionary spirit of the French Revolution which it inspired in various parts of Europe and which had been steadily growing more ominous. To defeat the progress of this secularist movement, the ARP posited a new Christian understanding of the state. From its viewpoint, none of the existing ideologies provided an acceptable option. Groen and Kuyper rejected the entire spectrum of the prevalent liberal/secular political approaches, and called instead for a radical Christian alternative.

This did not mean that Kuyper advocated a theocracy. Rather, he pleaded for a Christian society existing within a larger pluralistic society, one in which each of its parts or groups would maintain its own churches, schools, newspapers and political parties. And, indeed, until the 1960s, Dutch politics was shaped by these "pillars," as they were called. However, attempts were later made to transplant what worked in the Netherlands to other nations, but with only limited success. In South Africa, for example, this approach became perverted and led to the institution of apartheid.

The French Revolution of 1789 and, to a lesser degree, the Russian Revolution of 1917 provide the two outstanding negative examples of revolution. Undoubtedly, the revolutionary spirit spawned by these events came to prevail in numerous subsequent revolutionary events. Countries have been torn apart by revolutions, and millions have died in the name of the revolution. But does this mean that all revolutions after the French one must be labeled as evil?

My experience of EDSA led me to question this view. I had to revise my stance as a result. This change was important; it caused me to reflect more on the nature of revolution. My reflection is, I hope, useful, not only for me personally but also for others who have struggled over the years with the question of what makes a revolution good.

A Good Revolution?

What is a "revolution"? Aristotle's study of many existing polities (or constitutions, as we might call them) led him to conclude that the term "revolution" involved either a change in the constitution itself, such as a change from monarchy or oligarchy, for example, to something else, or a change in the ruling power that did not lead to a new constitution.

EDSA falls into the first category since a new constitution was produced soon afterward. In spite of the many differences with EDSA, the American Revolution is often cited as an example of a good revolution. The question remains: What makes a revolution "good"?

I want to devote much of the rest of this essay to an examination of this question. Before I begin, however, I need to make it clear that in so doing I am not approaching the question as a political scientist or historian (I am neither), and I do not intend to discuss a typology of revolutions. Instead, I want to examine a "good" revolution through the lens of violence versus nonviolence.

Kuyper's and Groen's condemnation of many revolutions as inherently violent and godless is understandable. For them, the French Revolution was the archetype of such a revolution since not only was it bloody, but also it was motivated by purely secular ideas. Later they could point to other similar revolutions in Europe. The Russian Revolution in 1917 came too late for their analysis. But their understanding would have been confirmed even more had they known that the total number of deaths to be attributed to twentieth-century communist revolutions in Russia and China are estimated conservatively at more than 100 million. Therefore, there can be no question about the evil character of some of these revolutions.

But how, then, are we to evaluate nonviolent revolutions, such as EDSA, along with several other revolutions elsewhere that followed its pattern? How does the Dutch analysis fit the experience of EDSA and these later revolutions? Are revolutions "good" as long as they are not violent and do not share a spirit of godlessness? The American Revolution clearly was violent, but it was not motivated by godlessness. The absence of violence should not be the only deciding factor. But the use of active nonviolence, as exemplified at EDSA, plays a key role in deciding whether a revolution is good.

The adoption of active nonviolence means that the use of violence can no longer be justified, even for the overthrow of corrupt and evil regimes. On the contemporary scene, warfare cannot be justified anymore. Even the use of violence in a civil war intended to hold a political entity together is not warranted. Active nonviolence, by definition, precludes the use of violence, yet it is active, meaning it does something. It is not passive. No matter what the goal is, violence is not permitted. But revolution is not excluded, since change is what is desired and is being actively pursued – nonviolently, of course.

EDSA was both nonviolent and bloodless. Who can forget the dialogue between General Ver and Marcos during EDSA? Ver urged the use of violence, but Marcos restrained him, deciding against it. Even this reflex fits the nonviolent nature of this revolution. EDSA provided a nonviolent template, especially for the largely bloodless revolutions of 1989 when a number of East European states dissociated themselves from the USSR (Romania being the sole exception).

There were few precursors for EDSA. The Glorious Revolution of 1688 in England, sometimes erroneously called the Bloodless Revolution, is often cited as an example, but it was not truly bloodless. Also, it was more an invasion by William III, the Dutch king, to build an Anglo-Dutch alliance against France. The few other legitimate examples of bloodless revolution, as in Portugal or Iran, never gained the influence that People Power in the Philippines did. The iconic image of nuns offering flowers to soldiers manning tanks became an inspiration for other nations. Nonviolent revolutions became the rage in Europe and beyond.

EDSA proved that a nonviolent revolution was possible, but it did not demonstrate that nonviolent revolutions are necessarily better in terms of results. The successful ouster of Marcos did not usher in solutions to the basic problem of gross social and economic inequality in the Philippines. Nor would that have been possible. EDSA was a political revolution, not a social one. The introduction of a new Philippine constitution did not bring about the further changes that were still needed.

The drama of EDSA captured the imagination of the world for many months, but the revolution eventually took a tragic turn. EDSA clearly did not put an end to graft and corruption. It did not end the political and economic control by the elite families that have traditionally controlled the country. Nor did it put an end to the drugs trade, which is now rampant. And, above all, it did not end the growing inequity between the rich and the poor. The last signals a universal problem for which there is no easy solution. More recently, prominent politicians in Europe and America have used populist appeals to gain power, but they evidently do not have the solution either. On the contrary, their approach presents a major threat to democracy.

EDSA, of course, cannot be blamed for the rise of populists like Duterte (or Trump), but the passing years have indicated how incomplete EDSA was as a revolution. Perhaps we should conclude that the use of nonviolence by itself does not make a revolution "good." Kuyper and Groen were certainly correct in rejecting the godless, secular spirit of revolution. Nonviolence, as such, does not sanctify a revolution, and also prayers, by themselves, are not sufficient – but that does not mean that promoting nonviolence and prayers is not necessary. EDSA proved otherwise.

It is important to note that, as history shows, all revolutions carry within them the seeds of further conflict. So the underlying problem is not only the inherent godless nature of some revolutions, but, more importantly, that revolutions inevitably turn out to be incomplete. The underlying issues that led up to revolution can never be dealt with adequately by the revolution itself. As EDSA indicates, there were serious underlying issues of corruption and socioeconomic inequality that still remained, thus necessitating further revolution. Thus the Philippines has also witnessed EDSA 2. Today, the country has a president whose crude remarks and violent behavior have been compared with those of Trump. The Philippines needs a further, social, revolution to deal with the issues of inequality and corruption. Even if we recognize that these issues can never be solved entirely, they do need to be addressed honestly and as soon as possible. To neglect them will guarantee further revolutions, and there is no guarantee that these will be nonviolent.

Closing Theological Observations

As a theologian, I feel compelled to make a few final remarks of a theological nature. I should hardly need to comment that any occurrence of revolution is the result of sin. Without sin, no revolution would be necessary. Because of our imperfection, no perfect polity is possible.

Sin is not just breaking God's commandments or rules; sin is more serious than that. Sin lies deep within our human nature. It infects each and every one of us. At its root, sin is the rejection of God. It is idolatry. We are all guilty of elevating something that God has made over God himself. Our idols are too numerous to cite: money, sex, power, and so on. These false gods can tempt all of us; no one is entirely immune from them. The Old Testament prophets railed against idol-worship. They accused their leaders of leading the country astray. We need prophets today to expose our idolatry and fearlessly condemn that of our leaders.

Too many people in too many countries have bought into the message of demagogues. In Canada, when I hear Filipinos praise Duterte for cleaning up the drugs trade while overlooking all his faults, I am upset. Similarly, when I hear many people disregard Trump's immorality and corruption because of his stance on abortion, I am enraged. In both countries people need to cry out: what is happening is idolatry!

Because of sin, all our political leaders are fallible; few, in fact, are capable of providing the quality leadership that God demands. On the contrary, the leadership of some leaders is so unacceptable that revolutions become necessary. And we, as citizens, are equally fallible. Even with the best of intentions, we are incapable of producing a perfect polity. The constitutions we write are imperfect; sooner or later another revolution is needed. And so the cycle continues.

Nonviolent revolutions have the merit of protecting lives on both sides of the political divide. That is clearly an important benefit. But they remain revolutions all the same, and share the same inherent weaknesses. After a nonviolent revolution, there is no guarantee that a new polity will be better. Problems will return. Even when we employ nonviolent means, we remain imperfect creatures who are incapable of governing ourselves as God intended.

EDSA demonstrates that. Those gathered on EDSA during the revolution had the best of intentions, but good intentions are never enough to satisfy God's demands perfectly. Sin makes that impossible. Sin is no longer in vogue today, but it is still the most appropriate word to describe the widespread mayhem and corruption that characterized the Marcos era and continues unabated now.

Yet we must not wallow in despair as a result. As believers, we know that Christ has already won the final victory over sin on the cross. The moment he died, a new world order began. The New Testament scholar N. T. Wright aptly describes Jesus's crucifixion as "the day the revolution began"; this is the title of his book published in 2016. Christ's death signals *the* Revolution. For us, it meant the forgiveness of our sins, but its significance extends far beyond saving individual sinners. His death embraces the whole creation, which has now been liberated. Because of the cross, sin no longer controls our world; the entire world and all its inhabitants have been set free to serve and worship God, even if this also is, for the moment, still done imperfectly.

So, rather than lamenting the ultimate failure of EDSA and other nonviolent revolutions, let us see them as signs of the present reality of God's kingdom. We ourselves cannot usher in that kingdom. Our revolutions are only signs of the much greater and more perfect revolution that took place on the cross. Just as sacraments are signs and seals of God's presence within his world, so the best revolutions too can be regarded as gifts from God. Only when we see this world in relation to God and his restorative work in us as part of the new creation can we appreciate the value that God accords our actions, no matter how tentative and imperfect they remain. EDSA could not bring heaven on earth. Nor was that really the intention of those involved during those heady days. Filipinos celebrated then because Marcos was sent packing. That was a good thing and is still worth celebrating even now after more than thirty years of further corruption.

The reunification of heaven and earth waits for Christ's return. Then the whole earth will serve God. Then God's will shall be fully realized on earth, just as it is accomplished in heaven. What we do now is preliminary. One day the entire creation will be able to fulfill its divinely given calling. Even now the Holy Spirit reveals something of God's will for this world to us as believers. As we respond in faith to his calling, we can recognize something of the role we play in God's dramatic production. From this perspective, we should not be discouraged by the tragic turn of present events. Through these events I began to realize that, like most things in creation, revolutions can have consequences for good or for ill. Not all revolutions are necessarily bad. We should rejoice in the small yet important role God allowed us to play in February 1986.

The perfect Revolution already took place almost two thousand years earlier. EDSA is at best a shadow of that great event, a sign given by God – an imperfect, yet significant sign. What happened on the cross was God's demonstration of his love for his creation and his forgiveness of every sin, even the sins of Marcos and his cronies that sent people to EDSA. God called them to go there. That is why I was there too. God called me. How else can I explain why I, a Canadian, joined the People Power Revolution with thousands of Filipinos? EDSA forms part of our loving response to the God who has called us to serve him in this world. Daily, God invites us to join him in the liberation of creation (including the environment). Even now, he is busy eliminating every injustice, and he wants us to participate in his redemptive work. That is what happened at EDSA and it continues today. Thanks be to God!

14

On Historical Babies, Paradigms and Miracles

Melba Padilla Maggay

Until now, analysts looking at the "People Power Revolution" of 1986 have been divided on what to make of its strange appearance on the scene.

A successful revolution, we are told, has a thousand fathers and mothers. True enough, in its early stages, there were many who posed as midwives to its birth. More than three decades after, the resurgence of corruption and the recycled faces of the Marcos regime have made people wonder whatever was really birthed during that time.

Those ideologically framed by Marxism say that no new thing had been born. The privileged ruling class remains entrenched, impervious to the plight of masses of our poor. More moderate elements say that something was born, but it was somewhat deformed. The new baby came out with a strong right arm and an underdeveloped left arm – a reference to the marginal presence of the Left and the military forces who happened to be at its maelstrom and subsequently mounted a series of coups, under the arrogant presumption of its right to direct the course of its future.

Still others, mostly external observers and religious communities present at the EDSA barricades, believe that what we are looking at is a wonder baby, a gorgeous and luminous bundle of life birthed by a people's grit and will to be free, aided by a somewhat miraculous intervention from on high.

That there is something odd about this baby is obvious enough. Unlike the secular humanism of the French Revolution, which spawned in its wake the Reign of Terror, and also unlike the atheistic underpinnings of the Russian and Chinese revolutions and other such upheavals, our "people power" revolt was extraordinary in that it was bloodless. It did not come out kicking and screaming, but charmed charging soldiers by offering flowers. The people who stood boldly before tanks had a trusting, confident faith that all things are possible with fervent prayer and a little help from clerical friends.

In short, we are baffled and fascinated, instinctively aware that there is something here that is complex and mysterious enough to deserve the making of many books. Early on, a sociologist friend, Randy David, remarked to me, "I have been a student of revolutions. But this is the first time I have seen a revolt led by the Virgin Mary."

What was in this revolution which warms and charms the heart and makes us start? Why is it that we feel such a need to explain it to ourselves?

Part of the answer is the bright cloud of transcendence over it. We were surprised, awed, by that margin of mystery where all our calculations collapsed and we came face to face with an overruling power that eluded explanation from our hoard of social science tools. The tales of serendipities, of so-called "miracles," are too numerous to be dismissed as mere coincidences. The character of this revolution stops us in our tracks because it is untidy and irregular, outside the usual boxes by which we frame and analyze uprisings.

The events at EDSA in 1986 have been analyzed mainly within the categories of the liberal democratic tradition, mostly seen as a "return to democracy." They have also been critiqued from more Marxist premises – "no change in objective economic and social relations." Critical social theories have also weighed in, as well as populist interpretations by those who stand to gain politically by deriding or diminishing its historical significance.

The following is an attempt to frame this phenomenon as a new mode of democratic assertion, based on a tradition older than our long tutelage into an American-type democracy – the indigenous culture as the controlling context for the revolution.

Vox Populi?

Quite unnoticed, a new element in our political culture has begun to surface since the time of Benigno Aquino's assassination. Direct people pressure upon structures of power, a sort of Lockean "radical democracy," has evolved into a widely acceptable instrument for asserting popular will. It showed its strength at EDSA, and since then has had an inspirational force among peoples of the world seeking to overthrow entrenched powers.

From what seemed to be an inert mass, what we call "the people" rose to its political responsibility and displayed a remarkable voluntarism. That we could actually topple an iron-handed government in four days of unarmed siege developed an awareness of power outside of the usual structures, a sense of elasticity in our parameters of what can and cannot be done, and by which we measure probable success in our political ventures.

For once, we displayed a sense of "nation." We rose from our usual narrow regionalism and moved toward participation and a sense of control over forces once held to be invincible. It is in this sense that "people power" is not, as some have alleged, merely a bourgeois convention for laying claim to the achievement of having overthrown an oppressive regime. It was a sign that indicated a growing sense among our people that they had a stake in the political fortunes of this country.

A newfound political assertiveness is now seen among grassroots communities. This is both an advance from the culture of silence embedded by authoritarianism in the past, and a preferred alternative to the conflictive class struggle espoused by Leftist politics. An index of the free-floating citizen movements and community organizing happening below is the fact that some 60,000 NGOs mushroomed and registered at the Securities and Exchange Commission a year or so after the EDSA events. This does not count the many faith-based organizations affiliated with churches, a result of the faithful awakening to their social responsibility.

In place of the old quiescence is an emergent culture of protest, and instead of the fire and thunder of revolutionary rhetoric is the softer and modulated tones of what has come to be known as the "politics of the center," the middle forces that have turned out to be not at all middling in numerical power. Perceived as merely reformist, it is populist in the classic liberal sense and derives its inspiration from peoplehood rooted in a vague sense of "national identity" rather than in belonging to a class.

Those who view this from the standpoint of political theories that have evolved from social eruptions that rocked the Western world two hundred years ago would tend to interpret "people power" as continuous with our experience of formal democracy under the tutelage of the US. It is seen as a recovery and reassertion of our democratic heritage, or a trumpet call to freedom-loving peoples of the world to unite against the tyranny of arbitrary power.

However, subsequent events and political trends do not lend themselves easily to a purely liberal frame of analysis.

The rise of authoritarianism in spite of a libertarian tradition implanted by American colonialism has raised questions about the depth of our rootage in democratic norms. When martial law was declared and Marcos assumed absolute power, classic liberals were dismayed by the people's casual indifference.

I remember visiting in jail Amando Doronila, editor of the *Manila Chronicle*, which was one of the first newspapers to get shut down when martial law was imposed. He was one of those high-profile journalists who were quickly rounded up for what the government called "preventive detention." He asked me how things looked outside, how the people were responding to the sudden loss of our constitutional rights. With some embarrassment, I said the event had been received with nary a whimper; after a day or two of shock and dislocation, the people went back to business, or what passed for normalcy in those times.

It could be argued that this indifference is a function of the essentially alien character of the democracy that we inherited, an example of the basic unexportability of ideological and political systems, rather than an index of the people's democratic impulses. Then as now, elections and power transfers tended to be merely bread and circuses for our people, distracted as they were by the daily struggle for survival. Political "rights" as they have developed in the West have little meaning to a people barely able to eke out a fragile existence.

Religion in the Revolution

While the revolution of 1986 was not exactly a populist "revolt of the masses," it was also not like the uprisings that came in the wake of the French and Russian revolutions. It did not derive its motive force from the ideological influence of humanist rationalism, but from something deep in the indigenous culture and religious imagination of our people.

The spectacle of a defenseless people protecting the military and placating soldiers with peace offerings, the strong presence of the church as catalyst and moral sanction, the quality of celebration in the midst of tension: all these set this revolution quite beyond the usual pattern of political upheavals.

Parallels with other revolutions before this have been noted: Mahatma Gandhi's nonviolent campaign for independence from the British, the mix of military and Muslim fundamentalist resistance against the Shah of Iran, the agitprop struggle waged by radio broadcasts in Algeria's war of liberation from the French. However, no other revolution combined all these elements, nor had such emotional appeal that it felt like a sob story and a thriller all at once.

Much of the unusual had to do with the curious mix of religion and revolution. Rosary beads slung round an Armalite rifle, fervent women intoning prayers through the night by candlelight, statues of the Virgin Mary shadowed against the dying flares of a setting sun: these images of unblushing faith in the supernatural suffused the experience with an elfin quality, almost as if we were back to a distant past when twilight was prime time for the gods and the earth and altar touched.

In a world used to thinking of the universe as a humless machine[1] and the making of history as entirely a matter of political strategy and military hardware, the earnest invocation to the gods to assist and intervene was a strange reversion, a throwback to medieval quests where virtue and magic made a winning team.

Much has been said about this revolution's character as a morality play, in which good and evil forces were sharply delineated and ranged against each other, locked in a deadly struggle. Quite astonishingly, the script did read a bit like it: a frail widow, victim of a cruel regime, takes on the tyrant king and wages battle with a shining shield of political innocence and the helter-skelter but nevertheless winning improvisations of her people.

The presence of religion in this uprising was not merely in the organized churches as represented by Cardinal Sin, the clerics and the lay faithful who manned the barricades and hovered round the soldiers like guardian angels. It was not only in Radio Veritas, the town crier transported into the age of mass media, cheering and warning the people, nor in the wealth of symbol and ritual, the rich effluence of incense and gun smoke, prayers and flowers.

More deeply, it was in the warm and vital presence of a transcendent consciousness, of a belief system that was deeper than creed and broader than life itself: the sense that the earth is a battleground of epic struggles between unseen and mutually hostile forces, a seamless interweaving of the natural and the supernatural, the world as we ordinarily know it and as it comes to us in dreams and what the novelist F. Scott Fitzgerald calls "dark liquid nights."

This palpable sense of traffic between nature and grace, the interplay of human action and divine intervention, of politics as a cosmic war, is perhaps the Filipino's contribution to the history of revolutions. Up till now, this has been mostly a record of fissures traceable to the great crack of secular humanism which split the architectonic structures of Christendom.

From history demythologized, we move toward history sacramentalized, the electric sense that the earth vibrates with the doings of humans and angels, that the drama taking place in the land of the living is somehow caught up in a larger, more intricate plot being woven from behind the scene, a scenario utterly beyond our imagining, yet inextricably made up out of the humble warp and woof of everyday duty, choices and pain.

---

1. Without rhyme or poetry.

The fantastical synthesis of ritual and political action is consistent with the harmonizing bent of the indigenous consciousness.

Note that the Filipino does not make a sharp distinction between the secular and the holy. Her worldview is wholistic, able to mediate between the seen and the unseen, seeing the world as all of a piece: crop failure is a disturbance in nature ultimately caused by the wrath of the gods.

The idea that things on earth interconnect with things in heaven is not at all peculiar. Primal religious cultures down the ages always knew that a plague upon the land was sign of a divine curse. Ritual and incantation, on the surface unrelated to the cause of sickness or defeat in war, could be means of entrance into a world of power. What is extraordinary is the surfacing of this as a living collective memory, and not as a misty remnant of a primal consciousness scattered here and there in fragments of myths and legends.

Our patient pacifism in the face of conflict may also be accounted to the harmonizing instinct, a facility for subtle synthesis shared by other Asian cultures. Opposing forces are embraced and wedded together into an inclusive whole. We see this in the readiness to stand shoulder-to-shoulder with a feared soldier, or in efforts to conciliate in the standoff between advancing soldiers and determined barricaders.

But perhaps it is the continuing vitality of the religious element among our people that sets this off as an empowering and inspirational force in our time. In some other cultural context, it is possible to imagine the jittery men behind the guns and tanks simply bulldozing their way through the crowd and opening fire. This is what happened in Tiananmen Square.

A Question of Paradigm

The issue of whether this revolution marked a genuine advance for the cause of the poor is a question best left to empirical study. Whether it was a truly revolutionary turn in the life of this nation is a question of paradigm, of our fundamental vision of what makes history turn.

Some locate pivotal change in material conditions, that is, in whether economic structures are equitable, the social classes more mobile, the political apparatus more responsive and conducive to the flourishing of the whole society.

Some would place it in changing people's subjective consciousness, increasing awareness of why they are poor, what they are capable of doing, where they should be going.

Still others would locate it in the rise of individuals crucial to a historical moment, men and women of nerve and insight who are able to seize strategic opportunities and turn the tide toward their vision of a future.

Those viewing this from more religious lenses would put emphasis on internally generated changes. Eastern religions think they can make the world better with good karma – doing good deeds and sending good vibes or thought waves. Christian traditions insist on conversion as key to social transformation. For systems and structures to become workable, there has to be a radical reformation of the dark and perverse inclinations of the human heart.

As studied and formulated, history moves through either objective or subjective conditions, matter or spirit, towering individuals or a faceless collective. These polarities, opposed to each other in a kind of Manichaean struggle, have been the stuff of historical and political theory in modern times.

Certainly, collective action and material forces like superior technology and military might can change the balance of power within and among nations. The people's numerical force at EDSA had to be backed by a series of military defections to convince Marcos to leave Malacañang and flee to the safety of his US patron.

Likewise, decades of conscientization and organizing at the grassroots by social movements, and the experience of suffering in the hands of a brutal regime, gave rise to a critical mass of sentiment and protest that reached a tipping point, expressed in such terms as "*Tama Na, Sobra Na.*"[2]

"The people," long submerged and consigned to what the Latin Americans call "the underside of history," surfaced as a formidable force, surprising analysts who thought we were "a nation of 50 million cowards" by demonstrating the ability to get roused and assemble for a common historical project. The ensuing resurgence of fractious and entrenched interests did not dim the moving solidarity displayed by the mourners who quietly filed past the coffin of the murdered Ninoy Aquino and lined the streets with placards saying "*Hindi Ka Nag-Iisa.*"[3]

The return of traditional politics and renewed corruption in high places highlight the tragic persistence of sin in social life and the need to hedge it about with structural checks and balances.

Secularists impoverish their analysis by remaining impervious to the power of a consciousness alive to moral values and the mystery of transcendence.

---

2. Loosely translated, "Enough is enough, too much to take anymore."
3. "You are not alone."

Narrow religionists naively fail to take into account the complex nature of organized injustice.

That revolutions devour their own is testament to the monster that lurks in the human breast. We carry within us the seeds of our own destruction. There is a hardness to evil that we do well to recognize: "What is crooked cannot be made straight," said Ecclesiastes (1:15 RSV).

Those who have long been in the business of changing the world run themselves aground against this reality. As the eco-scientist Gus Speth describes it: "I used to think the top environmental problems were biodiversity loss, ecosystem collapse and climate change. I thought that with thrity years of good science we could address those problems. I was wrong. The top environmental problems are selfishness, greed and apathy, and to deal with these we need a spiritual and cultural transformation. And we scientists don't know how to do that."[4]

The church, at least, knows that change begins from the inside – in that place where the battle between good and evil is at first instance waged – and that it is only by the power of the Spirit that we all get turned around from our self-serving proclivities and are able to make right choices.

However, our formulaic prescription "change individuals, change society" fails to grasp that evil can be institutionalized and perpetuate itself in organizational cultures and systems.

The theologian Walter Wink wrote on the need to discern and "name the powers," those spiritual forces that have entrenched themselves in institutions. We talk of the "spirit of a place," of a certain corrupting element which eventually becomes autonomous and systemic and before which we feel powerless to change.

Clearly, one needs to wed the dry hardness of material forces to the soft intractability of the spiritual and the subjective in assigning historical significance.

The Magic of Miracles

In spite of the impact of modern physics in our thought life, we remain Newtonian in our approach to social problems.

We think of the world as a great machine, a tight system of cause and effect. Hence we feel trapped by overwhelming social forces, mere cogs in a

---

4. http://winewaterwatch.org/2016/05/we-scientists-dont-know-how-to-do-that-what-a-commentary/.

machine called social determinism. "Man in the mass" is said to be subject to the iron laws of class, economics and the environment. Social behavior can be engineered by applying the right dosage of carrot and stick, seeing to it that societies are regulated by a system of reward and punishment.

The startling discovery among physicists that subatomic particles behave in a profoundly uncertain and unpredictable way, yet miraculously do not collide and are held together mysteriously, cautions us against confusing regularity with law, and probability with predictability. What appears like a windowless universe of recurrent natural occurrences is now shown to be a wild dance of atoms following indeterminate cosmic rhythms.

What this suggests is that there is a force capable of making a cosmos out of chaos, a stable world out of infinite permutations of mere probabilities. I sense that the reason for this, as Scripture tells us, is that the universe is not really a machine that runs on its own laws. It is a personal reality held together breathlessly by a good God who is intimately involved with us. In Jesus, we are told, "all things hold together" (Col 1:17 RSV).

G. K. Chesterton long ago proposed that what we call "nature" is really "miracle routinized," divine creativity as well as consistency in familiar wonders and ordered beauty. The sun always rises in the morning, and daisies in a field all look the same. Yet it may be that every morning the sun is told, "Get up," and daisies all look alike because someone never tires of making copies of his beautiful handiwork. Not that he is incapable of variety – the world is littered by the sheer prodigality of his inventions. In his making there is both the rhythm of repetition and the off-key surprise of a new tone.

And so in the human world, there is fixity and rigid automatisms, hard bureaucratic habits and fossilized ways of doing things. But there is also choice and moral freedom, creative assertion in the face of systemic oppression. There is room for rattling the social machinery and inventing fresh solutions to its broken-down parts.

Certainly, there is a certain predictability in the power play of social forces. We assume that threatened interests will always behave in a certain way, and the working class and other disadvantaged groups will also always behave in a certain way. But then sometimes the protagonists do not act according to expectations, and we are treated to the electric perils of improvisation. This revolution has shown us that shrewd villains can miscalculate, military men can disobey and heed their conscience instead, and masses of quiescent people can rise from their usual stupor and feelingly add to the body count with dignity and grace.

The bonds of injustice can be broken, and a people reduced to silence and acquiescence can find its voice. The world moves, not merely by a complex of socioeconomic forces coming to a head, but by people making personal choices that defy predictability.

God in history is at work in the ordinary workings of social movements as well as in catastrophic *kairos* moments when he appears to directly intervene and "the axe is laid at the root of the tree," as John the Baptist puts it.[5] Belief in the ordering hand of God in human affairs need not mean suspension of belief in the effective significance of human action. In the quiet, hidden events that lead to historic upheavals, God is also at work. His is not an altogether alien force that breaks in and stops the machine, a kind of what literature calls *deus ex machina*, but an immanent grace that is present wherever there is a struggle against forces that demean and deform human life. Theology calls this the "presence of the kingdom," the reign of justice and righteousness set in motion two thousand years ago by the risen King Jesus.

It may be asked why this "presence" seems missing in a time of resurgent corruption and authoritarian politics. The parable of the wheat and the tares hints at an answer.

We are seeing in our time an intensification of the crisis between the seed of the woman and the seed of the serpent. For some mysterious reason, we are all bound up in one human community – the children of light and the children of darkness share the same social space. "Let both grow together," says the master, "until the harvest." And so growth in the kingdom of light is matched by growth in the kingdom of darkness; for every advance in society's flourishing, there is a challenge and a counterforce from the dark underside of things. Mao Tse-tung put a name to it: historical change moves dialectically – "two steps forward, one step backward." We make great leaps forward, but also suffer a backlash as recalcitrant forces fight back.

This is why Scripture tells us to "gird up your loins," for this will be a prolonged war of attrition. Not that it is a battle between equals: the kingdom of God is strong, even when it appears weak. While small and unseen, the mustard seed grows, and God is always capable of surprising. As with the death and resurrection of Jesus, in moments when the serpent seems to have won the day by bruising our heel, God enables us to crush its head (Gen 3:15).

---

5. Matt 3:10 RSV.

Concluding Remarks

So then we answer the question with which we began: "People Power 1986" did produce a baby, and it is not necessarily deformed. Like all things in our life, it has something old and something new, something that is continuous with the kingdom and discontinuous with it.

That the uprising at EDSA was a tentative coalition built on a cause as simple and as universal as the desire to get rid of an abusive power need not diminish its significance as a historic marker in our journey as a people. It was less a return to democracy as classically conceived than a witness to a more indigenous democratic impulse, an instinct for freedom that is older and parallel to but ultimately independent of the formal mechanisms that have been transplanted here from the West.

The event summoned a subterranean solidarity that seems to surface whenever the Filipino's empathetic sense of *kapwa*, or fellow-feeling, is roused. We see it now and again in the hordes of mourners that turned up for Aquino's funeral, or in the crowds that jammed the church where the remains of Flor Contemplacion were given burial rites. She was executed in Singapore for a crime that our people believed she did not commit, and so they came in droves, quietly protesting against what she had become: a symbol of the hapless plight of our workers overseas.

Political rights in much of the Majority World tend to get devalued against a backdrop of massive poverty. Democracy and human rights sound like mere Western inventions. Today, the civil liberties won at EDSA seem trifling beside the clamorous need for bread.

But then our people at EDSA showed that freedom is a commodity precious and universal enough to die for. We do not live by bread alone. It is an old truism that things common to all people must be more valuable than things peculiar to some people. Genuine populist commitment needs to stretch itself over the fact that most of our people do not care much for the symmetry of an idea.

In this uprising, our social theories got stumped and we came face to face with the reality that there is something marvelously eccentric and untidy about human beings. Moreover, we got to have a peek, though fleeting, of an earth that is not what it seems: not a closed system of forces that inevitably march toward collision and conflict, but a wide, open space where all manner of good and gentle things are possible. Deadly battles can take on a quality close to whimsy, full of wonder because, we are told, the earth hangs by God's mere breath, a fragile cosmos that would drop with a crash without the sustaining presence of him in whom all things hold together.

G. K. Chesterton once said that "a revolution really has no need of great men; a true revolution is a time when all men" – and, I may add, women and children, the elderly and disabled, rich and poor – "are great."

15

A Gift for Millennials

Mary Racelis

Those six memorable years of living under martial law in the 1970s brought many lessons to the fore.

Marcos proved that demagogues strive to close down the space for people to act freely, all the while conspiring to claim it for themselves. This means that all democracy-loving citizens must resist every effort by the state to narrow the democratic space – in the family, at school, at work and at large. Institutions like the Catholic Church, although frustratingly conservative in some ways, are also important forces for defending human rights, emphasizing the moral order, and building people's innate strengths and spirituality to inspire progressive action.

It is important as well to maintain international links with human rights NGOs like Oxfam, Save the Children, the Asian Coalition for Housing Rights; with progressive faith-based institutions like MISEREOR, the Canadian Catholic Organization for Development and Peace (CCODP), Bread for the World, the World Council of Churches; bilateral government support for local priorities; and United Nations organizations.

Leftist forces pursue ideologically oriented and often violent ways of generating their own brand of authoritarianism to overthrow the state in the name of justice for the masses. On the other hand, multiple and diverse civil society groups play strong and crucial roles in bringing about transformative nonviolent social change that builds on grassroots people's aspirations, voice and agency. Governments would do well to acknowledge the contributions of NGOs and people's organizations to overall well-being, as well as listen to them.

Lessons Learned

Key lessons learned from my martial law experience might be summarized as follows:

1. Academic institutions encompass a wide range of intellectuals with different points of view; mutual respect for diversity and free discussion keep the spirit of questioning alive, so long as the leadership remains true to university ideals of academic freedom.

2. Links between academics, NGOs and people's organizations need strengthening for mutually supportive effects.

3. Civil society groups must strive to keep the democratic space open when authoritarian forces threaten freedom and human rights.

4. Community organizing represents a powerful nonviolent force for enabling marginalized groups to assert their rights and gain power.

5. Women's leadership and participation in demand-making in poor informal settlements are especially noteworthy and deserve support.

6. Networks of like-minded groups championing people's empowerment, justice and human rights generate purposeful and united action.

7. Access to information, especially regarding government plans, projects and policies, is crucial for the reduction of fear and effective action by civil society groups.

8. When in danger, either physically or in terms of adhering to one's values, affected persons must find ways of satisfactorily addressing the situation, recognizing that family safety concerns also deserve high priority.

9. The spirituality entrenched in people's lives, especially when faced with situations gravely threatening their safety and well-being, must be nurtured and respected.

10. An authoritarian government that attacks the people's freedom and rights must be resisted in the spirit of "Never again!"

Where Do We Go from Here?

Quo vadis, then, Filipino youth in the days ahead? Where are you headed?

Let us examine the current situation affecting our country to discern what prospects and possibilities lie ahead, especially for younger civil society groups. Populist trends pose the latest set of challenges to millennials.

In a series of articles reviewing the early presidency of Rodrigo Roa Duterte, academics and other civil society commentators representing different generations, geographic locations and disciplinary backgrounds examined the social, economic and political contexts that gave rise to his astonishing electoral victory in 2016.

The authors represented in *A Duterte Reader* reflected further on the significance of his populist presidency for the Philippines today. Their conclusions highlighted five components instrumental to Duterte's ascendancy: (1) scaling up the Davao model of governance to a national level; (2) applying police efforts to the drugs situation, now framed as a war; (3) mobilizing the state's coercive apparatus; (4) projecting public support; and (5) weak accountability mechanisms for the drugs war.[1]

Heydarian[2] assessed further Duterte's rise as a product of democratic fatigue shared across emerging market democracies. Despite impressive economic growth rates, a disenchanted populace was expressing its discontent with elite-controlled liberal democratic regimes. These had apparently been proven as unable to reform slow-moving and corrupt bureaucracies. The fallout came in frustrations over the limited access to improved public goods and services. He points out that Duterte ably attracted the support of all social classes while bringing new hope to Mindanaoans long alienated by the politics of "colonial Manila." The populist leader's earthy language stimulates many.

His pivoting away from a United States-dominated foreign policy to embrace China and Russia augurs well for those seeking a more independent affirmation of Philippine nationalism. Add to this Duterte's open condemnation – indeed cursing – of revered institutions like the United Nations, the European Union and the Catholic Church and it shows that power can challenge the most sacred institutions and that traditional norms of respect need no longer apply. Such bravado has bolstered his image among many as a decisive leader able to

---

1. Nicole Curato, "We Need to Talk about Rody," in *The Duterte Reader: Critical Essays on Rodrigo Duterte's Early Presidency*, ed. Nicole Curato (Quezon City: Bughaw and Ateneo de Manila University Press, 2017), 1–2.

2. Richard Heydarian, *The Rise of Duterte: A Populist Revolt against Elite Democracy* (Singapore: Palgrave Macmillan, 2018).

establish a new identity for an independent Philippines now prepared to hold its own in a turbulent and globalizing world.[3]

Controversy over the carrying out of his electoral and post-inauguration promises has taken center stage since his inauguration. He promised (1) to resolve long-festering Muslim Mindanao demands for autonomy, peace and development; (2) to end the protracted rebel insurgency led by the National Democratic Front (NDF) and the New People's Army (NPA); (3) to provide acceptable housing and resettlement for thousands of eviction-threatened urban poor informal settler families (ISFs); (4) to end contractualization of workers with short-term appointments, low salaries and a lack of benefits (ENDO); (5) to address the violations of thousands of overseas Filipino workers (OFWs), most of them women, in Middle Eastern and Asian countries; (6) to decide whether and how to handle large-scale mining ventures involving foreign investors; (7) to get massive construction projects underway ("build, build, build"), ranging from a subway system for traffic-afflicted Metro Manilans to modern highways and bridges connecting the island republic; (8) to find a *modus vivendi* for use and control of the South China Sea; and (9) to shift from a unitary to federal form of government necessitating constitutional reform through charter change, which has in turn focused attention on political dynasties as poverty-promoting institutions. In addition, Heydarian cites chronic concerns that remain worrying for the majority of poor Filipinos, namely, wages, employment and inflation.

More recently, the Duterte Administration has (1) instituted a tax reform program – Tax Reform for Acceleration and Inclusion (TRAIN) – as the government's plan for restructuring economic priorities; (2) pledged to rebuild Marawi City after its near total destruction from government bombs and Maute rebel action to halt the latter's growth in Mindanao; (3) ordered the summary shutdown of Boracay to address severe environmental degradation, with additional tourist sites being similarly targeted; (4) sent a Filipino team of scientists to explore Benham Rise on the Pacific coast; and (5) announced a plan for joint Philippines–China exploration in the South China Sea framed as a "co-ownership" agreement, rather than contest China's construction of military bases on islands claimed by the Philippines.

His continuing misogynist comments about women and his punitive actions against strong women critical of him are generating great resentment among women and men alike. Further, whether his administration can bring

---

3. Richard Heydarian, cited in Prashanth Parameswaran, "Duterte's Rise in Perspective," *The Diplomat*, 15 November 2017, accessed 2 June 2018, https://thediplomat.com/2017/11/richard-heydarian-dutertes-rise-in-perspective/.

down poverty levels and reduce an income disparity picture showing 1 percent of the population controlling more than 50 percent of its resources remains to be seen.[4]

Most controversial, however, has been his war on drugs and the massive extra-judicial killings (EJKs) associated with them. From 1 July 2016 to 31 January 2017, *Rappler* reported over seven thousand deaths linked to the "war on drugs" – both from legitimate police operations and from vigilante-style unexplained killings (including deaths under investigation).[5] Suspected drugs personalities killed in police operations as of 31 January 2017 numbered 2,555. Numbers of victims in cases of deaths under investigation as of 9 January 2017 reached 3,603, while those where investigations had been concluded were 922. By 14 September 2017, the number of suspects reported by Philippine National Police Chief Ronald de la Rosa as killed in police operations had reached 1,506, which he later revised to "only" 1,105 deaths. The president's statements glorifying the killings of drugs-linked persons and defending the police perpetrators affirmed his authoritarian stance and contempt for the rule of law as defined in liberal democracy and human rights terms.

Civil Society Responses

Negative interpretations of these developments in the civil society sector have activated a widespread clamor denouncing these violations of human rights. At whichever level they are framed – internationally, as the International Convention on Human Rights and the Covenant on Civil and Political Rights; nationally, through the Philippine Constitution, Bill of Rights, Philippine Commission on Human Rights or Magna Carta of Women; or locally and nationwide through civil society groups – these voices remain strong and unfazed in their denunciations of EJKs.

Numerous NGOs, people's organizations (POs), professional associations, academics, media and faith-based leaders have attacked the unrelenting EJKs as unconscionable violations of human rights and confirmed the president's anti-democratic authoritarianism akin to the Marcos nightmare. Several among them are working meticulously with EJK victims to document the latter's experiences for possible future legal action. A number of them are

---

4. World Bank, *Making Growth Work for the Poor: A Poverty Assessment for the Philippines* (Washington DC: World Bank, 2018), 6.

5. Michael Bueza, "In Numbers: The Philippines' 'War on Drugs,'" *Rappler*, 23 April 2017, accessed 23 March 2018, https://www.rappler.com/newsbreak/iq/145814-numbers-statistics-philippines-war-drugs.

enabling victimized women, children and family members to restore their shattered lives through food security, improved livelihoods, safe shelter, trauma counseling and scholarships for partially orphaned children. On the other hand, government's responsibility for the "collateral damage" on families is hardly in evidence.

Civil society vigilance has even reached the International Criminal Court, which has announced an inquiry in connection with cases with the charge of crimes against humanity since Rodrigo Duterte began his war on drugs as mayor of Davao in 1988 up till today. Although his notification to the United Nations of the Philippines' withdrawal from the ICC and the Rome Statute that created it will not take effect until one year after, the case remains, making him still susceptible to the charges and investigations.

The Catholic Church has likewise taken a strong position against EJKs. Its framework for action draws on Catholic social principles as formulated by the Catholic Bishops Conference of the Philippines in 1992: (1) integral development – human dignity and solidarity; (2) universal provision of earthly goods and private property; (3) social justice and love; (4) peace and active nonviolence; (5) preferential option for the poor; (6) the value of human work; (7) integrity of creation; and (8) people empowerment.[6] Other Christian churches have taken similar exception to the regime's excesses.

While condemnation of EJKs draws the strongest concerted ire, other entities focus on the president's stance in relation to their particular concerns: labor unions protesting the jeepney-modernization program; indigenous people on military violence in their communities; women outraged by his sexist remarks and derogatory language; workers displaced by the sudden closure of Boracay; the beleaguered residents of bombed-out Marawi anxious to return home from evacuation centers and temporary housing with relatives; and the proliferation of trolls spewing out fake news on social media. Nonetheless, the majority of the population appears attracted by his unorthodox ways and insulting challenges hurled at liberal elites. Even as his approval ratings remain high, substantial numbers disapprove of or remain uneasy about people being killed and denied access to the protection of the law. Recent surveys of the Social Weather Stations indicate a decline in support among the lowest or E sector of the population.

---

6. *Catholic Bishops Conference of the Philippines: Acts and Decrees of the Second Plenary Council of the Philippines* (1992), 290–329, as quoted at "Catholic Social Principles," John J. Carroll Institute on Church and Social Issues (JJCICSI), http://www.jjcicsi.org.ph/catholic-social-teaching/catholic-social-principles/.

Among the most moving protests have been the urban poor public dramatizations at Christmas and Easter times of the impact of the killings in their communities. Acted out by the people of the communities themselves with the assistance of partner NGOs and especially PETA – the Philippine Educational Theater Association – these popular street dramas have searingly portrayed the devastating effects on poor people of the "War on Drugs" and other government policies. These protests likewise highlight the continuing experience of eviction threats, inadequate housing settlements, deplorable basic services and the latest indignity, rising prices of basic goods and transport fares attributed to TRAIN.

Populism versus Pluralism

What, then, constitutes populism in this evolving Philippine scenario? And what about pluralism?

One writer explains, "Populism is a thin-centered ideology that considers society to be ultimately separated into two homogenous and antagonistic groups, the 'pure people' and 'the corrupt elite' and which argues that politics should be an expression of the *volonte generale* (general will) of the people." Five defining aspects of populism have been identified:[7]

- Populist leaders and movements often seek legitimacy by going directly to the people instead of utilizing institutional, representative mechanisms.
- Populism presents a demoralized "us" (the people) against "them" (the elite, the foreigners or the other).
- In populism, "the people" is a "symbolic or normative construct" and not the usual democratic notion of the people as "a collection of individuals or a type of government"; thus, while democracy is a "regime," populism is an "ideology."
- Populism as "thin-centered" points to its "malleability" and thereby its applicability to many variations (i.e. Left and Right).
- Populism draws the line between "the people and the elite" and is therefore incompatible with liberal democracy that considers "both masses and the elite as part of the 'people.'"

This formulation differs from the current liberal democratic notion of "pluralism," located at one end of the scale, with populism placed at the other.

---

7. Carmel Veloso Abao, "Engaging Duterte: That Space in Between Populism and Pluralism," in *Duterte Reader*, ed Curato, 302, quoting Espejo (2015), 62.

Pluralism emphasizes "the rule of law," elected leaders representing "the people" and following particular rules and procedures. Populists, on the other hand, "embody" rather than represent the people. Where populists envision a homogenous "people" unified against an "other," pluralists see "the people" as heterogeneous.[8] Both populism and pluralism reflect positive values in that both espouse popular sovereignty. On the negative side, populism overvalues power and ends up producing authoritarianism represented by a "strongman"; pluralism undervalues power and lodges power in an elite.

Effective dissent will thus not likely come either from a weakened liberal democratic elite or from the Left (Communist Party, the National Democratic Front and the New People's Army, or CPP-NDF-NPA) co-opted by having taken on key Cabinet positions in the Duterte administration. Instead, a new set of forces lodged in civil society is predicted to move into the domain of opposition. The success of these groups in defending democracy will stem from their ability to reject both the authoritarianism of populism and the elitism of pluralism.[9]

Nonetheless, civil society as comprised in the past must reckon with nuances provided by the present political dynamic, including (1) the use of social media; (2) a political supermajority cobbled together by the Duterte administration which further dilutes opposition; (3) the looming prospect of charter change which includes a (possible) reconfiguration of local–national dynamics via a federal system; and (4) the foregoing narrative of "us" vs. "them" or "*dilawan*" (yellow) vs. "*dutertards*" (pro-Duterte) forces that colors political issues of the day.

In light of all this, what roles can millennials play, drawing strength from the lessons of martial law but also constantly discerning from reliable evidence today what strategies are best for embedding democracy for all Filipinos? The particular strengths of the youth lie in their effective use of social media in the context of their aspirations and actions. Here are some possible actions:

1. Establish partnerships with grassroots groups directly and/or through social media channels, enhancing trust and unity through interactive dialogues that foster joint decision-making, and defining issues and actions that can heighten people's participation and voices.

---

8. Abao, "Engaging Duterte," 303–304.
9. Abao, 314.

2. Keep abreast of and disseminate local and national developments publicized through multiple information channels, giving significant attention to the distinctions between truthful and fake news.

3. Recognize gender differences and talents that enhance discernment and action on the part of men, women and LGBT+s.

4. Develop social networks – local, national, regional and international – which aim at social reform and nonviolent transformation, simultaneously pursing the kinds of information and action needed.

5. Understand local and national power relations and structures that generate and sustain inequality.

6. Get involved in electoral politics.

7. Register to vote in local and national elections, or even put forward one's own candidacy for electoral positions.

8. Mobilize eligible voters, especially new voters from eighteen years and above, to exercise their political rights as citizens by registering to vote.

9. Define, discuss and prioritize the issues to be addressed by political and NGO leaders in voter-education drives, especially those relating to youth aspirations and the needs of marginalized sectors.

10. Campaign for electoral candidates likely to be honest and dedicated servant leaders and hold all elective officials accountable to their promises through regular interrogation during their terms of public service.

11. Engage with partner groups in lobbying Senators and Congresspersons for just laws beneficial especially to marginalized groups, as well as the equivalent in local officials and ordinances.

12. Lodge efforts at reform and change linked to human rights perspectives in the context of youth's spiritual strengths and idealism, whether linked formally to organized faith-based institutions and/or through participation in small discernment groups on the ground or online.

13. Identify and actually create programs and dissemination processes through which social media can be harnessed to generate, help implement, monitor and evaluate national and local government performance.

14. In focusing on social media as your special expertise, remember that, crucial as information is, it is *information and action* that will ultimately make the difference.

To our millennials, in closing, you may wish to reflect on what significant figures in history have said about youth and your aspirations. Perhaps their wise sayings will serve as enduring *gifts*, inspiring you to continue onward in taking your steps toward a bright future:

Jose Rizal: "The youth is the hope of our future."

Margaret Mead: "Never doubt that a small group of thoughtful, committed citizens can change the world; indeed, it's the only thing that ever has."

Mahatma Gandhi: "You may never know what results come of your actions, but if you do nothing there will be no results."

Rabindranath Tagore: "Age considers; youth ventures."

Martin Luther King: "The arc of the moral universe is long, but it bends toward justice."

Henry Wordsworth Longfellow: "Youth comes but once in a lifetime."

Benjamin Disraeli: "Almost everything that is great has been done by youth."

Qur'an 13:11: "Indeed, Allah will not change the condition of a people until they change what is in themselves."

And finally, Jeremiah 1:7–9: "But the LORD said to me, 'Do not say, "I am too young." You must go to everyone I send you to and say whatever I command you. Do not be afraid of them, for I am with you and will rescue you,' declares the LORD." (NIV)

Millennials, this is your time!

References

Abao, Carmel Veloso. "Engaging Duterte: That Space in Between Populism and Pluralism." In Curato, *The Duterte Reader*, 301–318.

Bueza, Michael, "In Numbers: The Philippines' 'War on Drugs.'" *Rappler*, 23 April 2017. Accessed 23 March 2018. https://www.rappler.com/newsbreak/iq/145814-numbers-statistics-philippines-war-drugs.

"Catholic Social Principles." John J. Carroll Institute on Church and Social Issues (JJCICSI). http://www.jjcicsi.org.ph/catholic-social-teaching/catholic-social-principles/.

Curato, Nicole, ed. *The Duterte Reader: Critical Essays on Rodrigo Duterte's Early Presidency.* Quezon City: Bughaw and Ateneo de Manila University Press, 2017.

Curato, Nicole. "We Need to Talk about Rody." In *The Duterte Reader*, edited by N. Curato, 1–36. Quezon City: Ateneo de Manila University Press, 2015.

Heydarian, Richard J. *The Rise of Duterte: A Populist Revolt against Elite Democracy.* Singapore: Palgrave Macmillan, 2018.

Parameswaran, Prashanth. "Duterte's Rise in Perspective." *The Diplomat*, 15 November 2017. Accessed 2 June 2018. https://thediplomat.com/2017/11/richard-heydarian-dutertes-rise-in-perspective/.

World Bank. *Making Growth Work for the Poor: A Poverty Assessment for the Philippines.* Washington, DC: World Bank, 2018.

Epilogue

Putting an End to Our Unfinished Revolutions

Months after the events at EDSA, leaders of faith-based organizations came together to celebrate and reflect on what we did right and what we could have done better as participants in our recent history.

When it came to my turn to speak, representing evangelicals in the ecumenical gathering, I said we had forgotten at least two resources that could have guided us better in making historical choices: our culture and our faith. We appropriated ideologies and political models from outside that had no real congruence with either our faith or the culture of our people.

After I sat down, a priest who had been detained for his work in the underground movement, Ed de la Torre, sidled up to me and said, "It is true. Even if we are priests we became NPA." I thought he meant that they became part of the New People's Army. But no: "*Naging* NPA kami – Not Praying Anymore," he said, with a slightly impish smile.

As the stories here show, confronting the powers requires not just social science but an openness to the wider reality that there are cosmic forces of good and evil that will either thwart or aid us in the struggle for justice and righteousness.

The setbacks and disappointments after our "People Power" revolution are sufficient evidence that social change requires marathon runners who have their ears to the ground and who are immersed in the life of our people, with eyes set on the God who alone can give power to triumph and endure.

Taking on the Shadows

There is a hardness to evil that we would do well to take into account when devising blueprints for social change. As the skeptical Teacher tells us, "What is crooked cannot be made straight, what is lacking cannot be numbered."[1] This side of Eden, there will always be that constant opposition, that recalcitrant force that always threatens to foil our best efforts at making something better of the world.

Most fatal to such projects is the enemy within. Agents of change are just as subject to corruption as the despots they want to replace. The old saying that "power corrupts, and absolute power corrupts absolutely" applies to all who monopolize power, be they elected autocrats or a communist party supposedly acting as "vanguard of the proletariat."

The stories here are witness to where the Faustian will to power can take us. We learned "habits of the heart" that continue to destroy the very foundations of our democratic institutions. Our soldiers, once always subordinate to civilian authority, began to stage coups in the name of reform, arrogating to themselves the role of guardians of the social order. The bureaucracy has been reduced to being mere instrumentalities at the service of whoever is in power. The party system collapsed and has never recovered, the two-party system splintering into fractious and free-forming alliances based merely on the desire to secure power.

As our most senior anthropologist, Mary, has shown, even academics learned to adjust to whatever was the "new normal," exercising self-censorship. Some even surrendered empirical rigor to align themselves either with the myths that supported the regime or with the then reigning ideology.

These are only some of the consequences of the meltdown of our institutions under one-man rule. It is important to recognize that the system of checks and balances in a democracy was instituted precisely to hold in check the terrible force of evil within us that goes haywire when the restraints are off.

The Christian tradition calls this "original sin," the tendency to choose evil rather than the good when faced with critical choices. There is in us a constant "war among the members" as described by Paul:

> I do not understand what I do. For what I want to do I do not do, but what I hate I do . . . I have the desire to do what is good, but I cannot carry it out . . . When I want to do good, evil is right there with me. For in my inner being I delight in God's law; but I see another law at work in the members of my body, waging war

---

1. Eccl 1:15.

against the law of my mind and making me a prisoner of the law of sin at work within my members.[2]

The poet-critic Allen Tate once said that there are really only two kinds of writers: those who believe in original sin, and those who do not. Similarly, there are really only two kinds of social theorists: those who optimistically believe in the perfectibility of human nature by improved genetics and allocating the right proportion of reward and punishment in the social environment, and those who pessimistically believe in the radicality of human frailty – what the Reformers call "total depravity" – seeing institutions and cultural tradition as merely ways of forming and disciplining us into something fairly decent. There is this constant sense that divine help is necessary, even for ourselves to get transformed, enabling us to humbly accept limits to power and our own capacity to wield it without succumbing to corruption.

Political realism requires recognition that there is always this shadow side which accounts for the contradictions that develop in all the good work we wish to do. It is also part of the reason why our revolutions remain unfinished.

We have, for instance, a certain inability to confront headlong the dark side of our revolutionary projects. We turn away from having to name the crimes committed against our people. We do not insist that wrongdoing be acknowledged and those who are guilty be punished. Willie's pointed question, "Who killed Ninoy?" remains unanswered to this day. For that matter, it is important to ask: Why has there been no redress for the killing of Andres Bonifacio, the very founder of the Katipunan, or even Antonio Luna, its most able general?

This country was the first in Asia to declare itself a democratic republic. Yet since 1896, it has waged a struggle, not only against foreign powers, but against its own internal weakness. Our national hero José Rizal saw with prescient insight that political independence without the moral courage to take on the demands of a vigilant citizenship will be rendered useless. As Padre Florentino tells the dying Simoun in *El Filibusterismo*:

> Our ills we owe to ourselves alone, so let us blame no one. If Spain should see that we were less complaisant with tyranny and more disposed to struggle and suffer for our rights, Spain would be the first to grant us liberty, because when the fruit of the womb reaches maturity, woe unto the mother who would stifle it! So, while the Filipino people has not sufficient energy to proclaim,

---

2. Rom 7:15–23.

with head erect and bosom bared, its rights to social life, and to guarantee it with its sacrifices, with its own blood; while we see our countrymen in private life ashamed within themselves, hear the voice of conscience roar in rebellion and protest, yet in public life keep silence or even echo the words of him who abuses them in order to mock the abused; while we see them wrap themselves up in their egotism and with a forced smile praise the most iniquitous actions, begging with their eyes a portion of the booty – why grant them liberty? With Spain or without Spain they would always be the same, and perhaps worse! Why independence, if the slaves of today will be the tyrants of tomorrow? And that they will be such is not to be doubted, for he who submits to tyranny loves it.[3]

For as long as this nation is unable to face the shadows of its history and wield the sword on the side of justice, we cannot truly move on and begin again.

Romania lined up Nicolae Ceausescu and his wife against the wall and shot them for crimes against their people after a quarter century of their ruling one of the most repressive regimes in totalitarian Europe. In our country, the Marcoses were allowed to return and had the temerity to run for office, and the people voted for them. The reasons for this are complex and many, but one of them is a profound moral softness, both in the culture and in the justice system.

This is seen in the moral obtuseness and vast carelessness with which the present regime sweepingly tries to airbrush the truths of our history. There are shallow calls to just get on with the business of moving on and to forget the past. We are in danger of what the prophet Jeremiah calls "healing the wound of people lightly, saying 'peace, peace' when there is no peace."[4] National reconciliation requires clarity in who precisely was guilty of what crime, and the readiness to own up to responsibility. Forgiveness is premised on repentance.

What It Cost Us

Our experience of authoritarianism decimated our ranks of some of the best and brightest of our generation. The trauma of it was such that many could not even bear to talk about it. The silence has raised a generation unaware

---

3. José Rizal, *The Reign of Greed*, English translation by Charles Derbyshire of the Spanish *El Filibusterismo* (Manila: Philippine Education Co., 1912), 361, http://www.gutenberg.org/files/10676/10676-8.txt.

4. Jer 6:14; 8:11.

of what it cost to return to political normalcy and walk the streets in relative safety. As Elizabeth tells it:

> Rolly and I didn't talk much about the martial law period in front of our children, an oversight in my reckoning, because when it was time for them to vote, embracing the right to suffrage wasn't a big thing for them as it was for us. I must confess that these millennial children grew up apolitical so when Kimi had cast her vote for the President in 2010, she shrugged her shoulders and indifferently remarked, "Is that all there is to it?"
>
> I then thought but couldn't bring myself to utter to her, "It might be all there is to it, but we spent fourteen years fighting to get that right to vote back into our lives after the dictator deprived us of it."
>
> In the aftermath of EDSA 1986, I remember thinking that our firstborn child, Kimi, would now grow in a climate of freedom, uncertain and flawed though it might be. Even if she on the surface is flippant about the importance of hard-won freedom and human rights, I know in my heart that she has an ingrained sense of right and wrong. Hopefully, this will help her guard freedom and human rights like my generation did when she reaches a crossroads where these are threatened again.

Our generation may have been misguided by a failed ideology, but this need not diminish the value of the great idealism and self-sacrifice poured into the struggle for a better society. The following story is an example.

Quite early on, I sensed that the student activist movement of which I was a part might be going in the wrong direction. As I surveyed the wreckage wrought in the wake of the Diliman Commune – classroom chairs burnt and piled up as barricades along the UP Oval, charred branches of trees, broken glass and bottles of Molotov cocktails concocted in the chemistry and physics labs, scattered placards and crumpled manifestos and litter everywhere – I asked my discussion group leader, Raquel Edralin, who was part of the Diliman Directorate that the rebel students had set up, if she thought this kind of disorder would bring about the society we were dreaming about. She did not answer. We walked together in silence until we had rounded the oval and neared the Oblation statue at the entrance of the university. Then she said, with a sigh that was almost melancholy, "I don't know. But this is where I have committed my life to."

Brought up in a convent school, her activism had alienated her from faith and family. She had cast her lot with the supposedly inexorable march of the forces massing together toward the revolution. I asked if she really believed there was such a thing as the dialectic in history, since I was beginning to sense that it might be just another of those imagined metaphysics, indemonstrable scientifically. With unflinching honesty, she said nobody could be sure. "But then," she said, "you can also never be sure about the truth of your newfound faith." I had become a young believer at that point, and had begun to question the premises of the ideology that I had signed up to. "Let history judge between you and me," she said. We embraced each other and parted in front of the Oblation, the silent witness to our mutual sadness at having to separate and take our chosen paths.

Two decades later, I was putting my hand luggage into the overhead locker of the plane taking me to a conference in the US, when the woman seated near the window called my name. I did not recognize her at first, as her face had been badly disfigured. "Raquel," I said, "is it you?" With great joy I asked the man seated between us to take the aisle seat so we could sit together. Once I was settled in my seat, Raquel immediately plunged into her story: "You are quite right," she said. "I have come to faith." She beamed at me, her eyes bright. "I am back with my family, and the revolution is going nowhere."

For eighteen hours of the flight, she recounted her detention, the sexual molestation and the tortures she went through. In the sheer anguish, isolation and pain of it, "there was no one I could call but God," she said. Her brain got badly damaged, and she had to go through a costly and risky operation to survive. Upon release, she established a women's crisis center. Then she found herself and her husband inexplicably watched, suspected of betraying the revolution by former comrades. It was then that she drifted away from the movement, the disillusionment cutting more deeply than the torture marks she had suffered.

Besides torture and imprisonment, many of those who went underground suffered estrangement from their spouses and families, their children raised in the brutal environment of jail cells or forever wounded and haunted by the loss of a parent or a separation, the cause of which they hardly understood. Fe and her husband, Roger, were both incarcerated, but this was a far lesser price paid than the toll on their own child:

> Our life as a family had steadily recovered since 1986 when tragedy struck. Our only child, Tagúm (by then aged twenty-two) was diagnosed with lymphoma (cancer of the lymph nodes, stage 3). Roger and I were devastated and went into deep spiritual crisis.

Just in time, women friends of the Christian evangelical group shared the Bible with us. Our Bible readings and reflections together gave Roger and me the spiritual and physical strength we needed as Tagúm underwent chemo and radiation therapy for a year.

One evening, after our family prayer and sharing with Tagúm, he told Roger and me that while growing up as a child, he had often felt alone and lonely. "And now," he said in pain, "I will not always be around." We felt stabbed to the heart by this grave revelation. Roger and I asked for his forgiveness. We tried to explain that we were always together in an "abnormal sort of way," though he must have failed to notice. We also told him how we missed him terribly while at work trying to build a more just and humane society for him and the next generation. With tears in our eyes we tightly hugged him with as much love as we could give him. It was our daily Bible readings and prayer together with Tagúm that helped us accept his gentle passing into the Light. Roger and I since then have been back to our faith. We were lost and were found by God's grace through our son's death. Since then Roger and I no longer separate the personal and spiritual from our political commitments.

People First

The Catholic priest and psychologist Henri Nouwen once said that what is most deeply personal is also what is most universal.

We took personally the outrageous fact that so many of our people were and are being ground to dust by poverty and injustice. We tried to respond, the best way we knew how. But somewhere along the way, we lost sight of the untidy and messy constraints of the personal and began to have it sidelined by the abstract symmetry and totalitarian demands of an idea. We took to doing social arithmetic, following the utilitarianism of calculating "the greater good for the greater number," and rationalizing the elimination of people who got in the way as inevitable "collateral damage."

The end justifies the means, we reasoned. But in letting loose means and methods unfettered by conventions of right and wrong, the cause got waylaid and ran itself aground. The trouble is that in straining for political correctness, people are depersonalized into an abstract entity that is significant only in so far as it is part of a collective and serves the cause. Arthur Koestler, a disillusioned

Marxist, speaks of how the individual in socialist experiments was reduced to "a multitude of one million divided by one million." From here, it was only a step toward a mass descent into hell, whether it went by the name of "killing fields," a "cultural revolution" or a "Gulag Archipelago."

Today, we are witnessing the extra-judicial killing of thousands of suspected drugs users and pushers, mostly poor. Some justify this as a form of social cleansing – cleaning up the streets of dangerous elements and ridding society of useless scum. It is an opinion held even by respectable and religious people who consider themselves God-fearing.

This echoes the sort of reasoning behind the genocidal disasters of recent history. We forget that we have a Shepherd who will leave his flock of ninety-nine sheep to search for the one lost sheep that has gone astray. The God we presume to worship cares for the one person who bears his image, no matter how broken and defaced.

The inviolability of the human person is enshrined in the very covenant that God renewed with Noah after the cataclysmic flood: "Whoever sheds the blood of man, by man shall his blood be shed; for God made man in his own image."[5]

Wounds are deeper and the social consequences more lasting and horrific when some essential part of what makes us human is violated. The idea of "human rights" is not, at bottom, a liberal idea being foisted on us by the West, with its over-developed language for "rights," but a dignity and value intrinsic to us as people made in the very image of the Creator.

The universe is first of all a personal reality. That there are ten thousand miles between this country and the US holds far less meaning than the fact that it is the distance that separates us from a brother or a daughter, a parent or a son. A personal tie binds us deeper than a common cause or ideology, and endures through time and space. This is why Alma writes nostalgically of the friends she and Mario made while in China, and Mario laments over his Turkish friend and their failed dreams. Ultimately, we walk together because we have met each other as people.[6] This is how movements endure. And movements fail once there is a lack of circles of trust at their relational core; the center will not hold.

Our generation woke up to the unreality of one-answer ideological systems. We discovered that a human being is much more than a product of heredity conditioned by the social environment. We cannot be flattened into

---

5. Gen 9:6 RSV.
6. Amos 3:3.

one-dimensional creatures – merely political animals unable to live beyond the *polis*, or consumers determined by economics. We can rise beyond our social conditioning, heal from psychological wounds dealt in childhood and break barriers of class and gender. Life is too complex and people are too intractable to be neatly labeled or boxed in by merely social or economic class.

The British journalist Malcolm Muggeridge once remarked that "in movies, there are the good guys and the bad guys; but in real life, there are no heroes nor villains, only men." The stories in this book show the truth of this. Ideologues out to change society reduce people to insects that need to be exterminated when they do not toe the party line or are in the way of their revolutionary project. Demagogues like Marcos are capable of eliciting loyalty, can miscalculate and can make critical decisions that stay the hand of bloodshed. A military made subservient to one man's will to power found it in themselves to quietly subvert the chain of command and eventually defect.

In the end, the real dividing line is not class or ideology, but whether we are on the side of the good or on the side of evil at any given point in our history. Battles between good and evil forces in society begin in the human heart and flow outward into the choices we make.

Our Choices Matter, and We Are Not Unaided

One major choice that we had to make was the decision to face the tanks and potentially add to the body count. For some of us, like Adrian, it meant not just danger but an abrupt end to his missionary career in this country. Was he in the wrong to stand in solidarity with us in a time of great crisis?

There is a very thin line between political interference and standing in the gap because, as a missionary, it is part of one's duty to accompany the people in their struggle. Part of the meaning of the incarnation is that, like Jesus, we enter into a people's story. We lay down whatever it is that gives us immunity, such as a foreign passport that enables us to flee out of a troubled country at a moment's notice.

During the days of the EDSA uprising, a missionary friend told me that they were all advised to pack their bags and get ready to fly out in the event that things took a turn for the worse. While I was grateful I had a few missionary friends praying for me during those days, I felt somewhat alienated at the thought that we would have been abandoned had things panned out badly.

When we look at Jesus, we see a God who walks with us through the dust and grime and heat of our struggles. Unlike avatars who make fleeting appearances lost in the mist of mythic tales and legends, you can pin him down on a calendar and trace his footprints in a particular time, culture and place. No other religion talks of God in this way.

Similarly, it is intrinsic to our missional engagement to "incarnate" ourselves in a particular context, to be subject to the constraints, risks, dangers and opportunities presented by the country of the people we serve.

The parting advice to Mario and Alma to forget all about China is undergirded by the same need to contextualize; a revolution can only succeed if it is genuinely rooted in the soil of the culture and the realities of a given sociopolitical context. Mao Tse-tung departed from the Leninist emphasis on the proletariat as vanguard of the revolution and instead built his socialist vision on China's vast peasantry. In the same way, we cannot copy, much less plagiarize, one another's social experiments.

At the same time, we need to ask: What is the shape of human solidarity in a world that has globalized, where distant events and distant others affect us, and those who flee from war and poverty in their homelands come knocking on our doors?

The Filipinos, like Israel, have become a diaspora people. Perhaps as a kind of psychological insurrection, we feel ourselves to be exiles in our own land, always pining for another country. God's word to the exiles in Babylon could well speak to us:

> Build houses and live in them; plant gardens and eat their produce. Take wives and have sons and daughters: take wives for your sons, and give your daughters in marriage, that they may bear sons and daughters: multiply there, and do not decrease.
>
> But seek the welfare of the city where I have sent you into exile, and pray to the LORD on its behalf, for in its welfare you will find your welfare . . . For I know the plans I have for you, plans for welfare and not for evil, to give you a future and a hope.[7]

Build your roots, says the Lord. Plant them deep. For while we look forward to a better country, we must not live in suspension. We must live as if this is all the world we have and we shall stay here forever. Whether we like it or not, our fortunes are bound up with the alien city.

We must stand in solidarity with its sin and its need. We are to pray, to besiege God for the powers of the age to come to break in and bring in his purposive future.

---

7. Jer 29:5–7, 11 RSV.

As the Body of Christ on earth, in our own place and time, we are being called to be people of history, to plant our roots deeply somewhere and make a difference among the people we are called to serve.

It is the growing faith of the people behind this book that compelled us to tell our stories. We are a group of people who, because of differences in background, ideology and faith commitment, will not naturally come together. But because we are all coming to know the Lion who is also a Lamb, the wolf and the lamb are able to feed and lie down together.[8] We are learning to build on each other's strengths and hopefully serve others in their weakness.

There are those of us who are well ahead on the journey, and some who turned their backs on the religion of their childhood but are now rediscovering the mystic power of what used to be mere ritual. Writes Mario:

> Daddy was a Freemason. He allowed Mamma and their children to hear Mass on Sundays, but not to go to confession. He believed, as most of his fellow masons did, that early preparations for the 1896 Revolution were exposed to the Spanish authorities by a priest who learned about it from the confession of a Katipunero's sister. Like my elder siblings, however, I secretly had my first confession and communion in grade school, with Mamma's blessing. She earned her college degree from a school in Intramuros run by Spanish nuns. The last time I went to confession, however, was in 1963, before I started attending the Assemblies of God Church. Fifty years after, I asked a poet-priest at the altar if I could have communion without having gone to confession. He raised the chalice and whispered: "Body of Christ." "Amen," I replied. I opened my mouth, and felt the host melt on my tongue.

As people of faith, we have learned that history is not just a succession of events running on a chain of mere cause and effect, but of choices we make, big and small, that unexpectedly turn the tide and make us aware that human agency matters, but also that we are not unaided. There is an unseen Power at work, and all that we are being asked to do is to simply put one foot in front of the other and trust him for the outcomes. We can confidently count on the Almighty who has come down to meet us in our need.

Realism means that we maintain a tragic sense, a tough-minded refusal to seek refuge in illusory sources of optimism, knowing that neither healthy economics nor a just and sober government will result from a mere

---

8. Isa 65:25.

rearrangement of the social furniture. At the same time, we believe that truth will out and the lie will rot, that as we hold fast to honor and the best that we believe we become signs of the reality that the kingdom has come, and it is making a new world where justice and righteousness are possible and no longer relegated to the margins.

In a time when our democracy is slowly dying, our institutions eroded bit by bit by a populist autocrat presiding over the systematic collapse of the rule of law once again, Padre Florentino's words to Simoun on his failed revolution remind us that our precarious liberties are not secured by armed might, but by the quality of our citizenry:

> I do not mean to say that our liberty will be secured at the sword's point, for the sword plays but little part in modern affairs, but that we must secure it by making ourselves worthy of it, by exalting the intelligence and the dignity of the individual, by loving justice, right, and greatness, even to the extent of dying for them, – and when a people reaches that height God will provide a weapon, the idols will be shattered, the tyranny will crumble like a house of cards and liberty will shine out like the first dawn.[9]

The gift of our hard-won democracy is that we are no longer cowering subjects ruled by arbitrary and tyrannical despots, but self-governing citizens of a republic ruled by law. Let us, once and for all, prove ourselves worthy of our citizenship by making our institutions work for the good of our people.

Melba Padilla Maggay

---

9. Rizal, *Reign of Greed.*

About the Contributors

Adrian Helleman served as a pastor in British Columbia before being called to serve as a missionary-teacher in the Philippines. He received a ThM from Calvin Theological Seminary and a PhD from St Michael's College at the University of Toronto. He and his wife, Wendy, later taught philosophy at Moscow State University in Russia, and then philosophy and theology at the University of Jos in Nigeria. They have also lectured in Canada, the United States, South Africa and Tanzania.

For most of the year, he lives in Toronto with his wife. They have three adult children: a daughter and son living in Toronto and another daughter near Boston. They have five grandchildren.

Elizabeth Lolarga is a journalist, poet and teacher. She finished her journalism at the University of the Philippines Diliman and fine arts at UP Baguio. She is the author of *Catholic and Emancipated*, a compilation of selected essays published by the University of Santo Tomas, and of three poetry collections in limited editions: *The First Eye, Dangling Doll: Poems of Laughter and Desperation* and *Big Mama Sez: Poems Old and New*.

Ms Lolarga used to teach English and creative writing to high school students at the Community of Learners Foundation in San Juan City. She is a member of the Baguio Writers Group and the Philippine Center of International PEN.

Melba Padilla Maggay is a writer and a social anthropologist, a consultant on culture and social development issues at the interface of religion, culture and development. A trained journalist, Dr Maggay writes occasional commentaries in mainstream media and is frequently tapped as a resource person for cultural, religious and sociopolitical issues. She is a three-time top-prize winner in the Don Carlos Palanca Memorial Awards, writes fiction and wrote a zarzuela, *Bayan, Isang Paa Na Lamang*, a prize winner in the 1998 National Centennial Literary Competition commemorating one hundred years of Philippine independence. She accompanies development practitioners and social activists seeking change and was cited for her outstanding leadership in organizing the evangelical Protestant presence at the barricades during the Philippine "People Power" uprising in February 1986.

She is President of the Institute for Studies in Asian Church and Culture (ISACC), a research, training and advocacy organization on church and culture issues, and Micah Global, an alliance of more than seven hundred faith-based development organizations working among the poor worldwide.

Fe B. Mangahas taught Philippine history and music history at the University of the East, and Philippine history and women's studies at St Scholastica's College, Manila. She obtained her degrees in music and history from the University of the Philippines, Diliman, and her MA in history from the Ateneo de Manila University.

She served as Chair of the Department of History, St Scholastica's College, and was member of the board of commissioners of the National Historical Commission (NHCP) and the board of the National Commission on the Role of Filipino Women (NCRFW); and she headed the Cultural Center of the Philippines (CCP) Women's Program. She is author and co-author of textbooks on Philippine history and social studies. Her essays on women and *babaylan* feminism are a significant grounding of feminism in Philippine culture and history.

Alma Cruz Miclat is a freelance writer and retired business executive. She is president of the Maningning Miclat Art Foundation, Inc. (www.maningning.com) which has held the Maningning Miclat Trilingual Poetry Awards (Filipino, English and Chinese) during odd-numbered years since 2003 and the Maningning Miclat Art Award during even-numbered years since 2004.

She is the author of the deluxe book *Soul Searchers and Dreamers: Artists' Profiles*, a compilation of articles published in the *Philippine Daily Inquirer's* Arts & Books section and other publications. She is co-author with Mario I. Miclat, Maningning Miclat and Banaue Miclat of *Beyond the Great Wall: A Family Journal*, which was granted a National Book Award for biography in 2007. She co-edited *Fairground: A Literary Feast* with Gemino H. Abad, and is a contributor to *The Writers' Wives* edited by Narita Gonzales and *The Fallen Cradle* edited by Agnes Prieto and Ricardo de Ungria.

Mario I. Miclat is an awarded fictionist, poet, essayist and translator. He served as dean of the University of the Philippines Asian Center and retired as UP full professor and Associate of Likhaan UP Institute of Creative Writing. He has been given lifetime achievement awards, including the Gawad Pambansang Alagad ni Balagtas for fiction in English and Filipino, and Patnubay ng Sining at Kalinangan of the City of Manila. He has won the Gawad CCP, the Palanca Awards for Literature and UP Centennial Professorial Chair Award and UP

Press Centennial Publications Award. His books include *Secrets of the Eighteen Mansions*, long-listed for the Man Asian Literary Prize, and *Beyond the Great Wall*, National Book Awardee for biography.

He served as director of the Sentro ng Wikang Filipino of the UP System from 1996 to 2001 and as head of the National Committee on Language and Translation of the National Commission on Culture and the Arts (NCCA).

Mary Racelis is Professorial Lecturer at the Department of Sociology and Anthropology at Ateneo de Manila University, a well-known research scientist and a specialist in urban poverty, development, social policy and civil society. She was former director of the Institute of Philippine Culture.

She joined the Ateneo faculty in June 1960, the first woman professor in the college. Fr Frank Lynch, S.J., then starting both the Institute of Philippine Culture (IPC) and the Department of Sociology and Anthropology (DSA), invited her to be among his first staff members.

Dr Racelis was born in Manila in 1932 of a Filipino father and American mother. She received her elementary education in the Philippines, and finished high school and college in New York at Cornell University in Sociology and Anthropology in 1954. She returned to the Philippines with her husband, Helmuth Hollnsteiner, in 1955, and completed her MA in sociology at the University of the Philippines in 1960. In 1975, De La Salle University awarded her a doctorate in the social sciences *honoris causa*. In 2003, the Ateneo de Manila University awarded her a doctorate in humanities *honoris causa*.

Rolando Villacorte was a journalist and freelance magazine writer who started out as news correspondent for *The Evening News* in the early 1950s. Besides *The Real Hero of EDSA*, he has written two other books, *Baliwag Then and Now* and *The Philippine Constitution*, which were adopted as textbooks for high school and college students. He won first prize in an essay contest sponsored by the International Labor Organization and the Philippine Management Association of the Philippines. As well as receiving a cash prize, he went on a study tour of vocational rehabilitation centers in various European countries. He had previously toured similar institutions in Japan, Hong Kong and Singapore under ILO auspices.

He has edited a number of community newspapers in Quezon City, and for more than ten years he served in the QC government as PRO-researcher-translator and subsequently as head of its barrio government office. His civil service also included a two-year stint at the Malacañang Press Office as chief research and special projects officer during President Diosdado Macapagal's tenure.

Wilfrido "Willie" Villarama, a former Congressman (2001–2004) and vice governor of Bulacan (1972–1980), served a number of cabinet ministers in various capacities, most notably as chief of staff and assistant minister to Labor Secretary and then Senator Blas F. Ople, and subsequently Vice President Gloria Macapagal Arroyo.

An astute politician, he was secretary general and campaign manager of Buhay Party List, the political arm of El Shaddai, the largest Catholic charismatic movement in the country, and was instrumental in its winning three seats in the 2004 election.

He holds a degree in Political Science from Ateneo de Manila, a master's degree in Public Administration from Harvard University, an MBA from Xavier University in Ohio, and a master's in Community Development from the University of the Philippines. As a public servant, he is a Career Executive Service Officer (CESO 2).

Active in politics and civil society, he continues to advocate for Christian engagement in the political arena and sits on the boards of various NGOs, civic and religious organizations, including the Institute for Studies in Asian Church and Culture.

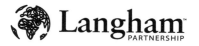

Langham Literature and its imprints are a ministry of Langham Partnership.

Langham Partnership is a global fellowship working in pursuit of the vision God entrusted to its founder John Stott –

to facilitate the growth of the church in maturity and Christ-likeness through raising the standards of biblical preaching and teaching.

Our vision is to see churches in the majority world equipped for mission and growing to maturity in Christ through the ministry of pastors and leaders who believe, teach and live by the Word of God.

Our mission is to strengthen the ministry of the Word of God through:
- nurturing national movements for biblical preaching
- fostering the creation and distribution of evangelical literature
- enhancing evangelical theological education

especially in countries where churches are under-resourced.

Our ministry

Langham Preaching partners with national leaders to nurture indigenous biblical preaching movements for pastors and lay preachers all around the world. With the support of a team of trainers from many countries, a multi-level programme of seminars provides practical training, and is followed by a programme for training local facilitators. Local preachers' groups and national and regional networks ensure continuity and ongoing development, seeking to build vigorous movements committed to Bible exposition.

Langham Literature provides majority world preachers, scholars and seminary libraries with evangelical books and electronic resources through publishing and distribution, grants and discounts. The programme also fosters the creation of indigenous evangelical books in many languages, through writer's grants, strengthening local evangelical publishing houses, and investment in major regional literature projects, such as one volume Bible commentaries like *The Africa Bible Commentary* and *The South Asia Bible Commentary.*

Langham Scholars provides financial support for evangelical doctoral students from the majority world so that, when they return home, they may train pastors and other Christian leaders with sound, biblical and theological teaching. This programme equips those who equip others. Langham Scholars also works in partnership with majority world seminaries in strengthening evangelical theological education. A growing number of Langham Scholars study in high quality doctoral programmes in the majority world itself. As well as teaching the next generation of pastors, graduated Langham Scholars exercise significant influence through their writing and leadership.

To learn more about Langham Partnership and the work we do visit **langham.org**